dBASE II®
A Comprehensive User's Manual

dBASE II®
A Comprehensive User's Manual
KERMAN D. BHARUCHA

TAB BOOKS Inc.
Blue Ridge Summit, PA 17214

FIRST EDITION

THIRD PRINTING

Copyright © 1985 by TAB BOOKS Inc.

Printed in the United States of America

Library of Congress Cataloging in Publication Data

Bharucha, Kerman D.
dBase II—a comprehensive user's manual.

Includes index.
1. dBase II (Computer program) 2. Business—Data
processing. I.Title. II.Title: dBASE two—a
comprehensive user's manual. III. Title: dBASE 2—a
comprehensive user's manual.
HF5548.4.D22B43 1985   001.64′25   84-23959
ISBN 0-8306-0884-2
ISBN 0-8306-1884-8 (pbk.)

Cover photograph by the Ziegler Photography Studio of Waynesboro, PA.

Contents

dBASE II®
A Comprehensive User's Manual

Introduction

dBASE-II is the name of a software package marketed by Ashton Tate, Inc., and is a powerful development tool for microcomputer business applications. If you utilize a microcomputer for personal or business needs but have never had the pleasure of working with dBASE-II, or if attempts at working with dBASE-II through the technical manual have proven frustrating, then the solution to both situations is contained in this book.

"dBASE-II—A Comprehensive User's Manual" discusses version 2.41, dated February 1, 1984, and has been written for the person who wants to get started *overnight* on serious development of business applications without going through the hassle and frustration of reading the technical manual on dBASE-II. You begin with the study of some fundamental computer concepts, including a general discussion on data-bases, before beginning your study of dBASE-II. Within the dBASE environment, you will learn how to create a data-base, edit/modify the data-base so as to guarantee the integrity of both data and structure, sort/index the data to rearrange it for reporting, pull off reports from the data, and write your own computer programs in dBASE to increase your power and flexibility with dBASE-II.

Obviously, no attempt has been made at any time to replace the manual. The full use of this book will take you a very long way towards effectively utilizing this powerful software, but the most complete repertory of commands is still the dBASE-II technical manual. The study of this book will guarantee your ability to understand, without further external assistance, any specific commands from the manual not explicitly covered here.

As each command is discussed, several "What-If" types of possibilities are explored for that command, so that you are not left in any doubt about multiple choices of action available, or their outcomes. Specific instructions are covered in one area of the book so you will not have to search through the whole book for answers. The index will direct you to the explanation for the various commands.

Literally zero data processing knowledge is presumed, and the approach taken has been that of guiding a novice through the paces of running and effectively utilizing dBASE-II. To that extent, the book has been formatted in three sections. Section 1 discusses some fundamental computer concepts and data-base concepts. Section 2 starts off with the study of dBASE-II Basic Features, and you will learn how to create, edit, modify, sort, index and report from any data-base. Section 3 is the Advanced Features section. In this section, you learn to write your own programs in dBASE-II, starting with the simplest of programs and working your way up to a high degree of programming sophistication.

The appendices contain the report generation program and all of the menu programs. They have been provided for your use without all the comments and explanations that were supplied in the text.

If you feel that you already know some dBASE-II, then follow through the table of contents down to the logical point you wish to pick up from. However, reading all the preliminary material will virtually guarantee even the experienced dBASE-II user of absorbing additional, useful information on this subject.

Part 1
Fundamentals

1. Data Processing Fundamentals

I n this chapter, I will introduce some definitions, explain some procedures, and answer some questions. If you are generally familiar with microcomputers and if you already use dBASE-II, you may prefer to skip all preliminary information and scan the table of contents for specific topics of interest.

Data Processing. *Data processing* is the systematic *collecting, analyzing, summarizing* and *reporting* of data. The function of data collection is, by far, the costliest of these four functions, and the most time-consuming, since it requires substantial human input into the process. Subsequent functions, of course, are purely mechanized by way of the computer.

Computer Program. A *computer program* is nothing more than a series of instructions to a computer. These instructions are, for the most part, *sequential* in nature. If you can manage to write a few instructions, in any computer language, and if you can manage to store these instructions in a module on an external device (say, a floppy diskette), then you have created a computer program. Computer programs can range from simple, to supersophisticated, depending on the output requirements of the program.

Hardware. The term *hardware* refers to the physical computer itself. Anything you can see and touch, the electronics of the machine, the various peripheral devices such as CRT (screen), keyboard, disk-drives, printer, and modem are all encompassed in the term hardware.

Software. *Software* refers to the computer program or programs that control a computer system at any point in time. The microcomputer usually runs only one program at a time, but in the case of main-frame computers, several hundred program modules could be executing simultaneously.

3

CPU. The basis of any computer system is the piece of hardware known as the *central processing unit* (CPU). This piece of hardware contains all the electronic circuitry required to perform the functions of *arithmetic, logic,* and *control.* It is the brains of the microcomputer system.

At any point in time, the CPU performs one of the following three functions:

1. It *obtains* the *next sequential instruction.*
2. It *interprets* that instruction.
3. It *executes* that instruction.

The cycle repeats, beginning again at step 1, for each instruction.

Memory. Another piece of hardware in a computer system is that known as the *main memory structure* of the system. For now, it is useful to visualize memory as being comprised of individual cells, like post office boxes, with each box being capable of containing one character.

The term *character* refers to a digit (0 through 9), a letter (a through z, or A through Z) or a special character (such as the @ # $ % & *, etc). The CPU has direct access to any memory-cell at random, and hence the main-memory structure is known as *Random(ly) Access(ible) Memory* or *RAM.* Since the CPU goes through life obtaining, interpreting and executing instructions, it stands to reason that the computer system must have a way of providing these instructions to the CPU. This is the function of main memory. In the case of a microcomputer system, the entire program that is currently executing needs to be in main memory, so that the program instructions can be accessed by the CPU. Also, main memory contains that portion of the data that the program is currently working on.

Peripherals. Surrounding the CPU and RAM are the external devices for permitting information to flow into and out of the computer system. The *keyboard* is the basic input device for placing information directly into a reserved area of memory. The *screen* is the basic output device for visual display of a reserved area of memory. The *disk drives* are used for permitting access to floppy diskettes on which information can be magnetically stored, or from which information can be retrieved. The *printer,* of course, is the basic output device for hard-copy displays.

Characters. If you want to store your name in a computer system, you will have to provide the system with the letters comprising your name. These are the individual *characters* of your name.

Suppose you also want to store your address in the computer system. You will have to supply to the system all the individual characters (letters and numbers) comprising your full address. So also, for your employee number, or organization, or salary, or any other *piece of information* you want to maintain for yourself.

Field. Each piece of information so created through the use of characters is called a *field* of information. Thus, you may have created your name-field, your organization-field, and your salary-field with the use of the appropriate characters.

Record. Now, if you have stored all the information you may want about yourself, in the form of fields of information, you have managed to create one *record* of information, about yourself.

File. As you may have guessed, if you can do the same for some of your colleagues working in the same department, you will have managed to create a *file* of information comprising several records of information.

These last four definitions can be summarized as follows:

A *file* is made up of individual records of information.
A *record* is made up of individual fields of information.
A *field* is made up of individual characters of information.
A *character* is any number, letter, or special character.

2. Operating System Fundamentals

An operating system is a collection of program modules that provide, among other things, an interface between an executing program's logical requests for input/output operations, and the physical aspects of carrying out the input or output request.

For example, your program has started execution, and at some point in time, it issues a logical read type of request. The operating system's module takes over, since it has to figure out where on the face of the disk the next block of data is located. Having obtained that information, it has to complete the task of loading that block into computer memory and then hand control back to your program.

Your program continues churning away, until it provides a request to write out to disk. Once again, the operating system takes over. It has to figure out where on the face of the disk there is space for the next block of information to be stored, and having figured that out, it has to complete the output operation and write the block out from memory to disk, and hand control back to your program.

Each time your program requests any kind of input or output operation to be performed, the modules of the operating system take over, and perform that task. This is how the operating system *interfaces* between your program's logical input/output requests and the physical aspects of carrying out the input or output request. Apart from providing this area of commonality for input/output for all programs, the operating system also handles disk-file maintenance and access procedures, and the physical loading and execution of programs. This, of course, is a very simplified explanation of some of the workings of an operating system, and depending on the computer system you are using, the operating system for that computer could be anything from basic to super complex.

Several operating systems for microcomputers are available with names such as CP/M, CP/M-86, PC-DOS, MSDOS, TRSDOS, Concurrent CP/M, CDOS, CROMIX, etc.

Since operating-system interfacing is required, you will first have to load the operating system into memory, before executing any other program. The process of loading the operating system into memory is also known as *booting* the system.

To load your computer system's operating system into memory usually requires a very simple task. The exact mechanics of the load process may differ from the explanation provided here, and if the process outlined here does not do the job for you, please consult your manual for the exact process of loading your particular operating system. The description here pertains to the Xerox 820-II computer hardware, and to the CP/M operating system.

When you first purchased your computer system, apart from the hardware that you received, you will have also received a floppy disk containing the operating system for your computer. That disk is referred to as the *systems disk*.

The systems disk should be inserted into the drive marked as the A:drive. (If you are not sure on how to load a floppy into a drive, again, consult your manual). Presuming you have correctly inserted a floppy containing the operating system into the A:drive, type in the letter A, or the letter L, and press the key on your keyboard that says enter or return, to start the process of loading. The loading takes only about a couple of seconds, at the end of which you should see the A >symbol on the screen.

> **Note:** If you get a load error type of message, either your floppy was not placed in correctly, or you forgot to close the drive latch, or the floppy does not contain an image of the operating system. Check out all possibilities!

When the A> appears on the screen, the operating system is asking you something to the effect, "Now what?" and is waiting for you to enter the name of the next program to be executed.

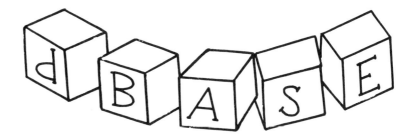

3. dBASE-II
Fundamentals

d BASE-II is the name of a software package, marketed by Ashton Tate, Inc., of
Culver City, California, and it is a very powerful tool for the development of microcomputer business applications. dBASE-II is a data manager! It is a piece of software that lets the user have full freedom in the conceptualization and creation of databases for all type of business applications. Since business depends on timely information dissemination, the value of a powerful utility for data-base generation, maintenance and query cannot be overstated.

dBASE-II can be executed on a variety of microcomputers under any one of the popular operating systems mentioned earlier. If you are inclined to use dBASE-II for your business needs, but are unsure of the compatibility of your computer system with dBASE, your dealer should be able to help you out.

WHAT IS A DATA-BASE?

A *data-base* is a central repository of related information. To translate this phrase very simply, a *data-base* is a physical grouping together of a collection of individual, but related, bits and pieces of information.

As an example, if you want to maintain information about each and every individual employed by you in your organization, you will need to create a *base of data* about all your employees, and this base will subsequently provide you with immediate access to the type of information you are seeking. Data-bases can be, and are being, maintained for every subject from astronomy to zoology. Computers, on account of their speed and accuracy, are the information processors, the physical means, of creating, and subsequently accessing, these data-bases.

WHO NEEDS THIS BOOK?

dBASE-II is a data manager. Anyone who has the need to create and maintain data needs to learn a package such as dBASE.

This book has been written for the person who wants to use dBASE-II for creating and maintaining and querying commercial data-bases (commercial, as opposed to scientific). If you own or use a microcomputer for personal or business applications but have found the dBASE manual too technical in its approach and too cryptic in its format, the study of this book will prove highly rewarding. Every software package needs some time spent in its study, and dBASE is no exception. This book will start you off with step 1, and guide you through a very logical path to a rather high level of dBASE sophistication. Experienced dBASE-II users also stand to gain much valuable information from this book.

WHICH VERSION IS DISCUSSED?

I will be discussing version 2.41, which is the latest release of the software (February 1, 1984). There is even a dBASE-III (written specially for the IBM-PC type 16-bit microcomputers). In the dynamic environment of software development, it is quite possible that further releases of dBASE-II will be announced before this book is available in print. However, just as one does not rush out to buy a new car every time a new model is announced, so does one not rush out to pick up every new release of a software package. Ashton-Tate has guaranteed that these releases will all be upward compatible, and so whatever you learn for the dBASE-II 2.41 version will hold good for the later versions.

> **Note:** dBASE-III is rather different from dBASE-II, and the upward compatibility references the versions within the dBASE-II and the dBASE-III series.

RELATIONAL DATA-BASE

dBASE-II is defined as a *relational data-base manager.* It will help you create and maintain relational data-bases. A *relational data-base* is one in which the data is arranged in the form of a *matrix,* with the rows of the matrix forming each individual record in the data-base, and the columns of the matrix forming the individual fields of information, across all records. An example of the structure of such a data-base follows:

	field-1	field-2	field-3	field-4	field-5
	(emp:num)	(emp:name)	(org)	(town)	(yr/hire)
record-1	xxxxx	xxxxx	xxxxx	xxxxx	xxxxx
record-2	xxxxx	xxxxx	xxxxx	xxxxx	xxxxx
record-3	xxxxx	xxxxx	xxxxx	xxxxx	xxxxx
record-4	xxxxx	xxxxx	xxxxx	xxxxx	xxxxx

The fields of information can, of course, be just about any field conceptualized by the user of dBASE. The (emp:num), (emp:name), etc., fields have been provided just as an example.

Through the use of dBASE-II, one can provide a relationship between more than one relational data-base such as the one shown above. You can, for example, access two or more data-bases to create a new one, and for the structure of the new data-base, you can specify any combination of fields from the input data-bases. You can even build entirely new fields, using the data from the input data-bases. dBASE, therefore, is a management system designed to create, maintain and query relational data-bases.

A WORD ON DOCUMENTATION

Let us take a moment here to emphasize that you must be prepared to maintain good documentation if you hope to work well with dBASE. The reason is that for every one data-base you create under control of dBASE, several supporting files will subsequently have to be produced. For example, you have a good, clean data-base, and now you are ready to start pulling off reports from this data-base. Well, before you can pull off any reports, your data-base will have to be either *physically sorted* or *logically indexed* to provide the proper *sequencing* of records for the report, and so you will have to develop either a *sorted file* or a *logical index* for your Master data-base. This can build up to quite a few files or indexes, especially if you want several reports, each requiring its own sequencing of records. Also, each type of *report format* required by you means the production of that specific format in the form of a *report format file,* and once again we have the possibility of several format files connected with one Master data-base. As you can appreciate, you will find yourself creating many different types of files in support of just one data-base, and you need to have a good method of documentation, naming, and keeping track of the various files you create. Obviously, this effect drastically multiplies, for each additional data-base you create.

STARTING UP WITH dBASE-II

To get started properly with dBASE-II requires three things: installing, copying, and loading. This chapter carefully explains each procedure for my computer system. Other computers may deviate slightly from this procedure but this dialogue should get you started. Consult the manual that came with your computer if you do not get the desired results.

Installation

Installation refers to the saving of certain parameters within the dBASE profile so that, during execution, the dBASE software can react with your computer hardware in an expected manner. Installation must be done before you can start using dBASE on your hardware.

As you can imagine, when you invoke the INSTALL program, the program will ask you a few questions about the kind of hardware you are working with, and a few other questions besides, after which it will give you an option of saving the parameters generated for your version of dBASE-II. The INSTALL program is found on your dBASE software disk. Let us go through an installation procedure. We will be looking at the INSTALL program, version 3.5B. If you find you have a different version, the description provided here may vary slightly, but for the most part this discussion will hold good.

At this point in time, you must have booted the system. Place your dBASE disk in the A:drive, and type INSTALL.

A>INSTALL
(Press "enter"/"return")

Now dBASE starts asking you some questions, to which you are to provide answers.

Are full screen operations wanted (Y/N)?

Hopefully, your system can support full-screen operations, (if unsure, check your manual), and the answer should be Y.

Select the terminal type.

The screen in front of you is not the full list of terminal types, and if you enter the X key, the second of the two screens shows you the rest of the terminal types supported by dBASE. Simply enter the appropriate letter to refer to your terminal type. If your terminal type is not listed in the two screens, you will have to define the individual characteristics of your terminal, using the appropriate option. Here, too, you will need to consult your computer system handbook, for full details of the attributes you will be entering.

Change macro, date, etc?

Type in Y.

Enter a character . . . . . . to designate . . . macro.

Press "enter"/"return".
This default will now mean that the & character will be used for macro definition. The term *macro* is explained fully in Chapter 10.

Error checking dialog?

This is important to understand. If you said yes, then later, during execution of any dBASE command, if you make an error in a command line, dBASE goes off into a small dialogue with you, asking you if you want to make corrections to whatever is wrong in the command line. If you respond Y to this question, then dBASE asks you what it is you want to change, and having obtained that, asks you what it is you want to change it to. The net effect is that you can make changes to a command line without having to retype the entire command.

However, the dialogue itself takes up a few seconds of time, and if you are a good typist, you would probably take less time retyping the entire command than going through the dialogue process to effect a change in a parameter in the command. This is particularly true if you had more than one error in the same command. The choice, of course, is entirely yours. I always opt for the nondialogue mode of operation.

Enter operating system choice.

Select the appropriate letter for CP/M, etc., depending on the operating system for your computer.

Select drive name for dBASE "overlay" and "help" files. . . .

Press "enter"/"return". This implies that you have now taken the default drive, from which dBASE is loaded, as the drive from which the "overlay" and "help" modules should also be loaded. In general, all dBASE software should be kept on one physical diskette, and all your data files on a physically separate disk. This point is also discussed at a later stage.

Change date format from mm/dd/yy to dd/mm/yy?

Usually, the response is N.

Change screen entry field-delimiters . . .?

Enter N, for no. This implies that you have selected the colon character as the default character to show the start and end of data fields whenever you have dBASE perform full-screen data-entry/edit type of operations. In place of the colon, you may opt for the [ ] pair of characters, or the < > pair of characters to specify the start and end of the data fields.

Now all you have to do is to type in a Y to save the control parameters you have selected. You have now installed dBASE to operate in your computer-system environment.

Making a Backup Copy

Remove the dBASE disk from the A:drive. Load the systems disk again from the A:drive. Now, apart from the operating system, your systems disk also contains other *utility* modules, which can be used, for example, to initialize (format) diskettes before usage, or create an image of your operating system on another disk, or make a complete backup copy of one disk to another, etc.

Your operating system is, of course, loaded into memory. You may now go about executing any program. Perhaps the first thing you want to do is to make a complete backup copy of your installed dBASE disk to protect yourself against accidental destruction of the dBASE Master disk.

If the following commands do not work for your particular system, consult your manual for the exact process of copying a disk. This copy-process relates to the Xerox 820-II computer system, running under CP/M. At the A> type in the COPY command.

A>COPY

Now press the "enter"/"return" key.

If the COPY command exists, the system will load the program, and hand control over to it, at which point the copy command will provide you with further instructions. If no further instructions appear on the screen, you will again have to consult your system manual for further action on your part.

For the most part, the instructions will tell you to place the Master disk (the dBASE master) in the A:drive, and a blank, formatted (initialized) disk in the B:drive, and press "enter"/"return" to start the copy process. Follow the instructions to complete the copy process.

If the COPY command does not exist on your disk, the system will inform you of that fact in no uncertain terms, and you should then proceed as follows. Place a blank, formatted (initialized) disk in the B:drive. Then type the following:

A>PIP B:=*.* [0V]

Press "enter"/"return". This command will selectively copy every module from your A:disk to the B:disk, in the same names.

If you can find neither the COPY nor the PIP command available to you, check your system's manual, or give your dealer a call.

Having made a backup copy of our installed dBASE disk, we now put the original away in a safe place, and play around with the copy. In fact, it may not hurt to make a second copy, and use one version of the copy as the *original*. That way, you don't have to touch the real original anymore.

Loading

The dBASE software should be on the same logical drive from which your operating system was loaded into memory. Presuming you have loaded the operating system into memory, now type in "dBASE", to load the software.

A>DBASE

Press "enter"/"return".

Date Check

In the case of 8-bit processors, dBASE will now ask you to enter today's date as follows:

ENTER TODAYS DATE OR RETURN FOR NONE
(MM/DD/YY) :

If you do make an entry for the date, dBASE will now check the date, and an entry such as 04/35/84 will cause the following song-and-dance routine to be executed:

Thirty days hath September
April, June and November
All the rest have thirty-one
Except February . . .

ENTER TODAYS DATE OR RETURN FOR NONE
(MM/DD/YY) :

14

Having entered a correct date, dBASE will, from now on, make two uses of that date.

1. If you now create a new file, or make any kind of change to an existing file, dBASE will pick up the date as the *date of last update* for that file.

2. If you now pull off any Report, the date will automatically appear on every page of the report, below the page number at the top left of the report.

If you wish to bypass entering the date at this time, you may simply press "enter"/"return" to go ahead. In that case, the "date of last update" will be accepted as 00/00/00, and the report outputs will show a blank where the date would have been.

Regardless of whether or not you have entered a date, dBASE will go ahead and present a dot on the screen.

> **Note:** In the case of 16-bit processors, dBASE picks up the date from the system clock, and so the loading for dBASE proceeds uninterrupted, until it presents you with a dot on the screen.

Dot Prompt

At the *dot prompt,* you are in pure dBASE, and now dBASE is asking you something to the effect of, "What Next?" At this stage, you may enter one of a number of commands available in the dBASE profile. As soon as the command is executed, dBASE again presents the dot prompt for the next command. Unless otherwise informed, dBASE will always present you with the dot prompt for the next command.

> **Please Note:** Never leave off a dBASE session by just pulling your disk out of the drive and walking away. If you do that, some of the last few records you had changed/created are still in memory, and your file will have lost these few records, which should have been written out to disk. To exit out of dBASE, always provide the QUIT command. This will ensure the integrity of the data-base last in use. Once you QUIT, you will find yourself back at the operating system level, at the A> symbol, at which point you may pull your disk out and walk away.

Help Feature

There will be times when you may forget the format of a specific command in dBASE-II and would like a quick reference to the manual. dBASE provides an on-line HELP feature, whereby at the dot prompt, you may type in "HELP XXXXX" (where XXXXX is a dBASE command). You will then be provided a brief description of the command, and an example of its use, on the screen.

GENERAL EXPLANATIONS AND CONVENTIONS

Before you get started on your study of dBASE, please note a few lines of explanation regarding syntax and other matters important to your clear understanding of some items provided in this book.

Syntax

At several places, we have provided the syntax of some dBASE command, an example of which could be as follows:

.COPY TO   <file>   [FOR <condition>]   . . . . <cr>

The word <file> implies that the name of a file (or date-base) must be provided in place of <file>. Without this entry, you will have committed a syntax error.

The phrase [FOR <condition>] specifies that the entire phrase is optional. Any entry in *square brackets* is an optional entry. Note, however, that within the optional entry, there is an entry like <condition>. This implies that *if* the FOR statement is used, there must be a condition provided with the FOR clause.

> **Note:** In dBASE-II, any command and/or any parameter of any command can be reduced to the first four characters. You do not have to type out the whole word. Also, you can use any combination of upper/lowercase, during entry of the command. For example, you may specify .MODIFY STRUCTURE or .MODI STRU to get the same effect.

<cr> Symbol

The <cr> symbol at the end of any command line refers to *carriage return,* and it is your cue that you should press the "enter" or "return" key on your keyboard. Obviously, if you do not <cr>, the command will stare right back at you without doing a thing.

Enter or Return

The words "enter" or "return" have been used interchangeably in this book to refer to the <cr> action.

Control Keys

At several places in this book, we have referred to either a dBASE function or a cursor-control movement, using the control-key-with-a-letter combination. For example, to inform you to use a control-key-and-W combination, we have mentioned either Ctrl-W or Ctrl+W, with the + or − sign used interchangeably.

The way this control action is to be performed by you at the keyboard is simple. Press the key marked Ctrl (or Ctl or Control) on your keyboard, and while you keep it depressed, press W!

There are several Ctrl-key-and-letter combinations provided throughout the book, and they all follow the above routine.

Specific Computer

I mentioned before that cursor-control explanations included in the book provide for a Ctrl-and-letter type of input from you. These control-key combinations will work properly regardless of the computer type used for executing dBASE!

However, in this book we have also provided alternative modes of cursor movement for much faster cursor response, and these alternative modes may or may not work for your particular computer hardware! This book was prepared with the XEROX 820-II computer system as the hardware, and these alternatives relate to this hardware.

I recommend that you first try out the regular *arrow keys* for movement of the cursor over the screen. If they work for your hardware, you need search no further. If the arrow keys do not function as you would expect, try the alternatives suggested in the book at appropriate places. If these alternatives work, well and good. Otherwise the Ctrl-key combinations will always work for cursor movement.

Disk-Drive Names

We have presumed that your disk drives have been assigned logical names of A: and B:. If this is not the case, please make mental substitutions as you proceed with the reading of this book, keeping your particular hardware in mind.

Files and Data-Bases

Throughout the course of this book, the terms file and data-base have been used interchangeably as referring to the same physical entity, the central repository of information.

File-Naming Conventions under the CP/M operating system dictate the following:

1. You must provide a primary name for the file from 1 to 8 characters in length.

2. You may or may not provide a secondary name. If you do provide a secondary name, it should be from 1 to 3 characters, and the two names must be separated by a period.

3. You may mention a drive name ahead of the filename as follows: B:filename. This would imply that you are accessing (creating, or reading from, or writing to) a file called <filename> on the B:drive. If no drive name is indicated, the default A:drive is selected.

The following list is an example of valid variations of a filename.

STUDENTS is a valid name for a dBASE data-base.
STUDENTS.DAT is also valid.
STUDENTS.FIL is also valid.
B:STUDENTS is also valid.

If you do not provide a secondary name for a file, then dBASE-II will provide its own default secondary name of .DBF (for dBASE file).

Part 2
Basic Features

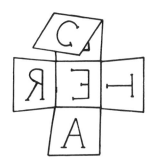

4. Creation Process

You are now ready to create your first data-base using dBASE-II. The process of creation is really the process of translating to dBASE-II the *structure* of the data you wish to create.

Let us say, for example, that you want to keep track of some information pertaining to the employees in your company. In your mind, let us suppose that you perceive that for each employee, you want to keep track of his/her Employee Number, Name, Organization, Year-of-Hire and Salary. Right at this point, you have conceived a *structure* for the information to be maintained for each employee. By deciding upon what fields of information you want to keep track of, you have taken the first step towards formalizing the structure of your proposed data-base.

So for now, let us say that your *conceptual structure* of the data for each employee looks like this:

Employee-Number	Employee-Name	Organization	Yr-of-Hire	Salary

The actual names of the fields in your conceptual structure will be decided later, but for now the above names will suffice. Now, you have to go one step further and let dBASE-II know what the contents of the fields are going to be. After all, the actual names really do not mean too much to dBASE-II, and it needs to be made aware of the kind of data it is dealing with, in each field.

You can define a field as being one of three types. Either the field is defined as character, or the field is defined as numeric, or the field is defined as logical. For now, we will concentrate on the character and numeric representations. The logical field will be covered later. The employee-number field will serve as a good example for realizing the difference between character and numeric.

Suppose you know for a fact that, at a later time, during actual data-entry into this structure, the data going into the employee-number field will only contain digits 0 through 9. That is, there will be no special characters (* $@, etc.) or letters needed in the employee-number fields. Would you now define the employee-number field as numeric?

The answer is No, since the only test needed to determine if the type of the field should be numeric is to ask yourself this question: "Do I foresee myself performing any kind of computation on this field? Will I ever be adding employee numbers together, or will I ever take an employee's record and add his employee number to his social-security number?" Since the answer to these questions is No, you should define the employee-number field as being of the character type.

As another example, take the Year-of-Hire field. Would you define the type of this field as numeric? Again, try and answer the same questions as before. Do you foresee performing any kind of computations against the Year-of-Hire field? The answer here is Yes. You may, perhaps, decide that you want to subtract the Year-of-Hire from to-day's date to obtain an employee's longevity in service. Since there is a possible computation in this case, the Year-of-Hire field should be defined as being numeric.

Other examples are a Social-Security field, which would be of the character type. A Salary field should, of course, be defined as numeric.

At this stage, your conceptual structure looks like this:

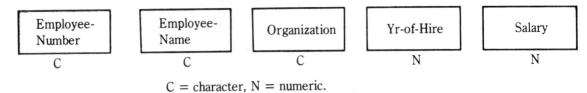

C = character, N = numeric.

One more piece of information needs to be provided before the proposed structure for each record of information is complete. As you may have guessed, you have to tell dBASE-II how large each of these fields is going to be. How many characters of information do you foresee going in as data for each employee number, or each employee name, etc.

Let us say that the employee-number fields will not contain more than 6 characters of data each, the employee-name fields can go up to 15 characters of data, and organization fields up to 3 characters of data. The year-of-hire fields can be provided 4 characters of data (for subsequent data being entered as 19xx).

The salary field needs to be looked at carefully. Suppose you visualize the actual data being entered into the salary fields as being of the form 99999.99 (5 digits before the decimal, and 2 after). This is, of course, adequate for salaries up to $99,999.99 per year, and will serve for the average salary. Now the length of this field should be defined as 8,2 (a total of 8 characters, inclusive of the decimal point, and comprised of 2 decimal places).

As a further clarification of this point, let us introduce a field which will not make any logical sense in the type of data-base we are considering, but has definite applications elsewhere. Let us consider a field like a Debit/Credit type of field, used in financial applications. In order to determine the length of this field, you again have to consider the kind of data that field will actually contain. As an example, suppose the field is to be designed to contain up to 3 digits before the decimal, 2 decimal places, and could possibly have negative values put in during data-entry. That is, you could possibly have a value such as −999.99. The length of this field should be defined as 7,2 [a total of 7 characters]; 3 (before the decimal), 2 (after the decimal), 1 (decimal point) and 1 (for a possible minus sign).

In our example, the formalized structure now looks like this:

Employee-Number	Employee-Name	Organization	Yr-of-Hire 19xx	Salary (5) . (2)
C	C	C	N	N
6	15	3	4	8,2

This, of course, is still our conceptual structure. We have not actually defined anything to dBASE-II yet.

You may define the employee-number field as ENO, if you like, but while this may make a lot of sense to you, it may make no sense at all to someone else picking up after you. So you may decide upon EMPNO. This is more readily comprehensible than ENO for employee number, but to make it precise, you should try something like EMP:NUM.

As another example, for the year-of-hire field, you may try something like YR:OF:HIRE, instead of YRHR. To break up the words for ease of reading, the *colon* is accepted. The *space* character, if used, will result in an error. The only rule to be satisfied is that the total length of the name itself cannot be more than 10 characters, inclusive of the colons. Do not confuse the length of the field-name with the length of the field itself. For example, the field called EMP:NAME has been defined as being 15 characters long, but the word EMP:NAME itself is only 8 characters long.

CREATING A DATA-BASE STRUCTURE

We shall now look at the actual mechanics of defining the structure of our data-base to dBASE-II. Having entered dBASE-II, the dot prompt is the signal that dBASE is waiting for you to enter a command. The command for creation of a structure is *CREATE*.

> **Caution:** Please be aware of what is perhaps the biggest drawback in the verson 2.41. If you tell dBASE-II to create a file, and by error you provide the filename of an existing file on the same disk, then dBASE-II will delete the existing file, both structure and data! No errors or warning messages will be issued!
>
> To ensure, therefore, that you don't make any kind of typos that would cause you to lose data, you may, perhaps, want to make a quick check of the directory listing of a disk to see the names of the files currently existing on that disk.

Directory Listings

At the dBASE-II dot prompt, you may enter a command as follows:

```
.LIST FILES              <cr>    or
.LIST FILES ON B         <cr>    or
.LIST FILES ON B:        <cr>
```

The first option will produce a listing on the screen of all the files on the A:drive (the logged-in drive) that have a secondary name of .DBF (for dBASE-formatted file). The second and third options, oif course, will provide a listing of all the .DBF files from the disk in the B:drive.

If you wanted to see all the files on any drive, regardless of the names of the files, enter the following commands:

```
.LIST FILES LIKE *.*                    <cr>   or
.LIST FILES LIKE *.*        ON  B       <cr>   or
.LIST FILES LIKE *.*        ON  B:      <cr>
```

This will produce the required listings from the drive mentioned in your command. If you wanted to see a particular group of files for example, all the index files, you may use:

```
.LIST FILES LIKE  *.NDX                  <cr>  or
.LIST FILES LIKE  *.NDX       ON  B      <cr>  or
.LIST FILES LIKE  *.NDX       ON  B:     <cr>
```

Here, the *.NDX is, of course, the *mask*, defining the type of files you want listed.

In case some clean-up is required, the following commands are useful. To delete .DBF files, use the following:

```
.DELETE FILE   ABC     <cr>
```

This will delete the file called ABC.DBF. To delete non-dBASE files, use the appropriate secondary filename.

```
.DELETE FILE   XXXXX.YYY      <cr>
```

This will delete the appropriately named file. To delete groups of files, for example, all the files ending in .NDX, use the following command:

```
.DELETE FILE ????????.NDX      <cr>
```

This will delete all files whose secondary name is NDX, regardless of the primary filename.

Note: You can only delete files with *status-codes* of read/write. Files with status-codes *read/only* cannot be deleted!

If it is necessary to rename files, use this command.

.RENAME   ABC   TO   XYZ   <cr>

This will rename the dBASE file called ABC(.DBF) to XYZ(.DBF). As before, you can rename only those files with status codes of read/write.

If you specify the secondary filename in the RENAME command, the file will be renamed accordingly.

.RENAME ABC.NDX TO PQR.NDX   <cr>

This will rename the file exactly as you had specified.

Software and Data Handling

You would be well-advised to keep to the following procedure. Always maintain your software and your data on separate disks. That is, do not get into the habit of creating your data on the same disk that contains the dBASE software, if for no other reason than that you may need the extra space on your disk, if you have several applications under dBASE. This recommendation is, of course, based also on logical and esthetic reasoning which dictates that software and data should be distinct and separate, which is how I always proceeded.

An argument could also be made to the effect that if one has software and data on the same disk, one only needs to carry one disk instead of two. To which, again, a counter can be made that the space requirement for two disks is virtually the same as that for one disk. Besides, if you are going to be at all serious about dBASE, you will find yourself requiring many more than just a couple of disks, and your dBASE software disk should be kept free of all data.

You may, of course, proceed as you wish, and use the appropriate version of the LIST command to find out what dBASE-files you already have on your data disk.

.LIST FILES   <cr>   or
.LIST FILES ON B   <cr>   or
.LIST FILES ON B: <cr>

This will produce a listing of all the .DBF files, from the appropriate disk.

> **Note:** If you do decide to keep to the recommendation of separating your software and your data, there is a useful feature in dBASE, which, if invoked, lets you log-on to the B:drive for data, but the dBASE software modules will continue to be accessed from the A: drive as and when needed. The following command invokes this feature:

.SET DEFAULT TO B   <cr>   or
.SET DEFAULT TO B: <cr>

From now on, you can refer to all your data files (and other files we shall be looking at, later on: on the B:drive without having to key in B: for each reference. The dBASE software, itself, will continue to operate from the A:drive.

Setting the Fields

Having decided on a filename, and having ensured that this filename for the proposed structure does not currently exist on the disk on which you wish to create that structure, you may now enter:

```
.CREATE                        <cr>        or
.CREATE <filename>             <cr>
```

If you do not enter a filename in the command line itself, then dBASE will prompt you for it in an intermediate step. Also, if you have not .SET DEFAULT TO B: then you will have to mention B:<filename>, if you want to create your file on the B:drive. This would be a good time for you to review the file-naming conventions under CP/M in Chapter 3 if you are not sure of how to name files created under control of CP/M.

Suppose we name our proposed file PERSNL. Naturally, after creation of this structure, its actual name in the system will be PERSNL.DBF, since dBASE-II will provide the .DBF secondary name. If you want to create your file on the B: drive, and you have not .SET DEFAULT TO B: specify B:<filename>. For now, I will assume that you have .SET DEFAULT TO B: so that all files (dBASE files and other supporting files) will be created and accessed on the B:drive without the necessity of mentioning B: for each reference.

```
.CREATE PERSNL                 <cr>
```

The effect of this action is that dBASE wants you to specify the structure of your proposed file in the following format:

field-name, type, width, decimals.

Having asked to CREATE a file, you may change your mind on this creation by simply hitting <cr> on the first blank line of the structure. dBASE-II will then delete this file.

Let us enter the fields of information for our proposed structure as follows. Please go along with the creation of the file called PERSNL(.DBF) as I explain it in this book. I will be using it throughout for examples.

field-name, type, width, decimals

001	EMP:NUM,C,6	<cr>
002	EMP:NAME,C,15	<cr>
003	TOWN,C,12	<cr>
004	ORG,C,3	<cr>
005	YR:OF:HIRE,N,4	<cr>
006	SALARY,N,8,2	<cr>
007	DUMMY,C,1	<cr>
008		<cr>

Observations on CREATE

1. You can ask to define a file either on the A:drive or on the B:drive. See the preceding paragraphs for a review of this option.

2. If you ask to CREATE <filename> and <filename> already exists on the same disk as your intended file, the existing file is completely zapped out! No errors or warning messges are issued.

3. You can change your mind on the creation, by <cr> on the first blank line, when dBASE-II asks you for the structure.

4. Having defined this structure, let us say that you decide on another field you would like to see entered between the ORG and YR:OF:HIRE field; that is, you would like to make a minor change to the above structure. Well, that's too bad! Please make a note of this: There is no edit capability, while you are defining a structure! You have to make either a physical or a mental note of the changes you want and finish defining the structure. Then, as a separate step, you can MODIFY the structure later on. But while you are defining a structure, the only editing that can be done is while the cursor is still on the same line. You can use the backspace key to erase your current entry, and retype the information for that field.

5. If you attempt to enter the same field on two different lines (in effect trying to create the same field again), dBASE-II prompts with the "Bad Name Field" error message.

6. The maximum length allowed for character fields is 254.

7. The maximum length for numeric fields is 10 digits of accuracy. You may ask for a numeric field larger than 10 digits, (up to 254, if you like!) but as soon as 10 digits of data have been (subsequently) entered in that field (regardless of whether these digits are before and/or after a decimal point, or regardless of the minus sign, if any), any more digits to the right are rounded off to zero. Hence the term 10 digits of accuracy.

8. You can define a maximum of 32-fields, for the structure of any one data-base. (For the advanced programmer who is well versed with programming in dBASE, I have provided in the last chapter the means for shattering this 32-field limitation myth. You can define any number of fields you want, if you know what you are doing. The novice, of course, will have to live with this limitation of 32-fields, for now.)

9. Within that limitation of 32-fields of data, you can only define a maximum of 1000 characters of data. For example, we have defined, in the 7 previous fields, a total of 49 characters of data. (6 for emp:num + 15 for emp:name + 12 for town + 3 for org + 4 for yr:of:hire + 8 for salary + 1 for dummy).

10. As soon as you have created 32-fields of information for a structure, dBASE-II will wrap up the definition process for you. Also, dBASE-II will not let you define more than 1000 characters in the structure. It does not automatically wrap up the structure if you have created less than 32-fields. You have to <cr> on a blank line.

11. When you have entered all the fields of the structure, include one more *dummy* field of either character or numeric type with a length 1. The reasons for this dummy field will be outlined later. This field will play a major role in your data-base. Obviously, this dummy field is possible only if you have defined a maximum of 31 real fields in the structure, since the dBASE limit is 32-fields in any data-base structure.

12. When you want to wrap up the definition process, hit <cr> on a blank line.

Let us wrap up the definition of our structure for now by <cr>. dBASE-II will ask you if you want to enter data into this structure at this point. Usually the answer should be N, for no, since you would normally want to review your structure first and make any changes to it before you actually go ahead and input data into it.

Please enter N for no. dBASE now wraps up defining the structure of the PERSNL.DBF file.

The complete sequence of the entries just explained is shown below. (The entries are, of course, a combination of the interaction between you, the user, and dBASE.)

```
. CREATE PERSNL                        <cr>
ENTER RECORD STRUCTURE AS FOLLOWS:

FIELD      NAME,TYPE,WIDTH,DECIMAL PLACES

001        EMP:NUM,C,6                 <cr>
002        EMP:NAME,C,15               <cr>
003        TOWN,C,12                   <cr>
004        ORG,C,3                     <cr>
005        YR:OF:HIRE,N,4              <cr>
006        SALARY,N,8,2                <cr>
007        DUMMY,C,1                   <cr>
008                                    <cr>
INPUT DATA NOW? N
```

Having CREATEd your data-base structure, at this point you may want to review the structure for accuracy before you actually go ahead and put data into it. Also, you will want to keep a hard copy of the structure for purposes of *documentation*.

Displaying and Documenting the Structure

At any time in the use of dBASE commands, if you want to start off the next command using a clean screen, type the following dBASE command:

```
.ERASE              <cr>
```

This will clear the screen and place the dot prompt at the top left of the screen. You may now proceed with another command.

To do any kind of processing on a data-base, you will first have to bring that data-base into USE by dBASE.

```
.USE     PERSNL               <cr>
```

Now to display the structure of this file, type in

```
.DISPLAY STRUCTURE        <cr>     or
.DISP       STRU          <cr>
```

This will bring the structure of the file up on the screen. Recall that any command and/or any parameter of any command can be reduced to the first-four characters.

If the file structure is short enough to fit on one screen without scrolling off the top of the screen, you can obtain a hard copy on the printer by typing Ctrl+HELP, or the appropriate combination of key input for your computer system. (Check your manual, if necessary.) If the file structure is too long to fit on one screen without scrolling off the top, then use the CP/M Ctrl+P option to activate the printer, and "dump out" the structure on the printer. Remember to do a Ctrl+P again, to deactivate the print function at the end of the structure printout.

Logical Fields

I started off our study of dBASE file structures by mentioning that you can define any field as being of the type called character or numeric or logical. I have discussed the character and numeric fields in detail. Now I shall explain what a logical field is.

A *logical field* is one which is of a predefined length, and the length is always 1 character. Suppose in our PERSNL file structure, we wanted to include a code for each employee in the form of a logical field, informing us of his/her exempt/nonexempt status. Somewhere in the structure, we would have included the following line:

```
---------
---------
EXEMPT,L,1
---------
```

I will be including a logical field in our structure later on, but for now you must understand the preliminaries about logical fields. Logical fields have to be defined with the letter L, and are not checked for length, since they have an implied length of only 1 character. In fact, any length supplied by you gets converted to length 1. As you may have guessed, if the implied length is always 1 character, you may even get by without mentioning any length at all. That is, the above line of code in the structure would also have been accepted as follows:

```
EXEMPT,L
```

Subsequent input of data into the logical field is restricted to one of the following 4 letters.

T	(for true)	Y	(for yes)
F	(for false)	N	(for no)

Note, however, that regardless of the Y or N entry into a logical field, the data in a logical field will always be stored as T or F. The Y entry gets converted to T and the N entry is stored as F. So much for the definition of a logical field. Its use will be covered later.

Modifying Structures

Having reviewed the structure of the file you have just created, it is logical for us to take the following stand: If you did want to make some kind of change to the structure of the data-base, now would be the time to do so, before you start putting in data. Perhaps, the type of change you envision entails the insertion of another field between, say, the ORG and YR:OF:HIRE fields, or perhaps you want to change the structure of one of the existing fields, (maybe a name change, or a type change, or a length change), or perhaps you want to delete one of the defined fields from the structure. Regardless of the kind of change you want, as we said before, it would be logical to make changes now. This does not mean that you cannot alter the structure of an existing data-base which contains data records. You can change structures at any time, in any data-base.

To modify the structure of the data-base you have just created, proceed as follows.

> **Caution:** Do not use the following procedure to modify struc-tures of existing data-bases that already have data-records in them, since the modification process, as it stands, destroys all existing data. (It is, after all, illogical to have old data residing under a new structure.) Since our data-base currently has a structure only, and no data, we can proceed with the modification process without any risk of loss. How-ever, *if you did want to modify the structure of an existing data-base that currently had data-records in them, please follow the procedure outlined in the Editing Section under the MODIFY command.*

.USE PERSNL	<cr>	If the file is already in USE, this is redundant.
.MODIFY STRUCTURE	<cr>	or
.MODI STRU	<cr>	

At this point, dBASE prompts you with the following message:

MODIFY ERASES ALL DATA RECORDS . . . PROCEED ? (Y/N)

We will, of course, boldly answer Y since we don't have any data records in our structure.

At this point, dBASE brings up the structure on the screen, in full-screen edit mode. It appears as follows:

	NAME	TYP	LEN	DEC	
FIELD 01	:EMP:NUM	C	006	000	:
FIELD 02	:EMP:NAME	C	015	000	:
FIELD 03	:TOWN	C	012	000	:
FIELD 04	:ORG	C	003	000	:
FIELD 05	:YR:OF:HIRE	N	004	000	:
FIELD 06	:SALARY	N	008	002	:
FIELD 07	:DUMMY	C	001	000	:
FIELD 08	:				:
FIELD 09	:				:

	NAME	TYP LEN DEC
FIELD 10	:	:
FIELD 11	:	:
FIELD 12	:	:
FIELD 13	:	:
FIELD 14	:	:
FIELD 15	:	:
FIELD 16	:	:
FIELD 17	:	:
FIELD 18	:	:
FIELD 19	:	:
FIELD 20	:	:
FIELD 21	:	:
FIELD 22	:	:

The cursor rests on the first character of the first field-name on the screen. One now has only to manipulate the cursor to the various screen positions, and put in the changes that one desires to the structure in view, and then save this new structure.

This is where a bit of complexity sets in, since you now have to learn *cursor controls* and *full-screen edit features* under dBASE. There is an initial learning phase to be gone through, until you get the feel of these cursor controls under your belt. It is not too difficult, however, and the advantage is that the cursor controls are identical all across the board. That is, regardless of the phase of operation you may be in (EDIT, BROWSE, INSERT, APPEND or MODIFY), these cursor-controls are the same. In order to get the maximum out of dBASE that the software has to offer, the sooner you get to learn these cursor controls, the better off you will be. Now is as good a time as any.

Cursor Controls

Please ensure that you try out all the cursor controls as they are being explained in the following few paragraphs, so that you can get to feel comfortable with the options.

Cursor Down. To get the cursor to run vertically down the various fields, use the *"return"* key (which will be designated as <cr>), or the *Ctrl-F* option. Notice that you only have to keep the <cr> key pressed down, and it moves the cursor vertically down the column of fields. If the Ctrl-F option is used, you have to hit Ctrl-F each time you want the cursor to move down. If you hold <cr> down too long and it goes beyond the 32nd field in the structure, dBASE will save whatever changes had been made until that point in time and get you out of the MODIFY mode and back to the dot prompt. If you have accidentally gone too far, and are back to the dot prompt, you can always get back in, with a .MODI STRU as before.

Cursor Up. To get the cursor to run vertically up the various fields, use the *Up-Arrow* key, or the *Ctrl-E* combination. Notice that you only have to keep the Up-Arrow key pressed down, and it moves the cursor vertically up the column of fields. If the Ctrl-E option is used, you have to hit Ctrl-E each time you want the cursor to move up. If you press the Up-Arrow key too long, the cursor comes to remain in the first field of the structure.

Cursor Right. Within a field, if you want the cursor to move right, use the *Left-arrow* key. You only have to hold this key down to have the cursor run to the right. You may also use the *Ctrl-D* combination. However, in this case you have to hit Ctrl-D each time you want the cursor to move (to the right).

Cursor Left. Within a field, if you want the cursor to move left, use the *Backspace* key. You only have to hold this key down to have the cursor run to the left. You may also use the *Ctrl-S* combination. However, in this case you have to hit Ctrl-S each time you want the cursor to move (to the left).

Ctrl-G. While in the middle of the field, each time you hit Ctrl-G, you will delete the character under the cursor (the cursor does not move), and the other characters to the right of the cursor will drop down by one position.

Ctrl-Y. While in the middle of a field, if you hit Ctrl-Y, that will erase the field to blanks, from the position of the cursor up to the end of the field, (an end-of-field effect), and the cursor will jump back to the beginning of the field. Hence, if you are in the middle of a field and you want to erase the contents of the entire field, entering Ctrl-Y twice will do the trick.

Ctrl-V. This pertains to the insert function. Suppose one of the fields was called EMP:NM instead of EMP:NUM as the intention had been. We now want to insert the U ahead of the M (we could, of course, just retype the whole name again, but the idea is to show the insert function here). Bring the cursor up to the M using the previous features described, and enter Ctrl-V. Notice the word INSERT appear at the top of the screen. This means that you are in the insert mode, as opposed to being in the over-write mode of operaton (which, of course, is always the default). Now key in the letter U and you will see it inserted into the field. The other characters are moved over to the right to make way for this character to come in. This movement of the other characters does not affect the field-definition as long as characters are not lost at the end of the field. If you insert too many characters into a field, characters could start spilling out of the field into never-never land. Try this out, to see the whole effect of the insert function. To get out of the insert mode, use Ctrl-V again. Ctrl-V is a toggle switch to get you in and out of the insert mode.

Rubout or Delete. The use of this key once will cause the cursor and the character under the cursor to move one character position to the left, overlaying, and thus deleting, that character. All other characters to the right of the cursor also move accordingly. Holding this key down will create a multiple, ripple effect, with the cursor running to the left, deleting characters in its path.

These controls are the basic cursor controls as they apply across the board, regardless of the function you may be performing.

There are other Ctrl-key combinations that perform specialized tasks, depending on the mode of operation you may be in. For example, we are currently in the MODIFY mode of operation. So a couple of more options follows.

Ctrl-T. To delete an entire line out of the structure, move the cursor anywhere in that line, and enter a Ctrl-T combination. That line entry is killed and the rest of the entries below that one move up one line to close the gap. In this way you may remove any number of entire fields out of the structure of the file.

Ctrl-N. To insert an entire new field in the existing structure, take the cursor anywhere in the field that is currently in the position where you want to define the new field in the structure. For example, if you want a new field inserted between the ORG and YR:OF:HIRE fields, take the cursor anywhere into the YR:OF:HIRE field, and hit Ctrl-N. A blank line opens up, the rest of the structure drops down one line, and you may now enter the name, type, width, and decimal places to complete the definition of the new field.

> **Note:** You do not have to stick to the column alignment when enterng the new field definition. However, commas cannot be used (as was possible during the original creation of the structure) to separate the various parameters of type, width, etc. Also, leading zeros for decimal places are not necessary.

If you use Ctrl-N to open up a space for a new field, but make no entry in it, it is as if you had not opened up the space at all. If you have, say, 10 fields in a structure, and you now move the cursor to the field-14 position (in the Modify Structure mode) and enter a new field there, the effect is the same as entering the new field in the field-ll position.

If you need to scroll back and forth in the structure (in the case of a long structure), use Ctrl-C (forward) and Ctrl-R (backward).

Using the combination of cursor controls you have seen so far, modify the structure of our file called PERSNL.DBF to include a new field called: EXEMPT,L after the ORG field. This field will be used to keep track of the employee's 'Exempt/Nonexempt' status. Note that this is a logical field, and has an implied length of 1 character.

When you are through modifying the structure, you now have one of two choices. Either you want to go ahead and have dBASE save this new modified structure, or you decide that you don't, after all, want this new structure, and that you could live with the previously created structure.

To highlight these two choices, two more across the board controls need to be introduced.

Ctrl-W. All across the board, Ctrl-W is how you can save whatever it was that you were currently doing, in dBASE.

Ctrl-Q. All across the board, Ctrl-Q is how you can negate whatever it was that you were currently doing, in dBASE.

Enter a Ctrl-W to save the new structure of our file. A Ctrl-Q, of course, would keep the original structure intact. At the end of the save process, dBASE comes up again with the dot prompt. To ensure that the change has taken place, and again, for the sake of documentation, use the following command and take a screen image, or use Ctrl-P for printing out the new structure on paper.

```
.DISP    STRU             <cr>
```

STRUCTURE FOR FILE:		A:PERSNL		.DBF
NUMBER OF RECORDS:		00000		
DATE OF LAST UPDATE:		00/00/00		
PRIMARY USE DATABASE				
FLD	NAME	TYPE	WIDTH	DEC
001	EMP:NUM	C	006	

FLD	NAME	TYPE	WIDTH	DEC
002	EMP:NAME	C	015	
003	TOWN	C	012	
004	ORG	C	003	
005	EXEMPT	L	001	
006	YR:OF:HIRE	N	004	
007	SALARY	N	008	002
008	DUMMY	C	001	
** TOTAL **				0051

At this point in your study of dBASE, you should be able to CREATE a structure, and, if need be, MODIFY the structure to come up with the exact data-base format you want.

The Extra Field

Look at the structure of the file again. Is there anything you see about the structure that does not quite click? (Try to find the discrepancy, before you read ahead.)

If you notice, dBASE informs you that your record structure is a total of 51 characters long, but you can swear that the individual field-lengths only add up to 50. That is, dBASE says that the length of all subsequent data records entered into this structure will be 51 characters, but you know you have only defined 50 characters in the structure. Why is dBASE obviously giving you an extra character position?

Suppose you had entered some data records into the structure, and then decided at some point in time that you did not like the looks of a particular record. You could ask dBASE to DELETE that record. Now, a delete request to dBASE does not end up in your record being physically zapped out right away, but rather in it's being logically deleted, that is, the record is flagged as deleted. dBASE uses an * ahead of the record to flag it as being deleted. Without an extra character position into which to place an *, dBASE would have no other option but to put the * in one of the existing data fields.

This capability of logically deleting records affords the user the luxury of a change of mind on a deleted record, and the user can always ask dBASE to reactivate any/all deleted records. dBASE obliges by simply removing the * from its position ahead of the record.

In summary, then, the extra character position is created by dBASE to handle a possible *delete indicator* (the *), should the need arise to delete/reactivate records. (You may rest assured this need will arise.)

I mentioned before that you can define a maximum of 1000 characters of data for a record structure. This does not include the extra position created by dBASE to handle deleted records. You, as a user, may define a full 100-character structure, as the structure of your data-base. The field to handle the delete indicator is a plus, from dBASE.

APPEND COMMAND

No what you are familiar with the mechanics of creating a structure and modifying it to suit our purpose, we shall proceed with the mechanics of entering data into the structure of our file.

Please read the previous discussion on creating a data-base structure before you go ahead and try the APPEND command. There are several points to be highlighted, before you actually start appending.

The APPEND command is used for entering data into our data-base. One uses this command regardless of whether or not our data-base currently contains data. That is, you can start entering data for the first time with the APPEND command, then continue entering more data on subsequent occasions also with the APPEND command. The new records simply get added on to the end of the existing data records.

```
.USE PERSNL              <cr>      (if not already in USE)
.APPEND                  <cr>
```

This will bring up the blank structure (mask) of the PERSNL file on the screen, as follows:

```
RECORD #      00001
EMP:NUM       :              :
EMP:NAME      :                    :
TOWN          :                :
ORG           :        :
EXEMPT        : :
YR:OF:HIRE    :            :
SALARY        :                :
DUMMY         : :
```

This is merely the *shell* (or *mask*) of the new record. You could now start entering data into it. The field-names are, of course, the names you had provided when you had created the structure. The colons indicate the lengths of the various fields, as defined in the structure. If you recall, in the installation phase of dBASE, we had opted for the colon as the field-delimiter character for depicting data-fields in full-screen operations. The record number at the top indicates which record you could currently enter data into.

Append Common Information

If you want to enter a lot of common information across the records (for example, most of the employees are in the same organization and in the same town, and it would be ridiculous to have to key in 'GSD' and 'ROCHESTER' across 300 records) you can make use of a feature that will help you maintain common information across records. This feature is invoked before you enter the APPEND mode.

```
.USE PERSNL              <cr>
.SET CARRY ON            <cr>
.APPEND                  <cr>
```

Now, instead of the blank structure of the next record coming up on the screen, the mask comes filled in with whatever had been keyed into the one previous record! (For the very first record APPENDed into an empty data-base structure, the mask is always blank.) You can now go through the record, making changes to the data, and you can skip those fields which contain the common, required, information.

Note that if you start off with invalid or false common information, you could end up with a couple of hundred records having to be subsequently edited! Also, you cannot pick and choose the fields on which you want the CARRY ON to function. It's an all-or-nothing proposition.

In either case, with/without the SET CARRY ON feature, we are in full-screen edit mode, and the cursor controls covered earler apply here with one exception. If you use the <cr> key when the cursor is in the first position of the first field, and no key depression has been made in the record, dBASE assumes you are through APPENDing, and gets you out of the APPEND mode. This is true even if you have SET CARRY ON. When this happens, the record currently on the screen is not saved. Records entered previous to this one, of course, will have been saved.

If you use the <cr> key when the cursor is in the first position of the first record, and data had been entered elsewhere in the record, dBASE saves that record and presents the structure of the next record. This is true even if you have SET CARRY ON.

Please read all the notes on the APPEND command, before you start entering the data into the data-base. The record number at the top of the screen tells you which record you are currently working with.

Observations On APPEND

1. This point is very important. When you are entering data into a numeric field, say, the SALARY field, it is imperative that you stick within the limitations of the structure that you yourself had defined for the SALARY field. That is, the decimal point must be allowed to fall (either explicitly or implicitly) where it was defined to fall.

The SALARY field had been defined as SALARY,N,8,2 since the expected salary in that field was presumed to be of the configuration 99999.99 (5 digits before the decimal, and 2 after). A salary amount of 1.23 should be entered just as is, without regard to right justification and when you <cr> to go to the next field, the right justification is automatic, since the decimal point in the data lines-up with the decimal point defined in the structure. A salary entry of 12.34 is fine and so is 123.45, or 12345 (all these entries still fall within your defined format). However, any attempt to insert salary data of the form 123456.7 will result in zero being accepted for the salary field, since you are violating the structure.

As another example of this, say you had defined a debit/credit type of field as follows:

DRCR,N,7,2   (the expected data is of the format −999.99)

Now, entering the following data gives these results:

1.23	is valid.
12.34	is valid.
123.45	is valid.

−123.45   is valid.

1123.45   is valid, since we are still within the length limitations defined in the structure of this field.

−1123.4   is not valid since we would be violating the structure, and zero would be accepted for our effort.

If a numeric field is the last field in the structure of a data-base, and during data-entry you fail to keep within the rules of the structure you defined, then as soon as you have keyed in the data in the (last) numeric field, dBASE takes off and saves the record just keyed in, and presents the shell of the structure for the next data record to be keyed in. This happens too fast for you to realize that you are keying in zero into all those numeric fields, since you are violating the structure. This can prove very frustrating after a long session with the APPEND command when you end up with zero in that numeric field for all records.

This is where the *dummy* entry as the last field in a structure plays its first important role, since if you had a dummy entry after the numeric field, you would have noticed the garbage entry into the numeric field as soon as the cursor left the numeric field to enter the dummy field. Another very important role of the dummy field will be outlined later. As you can appreciate, the dummy entry could save you hours of frustration.

> **Note:** If you attempt to key in character data letters, special characters, etc.) into a numeric field, it locks up the keyboard, and depending on your computer system, may ring a bell at the console.

2. When the cursor gets to the end of any one field, it automatically drops down to the start of the next field.

3. When the cursor is moved beyond the end of the last field, the record is saved, and the mask of the next record is presented for data-entry, on the screen.

4. You can make any number of changes to the data of the current record on the screen, by moving the cursor back and forth across the fields, using the cursor controls discussed earlier.

5. You don't have to get the cursor to the very end of the last field, in order to save a record. You may enter data only into a few chosen fields, if you like, and when you want to save that record, enter a Ctrl-W. This saves the partially-filled-in current record and presents the shell of the next record. If the record structure has more than 23 fields, you will have to Ctrl-W twice. The first Ctrl-W only brings fields 24 through 32 up on the screen (forward scroll). You cannot scroll back.

6. You can only enter a maximum of 65,535 records into the structure of any one data-base. This is, of course, more than sufficient for most practical applications.

7. Once a record has been saved and the blank structure (or filled-in structure, if SET CARRY ON was used) of the next record has been presented to you, it's a little too late to say "Oops!" You cannot make changes to existing records, while in the APPEND mode. You can only make changes to a record being APPENDed while it is still on the screen, in front of you. But once it has been saved, there are other commands to be used, (covered later) if you want to make changes to that record.

8. When you have made the last APPEND for the day, and dBASE has again

placed the blank (or filled-in) structure of the next record on the screen, you may exit out of the APPEND mode in one of several ways:

a. We mentioned before that the use of the <cr> key, when the cursor is on the first position of the first field will get you out of the APPEND mode. This is also true if you were using the SET CARRY ON feature.

b. You can enter a Ctrl-W. While a Ctrl-W is used in dBASE to save what you were doing, if you use the Ctrl-W on a blank structure, since there is nothing to save, dBASE gets you out of the APPEND mode. This is also true if you were using the SET CARRY ON feature.

c. Finally, of course, you can always Ctrl-Q (change your mind) on the next record being presented, and get out of the APPEND mode. This is also true if you were using the SET CARRY ON feature.

9. This brings up the obvious possibility, that you don't have to save the last record being worked on, in order to get out of the APPEND mode. If you had been entering data in a particular record, and you wanted to get out without saving this record, you can always Ctrl-Q to get this option.

10. If the record has many fields in the structure (maximum 32), then it is possible that the entire structure may not be visible on the screen all at once. When you enter the last character of the last field visible on the screen (field #23), the rest of the record structure appears into view. Or, if you want to skip a few fields when entering data, you may use Ctrl-W to scroll forward to bring fields 24 through 32 into view. (You cannot scroll back!)

11. If you are APPENDing with the SET CARRY ON mode active and each successive record structure appears with the information from the one-previous record in it, note that a simple Ctrl-W will not save the new record. That is, if no key depression has been made in the data of the record, dBASE will recognize the record as having only a mask of the information from the previous record, and Ctrl-W will cause an exit out of the APPEND mode. Also, at the end of the append process, do not forget to .SET CARRY OFF, else this mode remains active, regardless of the data-base in use.

Please proceed to enter data records for the structure of the PERSNL.DBF data-base. Use the following data records, since we will be using this data for examples throughout. Note that some of the data has been shown as a mixture of upper and lower case characters. Please enter them exactly as shown. The numbers to the left are the record numbers, which will be automatically provided by dBASE, as you proceed to APPEND the data.

Note also that the logical field called EXEMPT can only accept T, F, Y, and N as input, and that the input will finally rest in the logical field as either T or F only. Employee records of Exempt employees should contain T (true) for the Exempt field. Nonexempt employees should have an F (false) entered in the exempt field.

	EMP: NUM	EMP: NAME	TOWN	ORG	E	YRHR	SALARY
	---	--------	----	---	-	----	------
00001	070707	NINA BHARUCHA	WEBSTER	BSG	T	1980	33000.00

	EMP: NUM	EMP: NAME	TOWN	ORG	E	YRHR	SALARY
	---	--------	----	---	-	----	------
00002	7545AD	PETE JOHNSON	brighton	BSG	T	1976	27590.00
00003	987178	GLORIA PATEL	FAIRPORT	RMG	T	1982	27500.00
00004	232430	MAX LEVENSKY	HENRIETTA	RMG	F	1969	27550.00
00005	0989SD	KIM BRANDT	FAIRPORT	RMG	F	1977	36000.00
00006	AC9090	TIM MONTAL	ROCHESTER	RBG	F	1981	41900.00
00007	08FG09	WILLIAM PATEL	penfield	GSD	F	1971	28900.00
00008	091230	JAMES JAMESON	ROCHESTER	GSD	T	1977	29800.00
00009	438190	MORRIS KATZ	webster	BSG	F	1980	23450.00
00010	087FG0	PAUL BHARUCHA	BRIGHTON	BSG	T	1973	29100.00
00011	00707A	PHIL MARTIN	WEBSTER	RMG	F	1980	31000.00
00012	8745AD	JOHN PETERSON	BRIGHTON	RBG	T	1979	31480.00
00013	070970	JOY HARDY	fairport	RBG	F	1979	34200.00
00014	09890A	JAN MOREY	ROCHESTER	GSD	T	1967	18190.00
00015	087WRF	JOHN JONES	rochester	GSD	T	1970	25100.00

At this point in your study of dBASE, you should be able to CREATE a structure, MODIFY the structure if need be, DISPLAY and document the structure, and APPEND data into the existing structure.

DISPLAY COMMAND

Having put in some data into your data-base, you now want to be able to see that data in various shapes and forms, and to that end, we are going to look at a very powerful command in dBASE—the DISPLAY command.

Through the use of this command you may display on the screen or on paper the following:

All the data from a data-base	or
A single record from the data-base	or
A group of records from the data-base	or
Specified fields from selected records	or
Records which fulfill a simple condition	or
Records which fulfill a complex condition	or
Combinations of the above!	

As you can see, this command is very useful in all its creativity. Please follow closely on this section, since apart from being very useful and interesting, the parameters we shall be studying in this command appear across the board in many other dBASE commands, and understanding them here will guarantee your familiarity with the other commands as well.

The general format of the DISPLAY command is as follows:

.DISP   [scope]   [field-list]   [FOR <condition>]   [OFF]

As you can appreciate, all the parameters of this command are optional. This command is free form; the number of spaces between parameters is immaterial, provided you have left the minimum of 1 space.

The first point to be emphasized is that the DISP command, without any parameters, will always display the entire record that dBASE happens to be pointing to when the command is entered. If the record length is greater than screen size, the record will wrap around on the screen.

If you used the following combination, the first record in PERSNL will be displayed.

```
.USE PERSNL          <cr>
.DISP                <cr>
```

The USE command opens the PERSNL data-base and puts dBASE in control over the first record (i.e., dBASE is pointing to the first record). The DISP command will display the first record.

00001   070707 NINA BHARUCHA   WEBSTER   BSG T 1980 36300.00

Moving the Record Pointer

We can make this record pointer move around to any record we want. The following commands can make the pointer move around.

```
.SKIP      <cr>      will move the pointer to the next record from the previous
                     position. (In this case, to record #2.)
.SKIP 5    <cr>      will move the pointer from record #2 to record #7.
.SKIP −3   <cr>      will move the pointer from record #7 to record #4.
```

After any one of the above commands, a DISP command will display the appropriate record currently being pointed at. If you knew which record number you wanted to transfer control to (say, record #15), you could use the following commands:

```
.GO 15     <cr>      or
.GOTO 15   <cr>      or
.15        <cr>      This is the easiest method.
```

Any one of these will transfer control to record #15, and a DISP command issued now will display record #15. To transfer control very quickly to the first record in the data-base, use these commands:

```
.GO TOP    <cr>      or
.GOTO TOP  <cr>      or
.1         <cr>      Since the first record will always be record #1,
                     this is the fastest way to get quickly to the top
                     of the data-base.
```

To transfer control very quickly to the last record in the data-base, a similar form is used.

```
.GO BOTTOM       <cr>    or
.GOTO BOTT       <cr>    or
.GO BOTT         <cr>
```

Again, the point has to be emphasized that in the absence of any of the parameters, the DISP command will always display the entire record that dBASE happens to be pointing at when the command is issued.

Note: If you try the following stunt, you move the pointer to the last record.

.10	<cr>	This places the pointer at record #10.
.SKIP 9999	<cr>	Since you don't have so many records in your data-base, dBASE moves the pointer to the last record in the file.

Note: If you try the following, you move the pointer to the first record.

.10	<cr>	
.SKIP −99	<cr>	In this case the pointer is set to record #1 in the file.

Note: The DISP command automatically outputs 1 blank column ahead of character data or logical data, and 2 blank columns ahead of numeric data in the display.

We shall now proceed with the rest of the parameters of the DISPLAY command. Please note that the DISPLAY command only displays the data, without any column headings, and so you may want to use a combination of DISP STRU and DISPLAY (data) commands, to correlate the structure with the data.

DISPLAY	[scope]	[field-list]	[FOR <condition>]	[OFF]
	ALL	(emp:num	FOR TOWN = 'ROCHESTER'	
		emp:name		
	RECO n	org)		
	NEXT n			

The Scope Parameter

The [scope] parameter tells dBASE what the *scope* of the operation is supposed to be; that is, how many records you want included in the DISPLAY. You may have one of 3 entries for the scope field:

ALL. Obviously, this means you want all the records diaplayed. However, a DISP ALL command will only display 15 records at a time on the screen, and then dBASE will wait for you to enter any key, at which point it will display the next block of 15 records, and so on. Also, if the record-length is longer than screen size, each record will take up more than one line across the screen, and so the 15 records will not all be visible completely, since the earlier ones will have scrolled off the top of the screen. To stop/restart the scroll, use the CP/M option Ctrl-S.

RECO n. To display a specific record by record number, you may say .DISP RECO 15   <cr>. This will display record #15 in full. However, you may recall that the following combination does the same trick, and you won't make typos:

.15	<cr>	This moves the pointer to record #15
.DISP	<cr>	This displays the record pointed at.

NEXT n. To display a block of records, say 10, starting with record #5, we can do the following:

.5	<cr>	This moves the pointer to record #5 <cr>.
.DISP NEXT 10		This displays 10 records, starting with, and including, the record being pointed at. In this case, therefore, records #5 through 14 will be displayed.

> **Note:** The NEXT n option refers to physical records, not logical occurrences! This point will be clarified later.

The following examples illustrate [scope]:

.DISP   ALL   <cr>

00001	070707	NINA BHARUCHA	WEBSTER	BSG	.T.	1980	33000.00
00002	7545AD	PETE JOHNSON	brighton	BSG	.T.	1976	27590.00
00003	987178	GLORIA PATEL	FAIRPORT	RMG	.T.	1982	27500.00
00004	232430	MAX LEVENSKY	HENRIETTA	RMG	.F.	1969	27550.00
00005	0989SD	KIM BRANDT	FAIRPORT	RMG	.F.	1977	36000.00
00006	AC9090	TIM MONTAL	ROCHESTER	RBG	.F.	1981	41900.00
00007	08FG09	WILLIAM PATEL	penfield	GSD	.F.	1971	28900.00
00008	091230	JAMES JAMESON	ROCHESTER	GSD	.T.	1977	29800.00
00009	438190	MORRIS KATZ	webster	BSG	.F.	1980	23450.00
00010	087FG0	PAUL BHARUCHA	BRIGHTON	BSG	.T.	1973	29100.00
00011	00707A	PHIL MARTIN	WEBSTER	RMG	.F.	1980	31000.00
00012	8745AD	JOHN PETERSON	BRIGHTON	RBG	.T.	1979	31480.00
00013	070970	JOY HARDY	fairport	RBG	.F.	1979	34200.00
00014	09890A	JAN MOREY	ROCHESTER	GSD	.T.	1967	18190.00
00015	087WRF	JOHN JONES	rochester	GSD	.T.	1970	25100.00

> **Note:** If you have many records to display, and if the DISP ALL option of showing only 15 records at a time is undesirable, you may use

the LIST command. This command is identical to the DISP ALL command, with the only exception being that the LIST will list all records without pausing in-between, while the DISP ALL displays only 15 records at a time on the screen.

Notice, also, that the data from the logical field has been preceded and succeeded by a period, letting you differentiate that data as being from a logical field, rather than from a character field.

.DISP   RECO   5   \<cr\>

| 00005 | 0989SD | KIM BRANDT | FAIRPORT | RMG | .F. | 1977 | 36000.00 |

.DISP NEXT 5   \<cr\>

Note that record #5 was also included in the display, since dBASE was pointing to record #5, at the end of the previous command.

00005	0989SD	KIM BRANDT	FAIRPORT	RMG	.F.	1977	36000.00
00006	AC9090	TIM MONTAL	ROCHESTER	RBG	.F.	1981	41900.00
00007	08FG09	WILLIAM PATEL	penfield	GSD	.F.	1971	28900.00
00008	091230	JAMES JAMESON	ROCHESTER	GSD	.T.	1977	29800.00
00009	438190	MORRIS KATZ	webster	BSG	.F.	1980	23450.00

The Field-List/Expression-List Parameter

The next parameter is the field-list parameter. This parameter lets you specify which fields you want listed out, from those records selected through the scope parameter, In the absence of the field-list parameter, all the fields are selected for display.

Note: The fields will be displayed in the order in which they are named in the command, with one space ahead of character or logical fields, and two spaces ahead of numeric fields, in the display. Note that the commas in the field-list are optional.

.DISP   ALL   EMP:NUM,EMP:NAME,TOWN   \<cr\>

    \<---scope---\>   \<-----field-list----\>

You are asking for a display of all records, but only for the fields mentioned in the command. The following listing will be obtained.

00001	070707	NINA BHARUCHA	WEBSTER
00002	7545AD	PETE JOHNSON	brighton
00003	987178	GLORIA PATEL	FAIRPORT
00004	232430	MAX LEVENSKY	HENRIETTA
00005	0989SD	KIM BRANDT	FAIRPORT
00006	AC9090	TIM MONTAL	ROCHESTER
00007	08FG09	WILLIAM PATEL	penfield
00008	091230	JAMES JAMESON	ROCHESTER

00009	438190	MORRIS KATZ	webster
00010	087FG0	PAUL BHARUCHA	BRIGHTON
00011	00707A	PHIL MARTIN	WEBSTER
00012	8745AD	JOHN PETERSON	BRIGHTON
00013	070970	JOY HARDY	fairport
00014	09890A	JAN MOREY	ROCHESTER
00015	087WRF	JOHN JONES	rochester

.DISP   ALL   TOWN,ORG,SALARY   \<cr>

        \<--scope-->   \<---field-list---->

00001	WEBSTER	BSG	33000.00
00002	brighton	BSG	27590.00
00003	FAIRPORT	RMG	27500.00
00004	HENRIETTA	RMG	27550.00
00005	FAIRPORT	RMG	36000.00
00006	ROCHESTER	RBG	41900.00
00007	penfield	GSD	28900.00
00008	ROCHESTER	GSD	29800.00
00009	webster	BSG	23450.00
00010	BRIGHTON	BSG	29100.00
00011	WEBSTER	RMG	31000.00
00012	BRIGHTON	RBG	31480.00
00013	fairport	RBG	34200.00
00014	ROCHESTER	GSD	18190.00
00015	rochester	GSD	25100.00

.DISP   RECO 5   YR:OF:HIRE,TOWN,EXEMPT   \<cr>

     \< --scope-- >   \<-----field-list----->

00005	1977	FAIRPORT	.F.

Note: The field-list parameters could also include expression-lists, if required.

For example, suppose the current record is #1.

.DISP NEXT 5   EMP:NUM,EMP:NAME, SALARY,SALARY*2,SALARY/2

The * implies multiplication and the / implies division. Salary*2 and Salary/2 are expressions.

00001	070707	NINA BHARUCHA	33000.00	66000.00	16500.00
00002	7545AD	PETE JOHNSON	27590.00	55180.00	13795.50
00003	987178	GLORIA PATEL	27500.00	55000.00	13750.00
00004	232430	MAX LEVENSKY	27550.00	55100.00	13775.00
00005	0989SD	KIM BRANDT	36000.00	72000.00	18000.00

You can start from a specific position in the data-base.

```
.5              <cr>
.DISP           NEXT 5          EMP:NUM,ORG,YR:OF:HIRE        <cr>
                <--scope-->     <-----field-list----->

00005   0989SD  RMG   1977
00006   AC9090  RBG   1981
00007   08FG09  GSD   1971
00008   091230  GSD   1977
00009   438190  BSG   1980
```

As noted before, "commas" in the field-list, in the command line, are optional.

The FOR Condition

The FOR <condition> parameter is very powerful. It lets you specify simple or complex conditions under which records may be selected for display.

> **Note:** If a scope parameter has not been specified in the command, but a FOR condition has been mentioned, then ALL is the default for scope. That is, all the records that satisfy the condition will be selected for display, unless a specific <scope> has been mentioned.
> **Note:** When you specify values to be satisfied in a condition, then in the case of character fields, the values will have to be supplied in quotes (single quotes or double quotes are both OK). In the case of numeric fields, the values supplied should not be in quotes.
> **Note:** When you specify values to be satisfied in a condition, then in the case of character fields, dBASE will take the value that you supply in the literal sense.

Some examples, using the FOR condition follow.

```
.DISP   FOR   TOWN = 'ROCHESTER'          <cr>
```

Since a [scope] of operation has not been specified, but a FOR condition has been mentioned, the default for [scope] is ALL. Note that only those records in which the TOWN-field had the literal value ROCHESTER are selected for display.

```
00006   AC9090   TIM MONTAL       ROCHESTER    RBG  .F.  1981   41900.00
00008   091230   JAMES JAMESON    ROCHESTER    GSD  .T.  1977   29800.00
00014   09890A   JAN MOREY        ROCHESTER    GSD  .T.  1967   18190.00

        .DISP   FOR   TOWN = 'rochester'          <cr>
```

Note that only those records in which the TOWN-field had the literal value rochester are selected for display.

```
00015   087WRF   JOHN JONES       rochester    GSD  .T .  1970   25100.00
```

You can provide a generic key. That is, the full key-value does not need to be provided. But again, the value you provide must be in quotes since TOWN is a character field. In this command, all the records that have a capital ROCH in the first four character-positions of the TOWN-field will be selected for display.

00006	AC9090	TIM MONTAL	ROCHESTER	RBG .F.	1981	41900.00
00008	091230	JAMES JAMESON	ROCHESTER	GSD .T.	1977	29800.00
00014	09890A	JAN MOREY	ROCHESTER	GSD .T.	1967	18190.00

.DISP   FOR   TOWN = 'R'   <cr>

This command gives the same result as before. All the records that have a town beginning with a capital R will be selected for display.

00006	AC9090	TIM MONTAL	ROCHESTER	RBG .F.	1981	41900.00
00008	091230	JAMES JAMESON	ROCHESTER	GSD .T.	1977	29800.00
00014	09890A	JAN MOREY	ROCHESTER	GSD .T.	1967	18190.00

.DISP   FOR   TOWN=   'R'   <cr>

This example highlights the fact that the commands are essentially free form. Spaces before/after the parameters and/or logical operators (in this case, the = sign) do not matter.

00006	AC9090	TIM MONTAL	ROCHESTER	RBG .F.	1981	41900.00
00008	091230	JAMES JAMESON	ROCHESTER	GSD .T.	1977	29800.00
00014	09890A	JAN MOREY	ROCHESTER	GSD .T.	1967	18190.00

.DISP   RECO 5   FOR   TOWN = 'R'   <cr>

Record 5 may or may not qualify for display, depending, of course, on the contents of record 5. In our specific examples, it does not qualify.

Study the following example carefully.

.USE PERSNL   <cr>
.DISP ALL   <cr>

00001	070707	NINA BHARUCHA	WEBSTER	BSG	.T.	1980	33000.00
00002	7545AD	PETE JOHNSON	brighton	BSG	.T.	1976	27590.00
00003	987178	GLORIA PATEL	FAIRPORT	RMG	.T.	1982	27500.00
00004	232430	MAX LEVENSKY	HENRIETTA	RMG	.F.	1969	27550.00
00005	0989SD	KIM BRANDT	FAIRPORT	RMG	.F.	1977	36000.00
00006	AC9090	TIM MONTAL	ROCHESTER	RBG	.F.	1981	41900.00
00007	08FG09	WILLIAM PATEL	penfield	GSD	.F.	1971	28900.00
00008	091230	JAMES JAMESON	ROCHESTER	GSD	.T.	1977	29800.00
00009	438190	MORRIS KATZ	webster	BSG	.F.	1980	23450.00

00010	087FG0	PAUL BHARUCHA	BRIGHTON	BSG	.T.	1973	29100.00
00011	00707A	PHIL MARTIN	WEBSTER	RMG	.F.	1980	31000.00
00012	8745AD	JOHN PETERSON	BRIGHTON	RBG	.T.	1979	31480.00
00013	070970	JOY HARDY	fairport	RBG	.F.	1979	34200.00
00014	09890A	JAN MOREY	ROCHESTER	GSD	.T.	1967	18190.00
00015	087WRF	JOHN JONES	rochester	GSD	.T.	1970	25100.00

Now type the following:

.1   <cr>
.DISP   NEXT 5   FOR TOWN = 'FAIR'   <cr>

Since the NEXT n parameter refers to physical records, not logical occurrences, dBASE will check the NEXT 5 physical records, starting with the current record, and out of those 5 records, any with TOWN='FAIR' will be displayed. dBASE will not look for any 5 (logical) records anywhere in the file, that have a TOWN = 'FAIR'. This is what we mean when we say that the 'NEXT n' parameter refers to physical records, not logical occurrences.

| 00003 | 987178 | GLORIA PATEL | FAIRPORT | RMG | .T. | 1982 | 27500.00 |
| 00005 | 0989SD | KIM BRANDT | FAIRPORT | RMG | .F. | 1977 | 36000.00 |

Effect of Sequencing

To the microcomputer, if data were sequenced in normal ascending sequence, then all numbers "come ahead of"(are "logically lower" than) all letters, and within the letter series, the capital letters "come ahead of" (are "logically lower" than) the lower-case letters. That is, if you asked for a display sequenced by town of all the records out of our file, we will obtain the following listing: [The record numbers are still the original numbers from the data-base; the records have only been resequenced, to show the result of ascending sequence. The exact processes of sequencing will be covered in detail, later.]:

00010	087FG0	PAUL BHARUCHA	BRIGHTON	BSG	.T.	1973	29100.00
00012	8745AD	JOHN PETERSON	BRIGHTON	RBG	.T.	1979	31480.00
00003	987178	GLORIA PATEL	FAIRPORT	RMG	.T.	1982	27500.00
00005	0989SD	KIM BRANDT	FAIRPORT	RMG	.F.	1977	36000.00
00004	232430	MAX LEVENSKY	HENRIETTA	RMG	.F.	1969	27550.00
00006	AC9090	TIM MONTAL	ROCHESTER	RBG	.F.	1981	41900.00
00008	091230	JAMES JAMESON	ROCHESTER	GSD	.T.	1977	29800.00
00014	09890A	JAN MOREY	ROCHESTER	GSD	.T.	1967	18190.00
00001	070707	NINA BHARUCHA	WEBSTER	BSG	.T.	1980	33000.00
00011	00707A	PHIL MARTIN	WEBSTER	RMG	.F.	1980	31000.00
00002	7545AD	PETE JOHNSON	brighton	BSG	.T.	1976	27590.00
00013	070970	JOY HARDY	fairport	RBG	.F.	1979	34200.00
00007	08FG09	WILLIAM PATEL	penfield	GSD	.F.	1971	28900.00

| 00015 | 087WRF | JOHN JONES | rochester | GSD | .T. | 1970 | 25100.00 |
| 00009 | 438190 | MORRIS KATZ | webster | BSG | .F. | 1980 | 23450.00 |

The FOR Condition, Continued

Keeping this in mind, let us now try the following experiments, with our original PERSNL file as input:

.DISP   FOR   TOWN   <   'R'   <cr>

(< is the less than symbol)

All towns whose data begins with any letter below R in the alphabet series will be selected for display. Remember the quotes, and the rules for upper/lower case sequencing.

00003	987178	GLORIA PATEL	FAIRPORT	RMG	.T.	1982	27500.00
00004	232430	MAX LEVENSKY	HENRIETTA	RMG	.F.	1969	27550.00
00005	0989SD	KIM BRANDT	FAIRPORT	RMG	.F.	1977	36000.00
00010	087FG0	PAUL BHARUCHA	BRIGHTON	BSG	.T.	1973	29100.00
00012	8745AD	JOHN PETERSON	BRIGHTON	RBG	.T.	1979	31480.00

.DISP   FOR   TOWN > "R"   <cr>

(> is the greater than symbol)

All towns whose data begins with any letter above R in the letter series will be selected for display. Remember the quotes, and the rules for UPPER/lowercase. Single or double quotes are both OK.

00001	070707	NINA BHARUCHA	WEBSTER	BSG	.T.	1980	33000.00
00002	7545AD	PETER JOHNSON	brighton	BSG	.T.	1976	27590.00
00007	08FG09	WILLIAM PATEL	penfield	GSD	.F.	1971	28900.00
00009	438190	MORRIS KATZ	webster	BSG	.F.	1980	23450.00
00011	00707A	PHIL MARTIN	WEBSTER	RMG	.F.	1980	31000.00
00013	070970	JOY HARDY	fairport	RBG	.F.	1979	34200.00
00015	087WRF	JOHN JONES	rochester	GSD	.T.	1970	25100.00

.DISP   FOR   TOWN   < >   'R'   <cr>

(< > is the not equal to symbol)

Note: You cannot enter this symbol as < > (space in between). The <> sign, although made up of two keystrokes, is considered as one symbol without spaces in between.

All towns whose data begins with any letter not equal to R in the alphabet series will be selected for display. Remember the quotes. Single or double are both OK.

00001	070707	NINA BHARUCHA	WEBSTER	BSG	.T.	1980	33000.00
00002	7545AD	PETE JOHNSON	brighton	BSG	.T.	1976	27590.00
00003	987178	GLORIA PATEL	FAIRPORT	RMG	.T.	1982	27500.00
00004	232430	MAX LEVENSKY	HENRIETTA	RMG	.F.	1969	27550.00
00005	0989SD	KIM BRANDT	FAIRPORT	RMG	.F.	1977	36000.00
00007	08FG09	WILLIAM PATEL	penfield	GSD	.F.	1971	28900.00
00009	438190	MORRIS KATZ	webster	BSG	.F.	1980	23450.00
00010	087FG0	PAUL BHARUCHA	BRIGHTON	BSG	.T.	1973	29100.00
00011	00707A	PHIL MARTIN	WEBSTER	RMG	.F.	1980	31000.00
00012	8745AD	JOHN PETERSON	BRIGHTON	RBG	.T.	1979	31480.00
00013	070970	JOY HARDY	fairport	RBG	.F.	1979	34200.00
00015	087WRF	JOHN JONES	rochester	GSD	.T.	1970	25100.00

The # sign can also work as the not equal to symbol.

.DISP   FOR   TOWN   #   'R'   <cr>

You get the same result as before. This may be easier to type in for the not equal to condition.

.DISP   FOR   TOWN   <=   'R'   <cr>

This is the less than or equal to combination. Again, you cannot type this in as < = (spaces in between). The <= is considered as one symbol with space between them.

Note: <= works, but =< is invalid!

00003	987178	GLORIA PATEL	FAIRPORT	RMG	.T.	1982	27500.00
00004	232430	MAX LEVENSKY	HENRIETTA	RMG	.F.	1969	27550.00
00005	0989SD	KIM BRANDT	FAIRPORT	RMG	.F.	1977	36000.00
00006	AC9090	TIM MONTAL	ROCHESTER	RBG	.F.	1981	41900.00
00008	091230	JAMES JAMESON	ROCHESTER	GSD	.T.	1977	29800.00
00010	087FG0	PAUL BHARUCHA	BRIGHTON	BSG	.T.	1973	29100.00
00012	8745AD	JOHN PETERSON	BRIGHTON	RBG	.T.	1979	31480.00
00014	09890A	JAN MOREY	ROCHESTER	GSD	.T.	1967	18190.00

.DISP   FOR   TOWN   >=   'R'   <cr>

This is the greater than or equal to combination. Again, you cannot type this in as > = (spaces in between). The >= is considered as one symbol without space.

Note: >= works, but => is invalid!

00001	070707	NINA BHARUCHA	WEBSTER	BSG	.T.	1980	33000.00
00002	7545AD	PETE JOHNSON	brighton	BSG	.T.	1976	27590.00

00006	AC9090	TIM MONTAL	ROCHESTER	RBG	.F.	1981	41900.00
00007	08FG09	WILLIAM PATEL	penfield	GSD	.F.	1971	28900.00
00008	091230	JAMES JAMESON	ROCHESTER	GSD	.T.	1977	29800.00
00009	438190	MORRIS KATZ	webster	BSG	.F.	1980	23450.00
00011	00707A	PHIL MARTIN	WEBSTER	RMG	.F.	1980	31000.00
00013	070970	JOY HARDY	fairport	RBG	.F.	1979	34200.00
00014	09890A	JAN MOREY	ROCHESTER	GSD	.T.	1967	18190.00
00015	087WRF	JOHN JONES	rochester	GSD	.T.	1970	25100.00

Now let us play around with numeric fields.

> **Note:** When you specify values to be satisfied in a condition, then in the case of numeric fields, dBASE will take the value that you supply in the algebraic sense.

```
.DISP    FOR    YR:OF:HIRE = 19              <cr>
.
```

Notice that nothing qualifies, since we do not have any YEAR:OF:HIRE = 19 in our data-base. Also, when working with numeric fields, the value supplied should not be in quotes.

```
.DISP    FOR    YR:OF:HIRE  =  1980          <cr>
```

00001	070707	NINA BHARUCHA	WEBSTER	BSG	.T.	1980	33000.00
00009	438190	MORRIS KATZ	webster	BSG	.F.	1980	23450.00
00011	00707A	PHIL MARTIN	WEBSTER	RMG	.F.	1980	31000.00

```
.DISP    FOR    YR:OF:HIRE  <  1980          <cr>
```

00002	7545AD	PETE JOHNSON	brighton	BSG	.T.	1976	27590.00
00004	232430	MAX LEVENSKY	HENRIETTA	RMG	.F.	1969	27550.00
00005	0989SD	KIM BRANDT	FAIRPORT	RMG	.F.	1977	36000.00
00007	08FG09	WILLIAM PATEL	penfield	GSD	.F.	1971	28900.00
00008	091230	JAMES JAMESON	ROCHESTER	GSD	.T.	1977	29800.00
00010	087FG0	PAUL BHARUCHA	BRIGHTON	BSG	.T.	1973	29100.00
00012	8745AD	JOHN PETERSON	BRIGHTON	RBG	.T.	1979	31480.00
00013	070970	JOY HARDY	fairport	RBG	.F.	1979	34200.00
00014	09890A	JAN MOREY	ROCHESTER	GSD	.T.	1967	18190.00
00015	087WRF	JOHN JONES	rochester	GSD	.T.	1970	25100.00

```
.DISP    FOR    SALARY  <  25000            <cr>
```

00009	438190	MORRIS KATZ	webster	BSG	.F.	1980	23450.00
00014	09890A	JAN MOREY	ROCHESTER	GSD	.T.	1967	18190.00

```
.DISP    FOR    SALARY  #  25000            <cr>
```

00001	070707	NINA BHARUCHA	WEBSTER	BSG	.T.	1980	33000.00
00002	7545AD	PETE JOHNSON	brighton	BSG	.T.	1976	27590.00
00003	987178	GLORIA PATEL	FAIRPORT	RMG	.T.	1982	27500.00
00004	232430	MAX LEVENSKY	HENRIETTA	RMG	.F.	1969	27550.00
00005	0989SD	KIM BRANDT	FAIRPORT	RMG	.F.	1977	36000.00
00006	AC9090	TIM MONTAL	ROCHESTER	RBG	.F.	1981	41900.00
00007	08FG09	WILLIAM PATEL	penfield	GSD	.F.	1971	28900.00
00008	091230	JAMES JAMESON	ROCHESTER	GSD	.T.	1977	29800.00
00009	438190	MORRIS KATZ	webster	BSG	.F.	1980	23450.00
00010	087FG0	PAUL BHARUCHA	BRIGHTON	BSG	.T.	1973	29100.00
00011	00707A	PHIL MARTIN	WEBSTER	RMG	.F.	1980	31000.00
00012	8745AD	JOHN PETERSON	BRIGHTON	RBG	.T.	1979	31480.00
00013	070970	JOY HARDY	fairport	RBG	.F.	1979	34200.00
00014	09890A	JAN MOREY	ROCHESTER	GSD	.T.	1967	18190.00
00015	087WRF	JOHN JONES	rochester	GSD	.T.	1970	25100.00

.DISP   FOR   SALARY   =   25000   cr

00009	438190	MORRIS KATZ	webster	BSG	.F.	1980	23450.00
00014	09890A	JAN MOREY	ROCHESTER	GSD	.T.	1967	18190.00

.DISP   FOR   SALARY   >=   25000   <cr>

00001	070707	NINA BHARUCHA	WEBSTER	BSG	.T.	1980	33000.00
00002	7545AD	PETE JOHNSON	brighton	BSG	.T.	1976	27590.00
00003	987178	GLORIA PATEL	FAIRPORT	RMG	.T.	1982	27500.00
00004	232430	MAX LEVENSKY	HENRIETTA	RMG	.F.	1969	27550.00
00005	0989SD	KIM BRANDT	FAIRPORT	RMG	.F.	1977	36000.00
00006	AC9090	TIM MONTAL	ROCHESTER	RBG	.F.	1981	41900.00
00007	08FG09	WILLIAM PATEL	penfield	GSD	.F.	1971	28900.00
00008	091230	JAMES JAMESON	ROCHESTER	GSD	.T.	1977	29800.00
00009	438190	MORRIS KATZ	webster	BSG	.F.	1980	23450.00
00010	087FG0	PAUL BHARUCHA	BRIGHTON	BSG	.T.	1973	29100.00
00011	00707A	PHIL MARTIN	WEBSTER	RMG	.F.	1980	31000.00
00012	8745AD	JOHN PETERSON	BRIGHTON	RBG	.T.	1979	31480.00
00013	070970	JOY HARDY	fairport	RBG	.F.	1979	34200.00
00014	09890A	JAN MOREY	ROCHESTER	GSD	.T.	1967	18190.00
00015	087WRF	JOHN JONES	rochester	GSD	.T.	1970	25100.00

Using Logical Fields with DISPLAY

Note the following command:

.DISPLAY   FOR   EXEMPT   <cr>

Notice that we don't need any logical operators in this case, since we are dealing with a logical field. The implication is that we are asking for a display of all records in which EXEMPT = 'T'.

00001	070707	NINA BHARUCHA	WEBSTER	BSG	.T.	1980	33000.00
00002	7545AD	PETE JOHNSON	brighton	BSG	.T.	1976	27590.00
00003	987178	GLORIA PATEL	FAIRPORT	RMG	.T.	1982	27500.00
00008	091230	JAMES JAMESON	ROCHESTER	GSD	.T.	1977	29800.00
00010	087FG0	PAUL BHARUCHA	BRIGHTON	BSG	.T.	1973	29100.00
00012	8745AD	JOHN PETERSON	BRIGHTON	RBG	.T.	1979	31480.00
00014	09890A	JAN MOREY	ROCHESTER	GSD	.T.	1967	18190.00
00015	087WRF	JOHN JONES	rochester	GSD	.T.	1970	25100.00

.DISPLAY   FOR   .NOT.   EXEMPT   <cr>

The implication is that we are asking for a display of all records in which EXEMPT = 'F'.

00004	232430	MAX LEVENSKY	HENRIETTA	RMG	.F.	1969	27550.00
00005	0989SD	KIM BRANDT	FAIRPORT	RMG	.F.	1977	36000.00
00006	AC9090	TIM MONTAL	ROCHESTER	RBG	.F.	1981	41900.00
00007	08FG09	WILLIAM PATEL	penfield	GSD	.F.	1971	28900.00
00009	438190	MORRIS KATZ	webster	BSG	.F.	1980	23450.00
00011	00707A	PHIL MARTIN	WEBSTER	RMG	.F.	1980	31000.00
00013	070970	JOY HARDY	fairport	RBG	.F.	1979	34200.00

If the field called EXEMPT had been defined as a regular character field, then to obtain the above listings would have required the display commands to be as follows:

.DISPLAY FOR EXEMPT = 'T'   <cr>   or
.DISPLAY FOR EXEMPT = 'F'   <cr>

These commands depend entirely on the data that had been entered for the fields. Hopefully, this has clarified the difference in usage between character or numeric fields and logical fields.

Complex/Multiple Conditions

You can have more than one condition under which records may be selected for display.

.DISP   FOR   TOWN = 'ROCH'   .AND.   SALARY < 25000   <cr>

Note: There is always a period preceding and succeeding the logical operators. The logical operators are: AND, OR, and NOT.

00014	09890A	JAN MOREY	ROCHESTER	GSD	.T.	1967	18190.00

.DISP   FOR   ORG = 'BSG' .AND.   YR:OF:HIRE = 1980   <cr>

00001	070707	NINA BHARUCHA	WEBSTER	BSG	.T.	1980	33000.00
00009	438190	MORRIS KATZ	webster	BSG	.F.	1980	23450.00

```
.DISP    EMP:NUM,EMP:NAME    FOR ORG = 'BSG' .OR. ORG = 'GSD'    <cr>
         <--field-list-->                <----------condition-------------->
```

```
00001    070707    NINA BHARUCHA
00002    7545AD    PETE JOHNSON
00007    08FG09    WILLIAM PATEL
00008    091230    JAMES JAMESON
00009    438190    MORRIS KATZ
00010    087FG0    PAUL BHARUCHA
00014    09890A    JAN MOREY
00015    087WRF    JOHN JONES
```

You can have any combination of multiple ANDs and ORs.

```
.DISP FOR TOWN = 'ROCH' .AND. (ORG = 'BSG' .OR. ORG = 'GSD')
```

You must use parentheses, in order to clarify the intended logic of your command statement. In the absence of parentheses, dBASE will take its own default logic and proceed with an output that you may not have intended at all.

```
00008    091230    JAMES JAMESON    ROCHESTER    GSD   .T.   1977   29800.00
00014    09890     JAN MOREY        ROCHESTER    GSD   .T.   1967   18190.00
```

If you have too many logical operators, it is possible that you may not be able to fit your command all in one line on the screen. In order to continue a command line, at any appropriate point type in a *semicolon* character. This is the continuation character for dBASE. The maximum length of any command line is 254 characters.

Note: There must not be any space character entered after the semicolon.

```
.DISP FOR        TOWN = 'ROCH'        .AND.;            <cr>
                 (ORG = 'BSG' .OR.    ORG = GSD')       <cr>
```

```
00008    091230    JAMES JAMESON    ROCHESTER    GSD   .T.   1977   29800.00
00014    09890A    JAN MOREY        ROCHESTER    GSD   .T.   1967   18190.00
```

The OFF Parameter

The final parameter, for now, is the OFF parameter. This parameter simply removes the record numbers from display. If you have noticed, each of our previous displays had record numbers displayed. (These record numbers were provided by dBASE, as records were appended into the data-base.) The OFF parameter specifies that you do not want to see the record numbers.

```
.DISP  FOR  TOWN = 'ROCH'    OFF         <cr>
```

AC9090	TIM MONTAL	ROCHESTER	RBG	.F.	1981	41900.00
091230	JAMES JAMESON	ROCHESTER	GSD	.T.	1977	29800.00
09890A	JAN MOREY	ROCHESTER	GSD	.T.	1967	18190.00

LIST COMMAND

We had mentioned earlier that the DISP ALL command will only display up to 15 records at a time on the screen. Even if a FOR condition has been mentioned, if more than 15 records qualify for the condition, only 15 records at a time are displayed. There is another command called the LIST command, which is the same as DISPLAY ALL except that the LIST command has the advantage of not stopping after every 15 seconds. This is the only difference between DISP ALL and LIST.

A LIST command will list out the entire data-base on the screen in scroll mode. Using the Ctrl-P option to activate the printer, you can see that to obtain a quick and dirty listing of all the data in the data-base, one needs to use a combination of the LIST command and the Ctrl-P option. Also, if both structure and data are listed out, then you can correlate the structure with the data, if need be, since the LIST command itself only lists out the data, without any column headings.

> **Note:** On the Xerox 820-II system under CP/M, you can temporarily freeze the scroll movement, during LIST or DISP ALL, via the Ctrl-S option. Another Ctrl-S will restart the scroll movement. Ctrl-S is used as a toggle switch to stop/restart the scroll movement during either a DISP ALL or LIST execution.

```
.USE PERSNL      <cr>
.                <Ctrl-P>
.DISP STRU       <cr>
                 -----------
                 -----------        (structure is listed out
                 -----------           on paper)
.LIST            <cr>
                 -----------
                 -----------        (data is listed out
                 -----------           on paper)
```

Now the structure and data can be correlated.

SPECIAL FUNCTIONS

Using some special built-in functions of dBASE, one can really bolster the power of the DISPLAY (and other) commands. The special functions should be memorized as soon as possible on account of the increased capability they provide.

Substring Function

This applies only to character fields. It is to be used if you want to check for the occurrence of a required string of characters within a character field. For example, .DISP FOR TOWN = 'ROCH' <cr> will only select those records that have an uppercase ROCH in the first-four positions of the TOWN - field.

But if you wanted to select records which had an OCH in the 2nd through the 4th locations of the TOWN-field, you would have to specify the following:

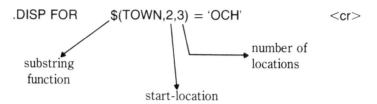

.DISP FOR $(TOWN,2,3) = 'OCH'   <cr>

substring
function

start-location

number of
locations

You are trying to substring the TOWN-field, and you want to specify the start location (character position 2), and you want to specify the number of locations (in this case, 3). that is, all those records that have an uppercase OCH in columns 2, 3, and 4 of the TOWN-field will be selected for display. As before, the value you supply, (in this case OCH) should be in quotes, since TOWN is a character field.

00006	AC9090	TIM MONTAL	ROCHESTER	RBG	.F.	1981	41900.00
00008	091230	JAMES JAMESON	ROCHESTER	GSD	.T.	1977	29800.00
00014	09890A	JAN MOREY	ROCHESTER	GSD	.T.	1967	18190.00

A much more powerful form of the substring option is available, which lets you find the character string you want anywhere within a field, instead of in certain locations only.

.DISP   FOR   'TER' $(TOWN)   <cr>

This will DISPLAY all records that have an uppercase TER anywhere in the TOWN-field.

00001	070707	NINA BHARUCHA	WEBSTER	BSG	.T.	1980	33000.00
00006	AC9090	TIM MONTAL	ROCHESTER	RBG	.F.	1981	41900.00
00008	091230	JAMES JAMESON	ROCHESTER	GSD	.T.	1977	29800.00
00011	00707A	PHIL MARTIN	WEBSTER	RMG	.F.	1980	31000.00
00014	09890A	JAN MOREY	ROCHESTER	GSD	.T.	1967	18190.00

Normally, the value supplied for numeric fields is considered to be the algebraic value.

.DISP FOR   YR:OF:HIRE = 19   <cr>

This command will find nothing since we do not have any data with an algebraic value of 19 in the YR:OF:HIRE field. However it is possible to have dBASE view a numeric-field as a character-field, so that we can take substrings off of that character field.

String Function

The expression STR(YR:OF:HIRE,4) will make dBASE look upon the YR:OF:HIRE field now as a character field. In general, to format a numeric field as a character field, you have to specify STR(field-name,field-length).

STR(SALARY,8,2) would be correct since the length of the salary field is defined as 8,2 in the structure of that field.

If we wanted to obtain a listing of all employees that had the character 7 in the 3rd position of the YR:OF:HIRE field, we can specify the following:

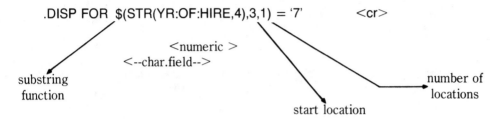

.DISP FOR $(STR(YR:OF:HIRE,4),3,1) = '7'   <cr>

substring function

<numeric >
<--char.field-->

start location

number of locations

The value supplied has to be in quotes, since you are now referring to a character field.

00002	7545AD	PETE JOHNSON	brighton	BSG	.T.	1976	27590.00
00005	0989SD	KIM BRANDT	FAIRPORT	RMG	.F.	1977	36000.00
00007	08FG09	WILLIAM PATEL	penfield	GSD	.F.	1971	28900.00
00008	091230	JAMES JAMESON	ROCHESTER	GSD	.T.	1977	29800.00
00010	087FG0	PAUL BHARUCHA	BRIGHTON	BSG	.T.	1973	29100.00
00012	8745AD	JOHN PETERSON	BRIGHTON	RBG	.T.	1979	31480.00
00013	070970	JOY HARDY	fairport	RBG	.F.	1979	34200.00
00015	087WRF	JOHN JONES	rochester	GSD	.T.	1970	25100.00

You realize, of course, that if you had wanted the above list of employees who had a '7' in the 3rd location of the YR:OF:HIRE field, i.e., all those hired in the 'seventies', you could have done it easier as follows:

.DISP FOR YR:OF:HIRE > 1969 .AND. YR:OF:HIRE < 1980   <cr>

However, the objective here was to show the substring function, on a numeric field strung as a character field. It's not as confusing as it sounds; it just takes a little doing!

Value Function

This is the opposite of the STRing function, since this function is used to derive numeric data out of a character field. Some examples are provided to clarify the workings of this function. Let us suppose we have some data stored in a character field called COUNTER:

Contents of the character field called COUNTER		Result of the expression: VAL(COUNTER)
(1)	1234	1234
(2)	12ABC	12
(3)	A212C	0
(4)	12ABC (leading spaces)	12
(5)	A123C (leading spaces)	0
(6)	123.456 (character data !)	123

The VAL function provides the leading numerical digits out of a character field, and the first nonnumeric stops the process.

Date() Function

When you first invoke dBASE, it asks you to provide today's date. This is in the case of 8-bit processors. For the IBM-PC type computers (16-bit), today's date is picked up from the system clock. In any event, either you have or have not provided the date to dBASE.

At any point in your processing, if you wish to enter a date, or change an existing date, you may:

.SET DATE TO MM/DD/YY

MM/DD/YY is the required date. Note that DATE is a character variable. If you now wish to refer to this date, you may use the special DATE() function. For example, .? DATE() will provide the entire date. If you wanted to pick up only the month out of the date, . VAL(DATE()) will provide the two leading numeric digits of the month, with the / stopping the operation. . $(DATE(),4,2) will provide you with the day. . $(DATE(),7,2) will provide you with the year.

Uppercase Function

So far we have noticed that in the case of character fields (or numeric fields strung as character), dBASE looks for the literal value we have provided in the expression. That is, if your data-entry procedure was not strictly followed for one or the other convention you established, it is possible that your data could end up being a mixture of upper and lowercase characters. That is, your DISPLAY commands would end up not finding some or all of the records that actually qualify, but have the wrong type of case for the literal equality.

If you suspect that this might be the case (no pun intended), you can ask dBASE to try and find a match regardless of upper or lowercase.

.DISP   FOR   !(TOWN)   =   'ROCH'   <cr>

This will now find all combinations of upper or lowercase of the ROCH characters, in the first four positions of the TOWN-field.

00006	AC9090	TIM MONTAL	ROCHESTER	RBG	.F.	1981	41900.00
00008	091230	JAMES JAMESON	ROCHESTER	GSD	.T.	1977	29800.00

| 00014 | 09890A | JAN MOREY | ROCHESTER | GSD | .T. | 1967 | 18190.00 |
| 00015 | 087WRF | JOHN JONES | rochester | GSD | .T. | 1970 | 25100.00 |

.DISP   FOR $(!(TOWN),2,3) = 'OCH'   \<cr\>

This will now find all combinations of upper or lowercase of the OCH characters, in positions 2, 3 or 4 of the TOWN - field.

00006	AC9090	TIM MONTAL	ROCHESTER	RBG	.F.	1981	41900.00
00008	091230	JAMES JAMESON	ROCHESTER	GSD	.T.	1977	29800.00
00014	09890A	JAN MOREY	ROCHESTER	GSD	.T.	1967	18190.00
00015	087WRF	JOHN JONES	rochester	GSD	.T.	1970	25100.00

.DISP   FOR   'TER' $(!(TOWN))   \<cr\>

This will now find all combinations of upper or lowercase, of the TER characters, anywhere in the TOWN-field.

00006	AC9090	TIM MONTAL	ROCHESTER	RBG	.F.	1981	41900.00
00008	091230	JAMES JAMESON	ROCHESTER	GSD	.T.	1977	29800.00
00014	09890A	JAN MOREY	ROCHESTER	GSD	.T.	1967	18190.00
00001	070707	NINA BHARUCHA	WEBSTER	BSG	.T.	1980	33000.00
00011	00707A	PHIL MARTIN	WEBSTER	RMG	.F.	1980	31000.00
00015	087WRF	JOHN JONES	rochester	GSD	.T.	1970	25100.00
00009	438190	MORRIS KATZ	webster	BSG	.F.	1980	23450.00

Important Note: The very nature of the uppercase function mandates that the value you supply should all be provided in uppercase only!! That is, .DISP FOR !(TOWN) = 'Roch'   \<cr\> will find nothing!. The value you provide must be in uppercase!! dBASE will then search for all combinations of cases, as specified in the command.

Record Number Function

The # is a special function, in dBASE, which means record number. As a simple example, at any point in time the dBASE pointer will always be positioned at a record within the file in use. If you quickly wanted to find out the record number of that record, you could always enter the following:

.DISP   \<cr\>

The entire record, including the record number, would list out. However, if you only wanted the record number to be accessed without the rest of the data being viewed, then this special function comes handy. Remember that you had nothing to do with the record numbers (they were provided by dBASE as you were APPENDing data), and so you do not have access to any field in the structure that will provide the record numbers directly. Hence this function. To view only the record number of the current record type the following:

.? #   <cr>

The ? can be interpreted to mean, "What is." In this example we are asking, "What is the record number of the current record?"

Type Function

At any time in the processing of our dBASE file, if you wanted to find out the TYPE definition of any field (character or numeric or logical), you could enter the following:

.DISP STRU   <cr>

This will display the entire structure, and you could get the information you wanted. If you only wanted to find out the type of the EMP:NUM field, you would enter the following:

. ? TYPE(EMP:NUM)   <cr>
C

The response is C or N or L for character or numeric or logical.

The + Function

Type in the following commands:

```
.1                                        <cr>
.DISP NEXT 5  EMP:NUM  EMP:NAME  TOWN      <cr>
```

00001	070707	NINA BHARUCHA	WEBSTER
00002	7545AD	PETE JOHNSON	brighton
00003	987178	GLORIA PATEL	FAIRPORT
00004	232430	MAX LEVENSKY	HENRIETTA
00005	0989SD	KIM BRANDT	FAIRPORT

This is one column of space between character fields. You may think you are seeing more columns, but that is only because the data in a field like the EMP:NAME field does not occupy the whole width of the field. In reality, there is only one column of space between fields. Note the single space between the EMP:NUM and EMP:NAME fields.

Now enter the following DISPLAY command using the plus signs.

```
.1                                              <cr>
.DISP NEXT 5  EMP:NUM + EMP:NAME + TOWN         <cr>
```

It would help if you interpreted the above + signs as: "EMP:NUM, *immediately followed by* EMP:NAME, *immediately followed by* TOWN", etc. Which means, without any spaces between the fields. Now the one blank column between the character fields has been eliminated. This is a *concatenation of fields*!

| 00001 | 070707NINA BHARUCHA | WEBSTER |
| 00002 | 7545ADPETE JOHNSON | brighton |

59

```
00003    987178GLORIA PATEL        FAIRPORT
00004    23243MAX LEVENSKY         HENRIETTA
00005    0989SDKIM BRANDT          FAIRPORT
```

> **Note:** The + function applies only to character fields, so if you do want to use the same option for numeric fields, you will have to specify the numeric fields as STRing functions.

```
.1                                                          <cr>
.DISP NEXT 5   STR(YR:OF:HIRE,4) + STR(SALARY,8,2)          <cr>
```

```
00001    198036300.00
00002    197630349.00
00003    198227500.00
00004    196927550.00
00005    197736000.00
```

The – Function

The minus function is used to remove trailing blanks from a field.

```
.1                                                          <cr>
.DISP NEXT 5    EMP:NUM – EMP:NAME – TOWN                   <cr>
```

This removes all trailing blanks from the EMP:NUM and EMP:NAME fields. It would help if you interpreted the above – signs as "EMP:NUM *minus all trailing blanks*, followed by EMP:NAME *minus all trailing blanks*, followed by TOWN", etc. Which means, a complete *concatenation of the data* of the named fields.

```
00001    070707NINA BHARUCHAWEBSTER
00002    7545ADPETE JOHNSONbrighton
00003    987178GLORIA PATELFAIRPORT
00004    232430MAX LEVENSKYHENRIETTA
00005    0989SDKIM BRANDTFAIRPORT
```

> **Note:** The – function applies only to character fields, so if you do want to use the same option for numeric fields, you will have to specify the numeric fields as STRing functions.

```
.1                                                          <cr>
.DISP NEXT 5    STR(YR:OF:HIRE,4) – STR(SALARY,8,2)         <cr>
```

```
00001    198036300.00
00002    197630349.00
00003    198227500.00
00004    196927550.00
00005    197736000.00
```

In summary, the + function results in a concatenation of the fields, while the − function results in a concatenation of the data within the fields.

You may also include literals in your parameters! Suppose you were positioned at record #1.

.DISP NEXT 5   EMP:NUM + ' ' + EMP:NAME + ' ' + TOWN \<cr>

00001	070707	NINA BHARUCHA	WEBSTER
00002	7545AD	PETE JOHNSON	brighton
00003	987178	GLORIA PATEL	FAIRPORT
00004	232430	MAX LEVENSKY	HENRIETTA
00005	0989SD	KIM BRANDT	FAIRPORT

The + function concatenate the fields to whatever is contained inside the single quotes. In this case, the literal is a space.

Trim Function

This command will result in familiar output.

.1   \<cr>
.DISP NEXT 5   TOWN ORG   \<cr>

00001	WEBSTER	BSG
00002	brighton	BSG
00003	FAIRPORT	RMG
00004	HENRIETTA	RMG
00005	FAIRPORT	RMG

By using the trim command, a slightly different result can be obtained.

.1   \<cr>
.DISP NEXT 5   TRIM(TOWN) ORG   \<cr>

00001	WEBSTER BSG
00001	brighton BSG
00003	FAIRPORT RMG
00004	HENRIETTA RMG
00005	FAIRPORT RMG

Now the output is different from the previous one. Notice that the TRIM function results in the removal of all but one of the trailing blanks of the trimmed field. This function is useful if data in the next field is required to slide over to the trimmed field. For example, in your file structure, you may have a field called TITLE,C,12 which would contain a salutation such as Mr. or Mr. and Mrs. or Mrs., etc. In this case, though, the length of the TITLE field is defined as 12 characters, but the data in that field could be variable in length. In such cases, the name that follows the salutation is required to slide over adjacent to the salutation, regardless of the length of the actual data in the salutation field. The TRIM function accomplishes this task.

.DISP ALL TRIM(TITLE)   TRIM(LASTNAME)   FIRSTNAM

Notice that even the LASTNAME field was trimmed, so that the firstname data could slide over adjacent to the last-name data.

Take a moment and consider the following relationships.

$$\text{TRIM(fieldA)} + \text{field B} = \text{fieldA} - \text{fieldB}$$

$$\text{TRIM(fieldA)} - \text{fieldB} = \text{fieldA} - \text{fieldB}$$

If you think about it, logically these relationships are correct, but we shall run a simple example to verify this.

```
.1                                          <cr>
.DISP NEXT 5 TRIM(TOWN) + ORG               <cr>

00001     WEBSTERBSG
00002     brightonBSG
00003     FAIRPORTRMG
00004     HENRIETTARMG
00005     FAIRPORTRMG

.1                                          <cr>
.DISP NEXT 5   TOWN − ORG                   <cr>

00001     WEBSTERBSG
00002     brightonBSG
00003     FAIRPORTRMG
00004     HENRIETTARMG
00005     FAIRPORTRMG
```

Notice that this output is identical to the one before, thus proving the equality of the two commands.

> **Note:** The TRIM function only applies to character fields. However, if you want to apply the TRIM option to numeric fields, simply STRing the numeric fields as character, and the TRIM function will work just fine.

```
.1                                          <cr>
.DISP NEXT 5   TRIM(STR(SALARY,8,2)) ORG    <cr>

00001     36300.00  BSG
00002     30349.00  BSG
```

00003	27500.00	RMG
00004	27550.00	RMG
00005	36000.00	RMG

LOCATE COMMAND

Since we have made ourselves quite familiar with the DISPLAY command, let us introduce an instruction, here, which is rather similar to the DISPLAY command, but which has its own niche in the dBASE set of commands.

```
.USE  PERSNL                                          <cr>
.LOCATE <scope>  FOR  <condition>                     <cr>
```

An example would look like the following one:

```
.LOCATE  FOR  TOWN = 'ROCH' .AND. ORG = 'BSG'   <cr>
```

dBASE starts at the top of the data-base and moves the pointer to the first record in the data-base that satisfies the condition, but will not display the record. You may DISPLAY, or EDIT (covered later) the record, and when you want dBASE to move on to the next such record (which satisfies the same condition as specified before), you may enter the following:

```
.CONT      <cr>  [for CONTINUE]
```

This will move the pointer to the next record satisfying the same condition as before. In this way, you may step through the entire data-base searching for selected records, and you may DISPLAY/EDIT them selectively along the way.

As before, you may use the special functions wthin your parameters, to enhance the power of the command:

```
.LOCATE  FOR  $(TOWN,2,3) = 'OCH'        <cr>
```

If you use the CONT parameter often enough, you will come across an "END OF FILE ENCOUNTERED" message. Further attempts to CONT will produce the same message.

SIMULTANEOUS DISPLAY OF DATA FROM TWO DATA-BASES

So far, we have studied in detail how data can be displayed in many shapes and forms. We shall now look at an enhancement that uses data from two data-bases, simultaneously.

Suppose we required a data-base that necessitated more than 32-fields in its structure. We would produce the structure of one data-base having the first 32-fields we needed, and we could now create the structure of another data-base, having the remaining fields, to account for our full requirement.

Now during data-entry, we would enter, in record #1 of the first data-base, the data for the first 32-fields and for record #1 of the second data-base, the data for the remaining fields, for that record. We would do this for all the records in the data-base.

That is, we would maintain a complete, one-to-one correspondence, between the records of both data-bases! It is just as if the second data-base was an extension of the first, and if we could have placed all the fields into one structure, we would have done so.

Having created such an arrangement, we now have to use both physical files, for the display of this one logical data-file. We start off by informing dBASE that one of these files is to be treated as the *primary file*, and the other file as the *secondary file*.

```
.SELECT PRIMARY
.USE FILEA
```

These two commands effectively designate FILEA as the primary file.

```
.SELECT SECONDARY
.USE FILEB
```

These two commands effectively designate FILEB as the secondary file. You complete the process with these last two commands.

```
.SELECT PRIMARY
.SET LINKAGE ON
```

From now on, dBASE will treat the two data-bases as one logical file. You can provide the DISPLAY commands as usual, specifying field-names from one or both data-bases, and dBASE will treat both files as belonging to one big structure.

> **Note:** After you are through using the LINKAGE arrangement, you should .SET LINKAGE OFF else dBASE tends to provide weird results, should you wish to use either file individually!
>
> **Note:** Under some circumstances, it is possible that your two file-structures could have some similar names. For example, you may have provided the same field EMP:NUM for both record structures. In that case, during the DISPLAY mode, if you wish to refer to any field from the secondary file which has the identical-named field in the primary, you should prefix the field-name with S.! For example:
>
> ```
> .DISP   EMP:NUM   S.EMP:NUM   ORG   S.TOWN
> ```
>
> This command would display for the current record(s), the EMP:NUM from the primary file record, the EMP:NUM from the secondary file record, the ORG from the primary file record, and the TOWN from the secondary file record.

By not providing any prefix, dBASE automatically assumes primary, since .SELECT PRIMARY was the statement you had ended up on before you issued the .SET LINKAGE ON command.

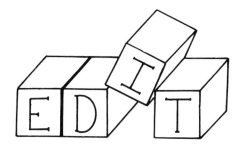

5. Editing Process

We are now moving into the realm of EDITING. We shall be studying several ways in which to change the contents of our data-base records and/or structures. In order to preserve the original data for subsequent reports, please execute the following commands.

```
.USE PERSNL          <cr>
.COPY TO PRESERVE <cr> (To be explained later)
```

The file in use is still PERSNL. Now we can go ahead and practice all we want against the PERSNL file with the editing features to be covered here, and later on we can restore the original PERSNL file.

EDIT COMMAND

The EDIT command permits us to make changes to our data-base, one record at a time. You have to decide which record it is that you want to edit. Your previous DISPLAY commands will help you obtain the record number of the record to be edited.

```
.USE PERSNL   <cr>
.EDIT 5       <cr>
```

This will bring up record #5 on the screen in full-screen edit mode and subject to the full-screen cursor controls as before. The data appears in vertical format, hence we can only edit one record at a time.

```
RECORD # 00005
EMP:NUM    :0989SD:
EMP:NAME  :KIM BRANDT      :
TOWN       :FAIRPORT  :
ORG        :RMG:
EXEMPT    :F:
YR:OF:HIRE :1977:
SALARY     :36000.00:
DUMMY      : :
```

> **Note:** In the edit mode of operation, the exception I mentioned
> before (during the APPEND command discussion) does not apply. That
> is, even if the cursor is in the first position of the first field in the
> structure, the use of the <cr> key simply moves the cursor down a
> field, and does not get you out of the EDIT mode.

Use the cursor controls studied before, and make any changes to the record.
Remember, the field EXEMPT is a logical field, and can only contain T, F, Y, or N for
data. Having made changes to the record on the screen in front of you, you now have one
of four choices of action:

1. You may want to save this record, and present the next one for similar changes.
Use Ctrl-C.

> **Note:** If your current record on the screen is the last record in the
> data-base, then Ctrl-C will save this record and get you out of the edit
> mode.

2. You may want to save this record, and present the previous one for similar
changes. Use Ctrl-R.

> **Note:** If your current record on the screen is the first record in the
> data-base, then Ctrl-R will save this record and get you out of the edit
> mode.

3. You may want to save this record and get out of the EDIT mode. Use Ctrl-W.
4. You may want to change your mind about the changes made (to the current
record, only!), and get out of the EDIT mode. Use Ctrl-Q.

> **Note:** In making the changes to a record, if the last character of
> the last field is changed OR if the <cr> key is kept depressed beyond
> the last field, the effect is the same as a Ctrl-C. That is, the next record
> is presented for edit. Also, if the record has many fields, and you are
> unable to see them all when the record is first brought up for edit, then
> these actions will cause the latter portion of the record to be brought
> into view, and a repeat of the same actions will cause the Ctrl-C effect.

66

Note: In making changes to a record, if the UP-ARROW key (or the Ctrl-E combination) is used to move up field by field, then trying to proceed beyond the first field has the same effect as a Ctrl-R. That is, the previous record is presented for edit.

Note: While in the edit mode, if you enter a Ctrl-U combination, you will be flagging the record as deleted! Another Ctrl-U will again unflag it. That is, Ctrl-U is a toggle switch for the delete indicator, while in the EDIT mode of operation.

Let us take some combinations of actions and see the results for several examples.

1. You make changes to record #5, then Ctrl-C. All changes to record #5 are saved, and record #6 is presented for edit.

2. Now you enter Ctrl-U, followed by Ctrl-C. Record #6 is flagged as deleted, then saved as such! Record #7 is on the screen.

3. You make changes to record #7, then enter Ctrl-W.

The net effect is that record #5 is changed, record #6 is flagged as deleted, and record #7 is changed, after which you got out of the edit mode. Let's try another example.

1. You make changes to record #5, then Ctrl-C. All changes to record #5 are saved, and record #6 is presented for edit.

2. Now you enter:

Ctrl-U,	Ctrl-C,	Ctrl-R,	Ctrl-U,	Ctrl-Q.
deletes record 6.	saves record 6. as deleted and presents record 7.	saves record 7. and presents record 6.	undeletes record 6.	change your mind on the change.

As you can see from the sequence of the commands, the net effect is that record #6 is flagged as deleted.

.LIST <cr> Ensures that your changes were correctly keyed in.

Note: If you wish to edit the current record that dBASE happens to be pointing at (say you have just APPENDed a record which you want EDITed), then without knowing the record number, you can get to that record by the command EDIT A.

BROWSE COMMAND

Despite what the name of this command may suggest, this command is a very powerful version of the edit command. With this command, you can edit up to 29 records simultaneously on the screen, and this time, of course, each record is presented horizontally across the screen. If the record length is longer than screen size, no wrap around occurs, and the rest of the record is beyond the screen.

Cursor controls and editing features here are virtually identical to what they were in the edit mode! The only obvious difference is, of course, in the fact that in the Edit mode we see each record vertically on the screen, and in the Browse mode we see up to 19 records in the horizontal format.

> **Note:** When the BROWSE command is issued, dBASE will bring up to 19 records on the screen, starting with the current record being pointed to. That is, if you wanted to browse from the top of the data-base, you would have to move the record pointer to record #1 first.

```
     .1            <cr>
    .BROWSE        <cr>
```

RECORD # :00001

EMP:NU	EMP:NAME-------	TOWN-------	ORG	E	YR:0	SALARY--D
070707	NINA BHARUCHA	WEBSTER	BSG	.T.	1980	33000.00
7545AD	PETE JOHNSON	brighton	BSG	.T.	1976	27590.00
987178	GLORIA PATEL	FAIRPORT	RMG	.T.	1982	27500.00
232430	MAX LEVENSKY	HENRIETTA	RMG	.F.	1969	27550.00
0989SD	KIM BRANDT	FAIRPORT	RMG	.F.	1977	36000.00
AC9090	TIM MONTAL	ROCHESTER	RBG	.F.	1981	41900.00
08FG09	WILLIAM PATEL	penfield	GSD	.F.	1971	28900.00
091230	JAMES JAMESON	ROCHESTER	GSD	.T.	1977	29800.00
438190	MORRIS KATZ	webster	BSG	.F.	1980	23450.00
087FG0	PAUL BHARUCHA	BRIGHTON	BSG	.T.	1973	29100.00
00707A	PHIL MARTIN	WEBSTER	RMG	.F.	1980	31000.00
8745AD	JOHN PETERSON	BRIGHTON	RBG	.T.	1979	31480.00
070970	JOY HARY	fairport	RBG	.F.	1979	34200.00
09890A	JAN MOREY	ROCHESTER	GSD	.T.	1967	18190.00
087WRF	JOHN JONES	rochester	GSD	.T.	1970	25100.00

The cursor always starts off at the first position of the first field. Notice that in the browse mode you do find column headings, made up of the field-names from the structure of the file, but limited to the width of the field from the structure.

Since record numbers are not presented, the top of the screen tells you which record you are currently on. The position of the cursor anywhere within a record identifies that record as the current record.

I mentioned before that the cursor controls and editing features are completely identical to those in the edit command.

1. Entering the <cr> key or Ctrl-F will make the cursor go forward field-by-field, in the horizontal direction.

2. Entering the up-arrow key or Ctrl-E will make the cursor go backward field-by-field in the horizontal direction.

3. Within a field, using the left-arrow key or Ctrl-D will make the cursor run to the right.

4. Within a field, using the backspace key or Ctrl-S will make the cursor run to the left.

5. Within a field, the Ctrl-V option can be used for the Insert feature.

6. Within a field, the Ctrl-G can be used to delete the character under the cursor.

7. Within a field, the delete key can be used to delete the character ahead of the cursor.

8. Having made changes to, say, record #5, entering Ctrl-C will drop the cursor down vertically into the next record. That has the effect of saving record #5 (just like in the edit mode).

9. Having made changes to, say, record #5, entering Ctrl-R will move the cursor up vertically into the previous record. That has the effect of saving record #5 (just like in the edit mode).

10. While in any record, if you decide to delete the record, you may simply Ctrl-U to flag the record for delete. Notice the DELETED indicator appear at the top of the screen. Now when you Ctrl-C or Ctrl-R, you have saved that record as deleted. Later on, if your cursor finds itself anywhere in that (deleted) record line again, the DELETED indicator again appears at the top, reminding you that this record has been flagged as deleted. At this point, of course, you can always Ctrl-U again, to undelete the record.

11. Having made the last changes you want to a record, you may now Ctrl-W to exit the BROWSE mode with a save of the last record changed, or Ctrl-Q to exit the BROWSE mode without a save of the changes made to the last record (to the last record, only!).

So as you can see, the cursor controls and editing features in the BROWSE mode are absolutely identical to those in the EDIT mode. The only items remaining to be covered are those pertaining to fields which are outside of the view of the screen, if the record length is more than 80 characters.

Two new controls need to be introduced here, for the scrolling options:

Ctrl-B<cr> will cause a scroll to the RIGHT, field-by-field.
Ctrl-Z <cr>will cause a scroll to the LEFT, field-by-field.

Scrolling

Scrolling, in the data processing environment, refers to the apparent movement (vertically or horizontally) of the data across a monitor screen. In scrolling, you have to visualize the data as being stationary, and the screen as moving across the data. If the screen moves to the left, you have scrolled left and if the screen moves up, you have scrolled up, and so on. In reality, of course, the screen does not move anywhere, and when you have scrolled left, that is, when the screen has moved left, the data appears to move to the right! Similarly, a scroll-up is only if the data moves down, and so on. This left and right and up and down definition could be confusing.

If you stick to the convention of the data being stationary and the screen moving across that data, then the scroll left or scroll up etc., will have a definite meaning, as outlined before. In this convention, a scroll left means that the data moves right, and vice versa.

Fields Subparameter

In those applications that have rather large record-lengths, if you wanted to make changes to field 1 and field 20 of many records, using the BROWSE mode, you can imagine the amount of time that would be wasted in scrolling between field 1 and field 20 for all the records. In such a situation, you can use a powerful extension of the BROWSE command, as follows:

.BROWSE FIELDS field-1,field-20   \<cr\>

> **Note:** Here the comma in the parameters is mandatory! Without the comma, only field-1 will be appreciated, and field-20 will be ignored! When in doubt, put in the comma!

Now only field 1 and field 20 appear on the screen, adjacent to each other, and you can browse from one field to the other in the usual way.

Please try the effect of the following command:

.1   \<cr\>
.BROWSE FIELDS   EMP:NUM,EMP:NAME,TOWN   \<cr\>

```
RECORD # :00001
EMP:NU  EMP:NAME-------        TOWN-------
070707  NINA BHARUCHA         WEBSTER
7545AD  PETE JOHNSON          brighton
987178  GLORIA PATEL          FAIRPORT
232430  MAX LEVENSKY          HENRIETTA
0989SD  KIM BRANDT            FAIRPORT
AC9090  TIM MONTAL            ROCHESTER
08FG09  WILLIAM PATEL         penfield
791230  JAMES JAMESON         ROCHESTER
438190  MORRIS KATZ           webster
087FG0  PAUL BHARUCHA         BRIGHTON
00707A  PHIL MARTIN           WEBSTER
8745AD  JOHN PETERSON         BRIGHTON
070970  JOY HARDY             fairport
09890A  JAN MOREY             ROCHESTER
087WRF  JOHN JONES            rochester
```

DELETE COMMAND

This command is used to flag one or more records as logically deleted. The flag is an asterisk in the extra field that was supplied to us by dBASE (the delete-indicator field), when we first created the structure under dBASE. This logical delete, as opposed to a physical delete, affords us the luxury of a change of mind, in case we decide to activate some/all of our deleted records.

.DELETE [scope] [FOR \<condition\>] \<cr\>

The parameters are optional. In the event of a DELETE command without parameters, the current record pointed to by dBASE gets deleted.

Note: In the sets of examples that follow, each group of instructions is independent of any other. That is, we shall presume that a fresh copy of the data-base records was available for each group of instructions.

Try out the following sequence of commands:

```
.5              <cr>
.DELETE         <cr>
.LIST           <cr>
```

Notice the * alongside record #5. This record is now logically deleted.

00001	070707	NINA BHARUCHA	WEBSTER	BSG	.T.	1980	33000.00
00002	7545AD	PETE JOHNSON	brighton	BSG	.T.	1976	27590.00
00003	987178	GLORIA PATEL	FAIRPORT	RMG	.T.	1982	27500.00
00004	232430	MAX LEVENSKY	HENRIETTA	RMG	.F.	1969	27550.00
00005	*0989SD	KIM BRANDT	FAIRPORT	RMG	.F.	1977	36000.00
00006	AC9090	TIM MONTAL	ROCHESTER	RBG	.F.	1981	41900.00
00007	08FG09	WILLIAM PATEL	penfield	GSD	.F.	1971	28900.00
00008	091230	JAMES JAMESON	ROCHESTER	GSD	.T.	1977	29800.00
00009	438190	MORRIS KATZ	webster	BSG	.F.	1980	23450.00
00010	087FG0	PAUL BHARUCHA	BRIGHTON	BSG	.T.	1973	29100.00
00011	00707A	PHIL MARTIN	WEBSTER	RMG	.F.	1980	31000.00
00012	8745AD	JOHN PETERSON	BRIGHTON	RBG	.T.	1979	31480.00
00013	070970	JOY HARDY	fairport	RBG	.F.	1979	34200.00
00014	09890A	JAN MOREY	ROCHESTER	GSD	.T.	1967	18190.00
00015	087WRF	JOHN JONES	rochester	GSD	.T.	1970	25100.00

If you recall, the [scope] parameter could be ALL, RECO n, or NEXT n. Try the following steps:

```
.5                  <cr>
.DELETE NEXT 5      <cr>
.LIST               <cr>
```

Record numbers 5 through 9 are flagged as deleted.

00001	070707	NINA BHARUCHA	WEBSTER	BSG	.T.	1980	33000.00
00002	7545AD	PETE JOHNSON	brighton	BSG	.T.	1976	27590.00
00003	987178	GLORIA PATEL	FAIRPORT	RMG	.T.	1982	27500.00
00004	232430	MAX LEVENSKY	HENRIETTA	RMG	.F.	1969	27550.00
00005	*0989SD	KIM BRANDT	FAIRPORT	RMG	.F.	1977	36000.00
00006	*AC9090	TIM MONTAL	ROCHESTER	RBG	.F.	1981	41900.00
00007	*08FG09	WILLIAM PATEL	penfield	GSD	.F.	1971	28900.00

00008	*091230	JAMES JAMESON	ROCHESTER	GSD	.T.	1977	29800.00
00009	*438190	MORRIS KATZ	webster	BSG	.F.	1980	23450.00
00010	087FG0	PAUL BHARUCHA	BRIGHTON	BSG	.T.	1973	29100.00
00011	00707A	PHIL MARTIN	WEBSTER	RMG	.F.	1980	31000.00
00012	8745AD	JOHN PETERSON	BRIGHTON	RBG	.T.	1979	31480.00
00013	070970	JOY HARDY	fairport	RBG	.F.	1979	34200.00
00014	09890A	JAN MOREY	ROCHESTER	GSD	.T.	1967	18190.00
00015	087WRF	JOHN JONES	rochester	GSD	.T.	1970	25100.00

     .DELETE FOR TOWN = ROCH'   <cr
     .LIST   <cr>

As before, if no [scope] has been mentioned, but a FOR condition exists, then ALL is the default for the scope. The above command will flag all the records that satisfy the condition.

00001	070707	NINA BHARUCHA	WEBSTER	BSG	.T.	1980	33000.00
00002	7545AD	PETE JOHNSON	brighton	BSG	.T.	1976	27590.00
00003	987178	GLORIA PATEL	FAIRPORT	RMG	.T.	1982	27500.00
00004	232430	MAX LEVENSKY	HENRIETTA	RMG	.F.	1969	27550.00
00005	0989SD	KIM BRANDT	FAIRPORT	RMG	.F.	1977	36000.00
00006	*AC9090	TIM MONTAL	ROCHESTER	RBG	.F.	1981	41900.00
00007	08FG09	WILLIAM PATEL	penfield	GSD	.F.	1971	28900.00
00008	*091230	JAMES JAMESON	ROCHESTER	GSD	.T.	1977	29800.00
00009	438190	MORRIS KATZ	webster	BSG	.F.	1980	23450.00
00010	087FG0	PAUL BHARUCHA	BRIGHTON	BSG	.T.	1973	29100.00
00011	00707A	PHIL MARTIN	WEBSTER	RMG	.F.	1980	31000.00
00012	8745AD	JOHN PETERSON	BRIGHTON	RBG	.T.	1979	31480.00
00013	070970	JOY HARDY	fairport	RBG	.F.	1979	34200.00
00014	*09890A	JAN MOREY	ROCHESTER	GSD	.T.	1967	18190.00
00015	087WRF	JOHN JONES	rochester	GSD	.T.	1970	25100.00

As before, the condition may be as simple or as complex as you may want to make it. You may, if you like, also include the special functions we learned earlier.

     .DELETE FOR $(TOWN,2,3) = 'OCH'   <cr>
     .LIST   <cr>

00001	070707	NINA BHARUCHA	WEBSTER	BSG	.T.	1980	33000.00
00002	7545AD	PETE JOHNSON	brighton	BSG	.T.	1976	27590.00
00003	987178	GLORIA PATEL	FAIRPORT	RMG	.T.	1982	27500.00
00004	232430	MAX LEVENSKY	HENRIETTA	RMG	.F.	1969	27550.00
00005	0989SD	KIM BRANDT	FAIRPORT	RMG	.F.	1977	36000.00
00006	*AC9090	TIM MONTAL	ROCHESTER	RBG	.F.	1981	41900.00
00007	08FG09	WILLIAM PATEL	penfield	GSD	.F.	1971	28900.00
00008	*091230	JAMES JAMESON	ROCHESTER	GSD	.T.	1977	29800.00

00009	438190	MORRIS KATZ	webster	BSG	.F.	1980	23450.00
00010	087FG0	PAUL BHARUCHA	BRIGHTON	BSG	.T.	1973	29100.00
00011	00707A	PHIL MARTIN	WEBSTER	RMG	.F.	1980	31000.00
00012	8745AD	JOHN PETERSON	BRIGHTON	RBG	.T.	1979	31480.00
00013	070970	JOY HARDY	fairport	RBG	.F.	1979	34200.00
00014	*09890A	JAN MOREY	ROCHESTER	GSD	.T.	1967	18190.00
00015	087WRF	JOHN JONES	rochester	GSD	.T.	1970	25100.00

.DELETE FOR ORG = 'BSG' .AND. YR:OF:HIRE >= 1980   <cr>
.LIST   <cr>

Again, all records that satisfy the condition will be deleted.

00001	*070707	NINA BHARUCHA	WEBSTER	BSG	.T.	1980	33000.00
00002	7545AD	PETE JOHNSON	brighton	BSG	.T.	1976	27590.00
00003	987178	GLORIA PATEL	FAIRPORT	RMG	.T.	1982	27500.00
00004	232430	MAX LEVENSKY	HENRIETTA	RMG	.F.	1969	27550.00
00005	0989SD	KIM BRANDT	FAIRPORT	RMG	.F.	1977	36000.00
00006	AC9090	TIM MONTAL	ROCHESTER	RBG	.F.	1981	41900.00
00007	08FG09	WILLIAM PATEL	penfield	GSD	.F.	1971	28900.00
00008	091230	JAMES JAMESON	ROCHESTER	GSD	.T.	1977	29800.00
00009	*438190	MORRIS KATZ	webster	BSG	.F.	1980	23450.00
00010	087FG0	PAUL BHARUCHA	BRIGHTON	BSG	.T.	1973	29100.00
00011	00707A	PHIL MARTIN	WEBSTER	RMG	.F.	1980	31000.00
00012	8745AD	JOHN PETERSON	BRIGHTON	RBG	.T.	1979	31480.00
00013	070970	JOY HARDY	fairport	RBG	.F.	1979	34200.00
00014	09890A	JAN MOREY	ROCHESTER	GSD	.T.	1967	18190.00
00015	087WRF	JOHN JONES	rochester	GSD	.T.	1970	25100.00

List Deleted Records

The next command will give you a listing, on the screen, of all the deleted records only. The * is a special function, which refers to deleted record.

.LIST   FOR   *   <cr>

| 00001 | *070707 | NINA BHARUCHA | WEBSTER | BSG | .T. | 1980 | 33000.00 |
| 00009 | *438190 | MORRIS KATZ | webster | BSG | .F. | 1980 | 23450.00 |

List Active Records

This version of list will provide a listing of all the good, valid records.

.LIST FOR   .NOT. *   <cr>

00002	7545AD	PETE JOHNSON	brighton	BSG	.T.	1976	27590.00
00003	987178	GLORIA PATEL	FAIRPORT	RMG	.T.	1982	27500.00
00004	232430	MAX LEVENSKY	HENRIETTA	RMG	.F.	1969	27550.00

00005	0989SD	KIM BRANDT	FAIRPORT	RMG	.F.	1977	36000.00
00006	AC9090	TIM MONTAL	ROCHESTER	RBG	.F.	1981	41900.00
00007	08FG09	WILLIAM PATEL	penfield	GSD	.F.	1971	28900.00
00008	091230	JAMES JAMESON	ROCHESTER	GSD	.T.	1977	29800.00
00010	087FG0	PAUL BHARUCHA	BRIGHTON	BSG	.T.	1973	29100.00
00011	00707A	PHIL MARTIN	WEBSTER	RMG	.F.	1980	31000.00
00012	8745AD	JOHN PETERSON	BRIGHTON	RBG	.T.	1979	31480.00
00013	070970	JOY HARDY	fairport	RBG	.F.	1979	34200.00
00014	09890A	JAN MOREY	ROCHESTER	GSD	.T.	1967	18190.00
00015	087WRF	JOHN JONES	rochester	GSD	.T.	1970	25100.00

All the major commands of dBASE will ignore deleted records. For example, if you want to copy records from one data-base to another, the deleted records in the from data-base are ignored. Commands that ignore these deleted records (as they should rightly do) are: APPEND, COPY, REPLACE, SORT, REPORT, etc.

However, as we have already seen, there are some commands (like the DISP ALL or LIST command) that do not ignore deleted records. Commands that will not ignore deleted records are: LIST (DISP), FIND, INDEX, COUNT, etc.

RECALL COMMAND

This command is the opposite of the DELETE command, in that it removes the logical indicator of * (the delete flag) from deleted records. It is identical in format to the DELETE command.

.RECALL   [scope]   [FOR <condition>]   <cr>

The example that follows illustrates the use of the parameters.

.DELETE ALL   <cr>   Deletes all records.
.LIST   <cr>

00001	* 070707	NINA BHARUCHA	WEBSTER	BSG	.T.	1980	33000.00
00002	* 7545AD	PETE JOHNSON	brighton	BSG	.T.	1976	27590.00
00003	* 987178	GLORIA PATEL	FAIRPORT	RMG	.T.	1982	27500.00
00004	* 232430	MAX LEVENSKY	HENRIETTA	RMG	.F.	1969	27550.00
00005	* 0989SD	KIM BRANDT	FAIRPORT	RMG	.F.	1977	36000.00
00006	* AC9090	TIM MONTAL	ROCHESTER	RBG	.F.	1981	41900.00
00007	* 08FG09	WILLIAM PATEL	penfield	GSD	.F.	1971	28900.00
00008	* 091230	JAMES JAMESON	ROCHESTER	GSD	.T.	1977	29800.00
00009	* 438190	MORRIS KATZ	webster	BSG	.F.	1980	23450.00
00010	* 087FG0	PAUL BHARUCHA	BRIGHTON	BSG	.T.	1973	29100.00
00011	* 00707A	PHIL MARTIN	WEBSTER	RMG	.F.	1980	31000.00
00012	* 8745AD	JOHN PETERSON	BRIGHTON	RBG	.T.	1979	31480.00
00013	* 070970	JOY HARDY	fairport	RBG	.F.	1979	34200.00
00014	* 09890A	JAN MOREY	ROCHESTER	GSD	.T.	1967	18190.00
00015	* 087WRF	JOHN JONES	rochester	GSD	.T.	1970	25100.00

.RECALL FOR TOWN ='ROCH' .AND. ORG = 'GSD' <cr>

All the records that satisfy the condition will have the delete flag removed, thus activating them again.

.LIST   <cr>

00001	* 070707	NINA BHARUCHA	WEBSTER	BSG	.T.	1980	33000.00
00002	* 7545AD	PETE JOHNSON	brighton	BSG	.T.	1976	27590.00
00003	*987178	GLORIA PATEL	FAIRPORT	RMG	.T.	1982	27500.00
00004	* 232430	MAX LEVENSKY	HENRIETTA	RMG	.F.	1969	27550.00
00005	* 0989SD	KIM BRANDT	FAIRPORT	RMG	.F.	1977	36000.00
00006	* AC9090	TIM MONTAL	ROCHESTER	RBG	.F.	1981	41900.00
00007	* 08FG09	WILLIAM PATEL	penfield	GSD	.F.	1971	28900.00
00008	091230	JAMES JAMESON	ROCHESTER	GSD	.T.	1977	29800.00
00009	*438190	MORRIS KATZ	webster	BSG	.F.	1980	23450.00
00010	*087FG0	PAUL BHARUCHA	BRIGHTON	BSG	.T.	1973	29100.00
00011	*00707A	PHIL MARTIN	WEBSTER	RMG	.F.	1980	31000.00
00012	*8745AD	JOHN PETERSON	BRIGHTON	RBG	.T.	1979	31480.00
00013	*070970	JOY HARDY	fairport	RBG	.F.	1979	34200.00
00014	09890A	JAN MOREY	ROCHESTER	GSD	.T.	1967	18190.00
00015	*087WRF	JOHN JONES	rochester	GSD	.T.	1970	25100.00

Incidentally, if you want to delete and recall records, you should use the DELETE and RECALL commands, as opposed to going into the EDIT or BROWSE modes with the Ctrl-U option. (If you remember, the Ctrl-U option under EDIT or BROWSE also flags records as deleted/recalled). The Ctrl-U feature is merely a plus feature of the EDIT or BROWSE commands, so that if you were in the EDIT or BROWSE mode of operation and if you wanted to delete/recall records, you could use Ctrl-U. But you would not want to go out of your way to enter the EDIT/BROWSE mode just to delete/recall records.

PACK COMMAND

This command is responsible for physically removing records that had, until now, been logically flagged as deleted.

.PACK   <cr>

Note that the PACK command has no parameters. This means that you cannot pick and choose the deleted records to be PACKed. It, too, is an all-or-nothing type of proposition. All deleted records will be physically zapped out.

Please understand very clearly that once you have packed it in, there is no way that you can ever bring those records back into your control again. So before you PACK it in, please take a moment to reflect upon the wisdom of your action.

After the PACK operation, your data-base will be reduced by the number of deleted records that had been removed. The record numbers in your data-base will have been readjusted to provide for consecutive numbering, starting from 1. Usually, before you do go ahead and PACK things in, you may want to make a record of your deleted records, perhaps a listing on paper, so that if you ever decide that you had made an error, you can always have access to the original data.

.LIST FOR *   \<cr\>

00001	*070707	NINA BHARUCHA	WEBSTER	BSG	.T.	1980	33000.00
00002	*7545AD	PETE JOHNSON	brighton	BSG	.T.	1976	27590.00
00003	*987178	GLORIA PATEL	FAIRPORT	RMG	.T.	1982	27500.00
00004	*232430	MAX LEVENSKY	HENRIETTA	RMG	.F.	1969	27550.00
00005	*0989SD	KIM BRANDT	FAIRPORT	RMG	.F.	1977	36000.00
00006	*AC9090	TIM MONTAL	ROCHESTER	RBG	.F.	1981	41900.00
00007	*08FG09	WILLIAM PATEL	penfield	GSD	.F.	1971	28900.00
00009	*438190	MORRIS KATZ	webster	BSG	.F.	1980	23450.00
00010	*087FG0	PAUL BHARUCHA	BRIGHTON	BSG	.T.	1973	29100.00
00011	*00707A	PHIL MARTIN	WEBSTER	RMG	.F.	1980	31000.00
00012	*8745AD	JOHN PETERSON	BRIGHTON	RBG	.T.	1979	31480.00
00013	*070970	JOY HARDY	fairport	RBG	.F.	1979	34200.00
00015	*087WRF	JOHN JONES	rochester	GSD	.T.	1970	25100.00

Now, a combination of this command with the Ctrl-P option will work wonders at giving you a listing, on paper, of only the deleted records. Now you may feel confident enough to go ahead and PACK it in. But Wait! If you ever wanted your data back into your Master file, you would have to go through the hassle of keying-in, again, all the records that have been listed out! This is, obviously, not a very sensible way of keeping track of the deleted records.

Later on, after we have covered the necessary commands, we shall look at a way of saving your deleted records in another data-base of the same structure as the Master data-base, prior to issuing the PACK command. In case you ever want to bring those deleted records back in, it would only take a couple of dBASE commands to do so.

> **Note:** The PACK command does not reduce the size of your file! That is, although the file has been shortened by the removal of the deleted records, the file disk space is not released, and to the system, it appears that the data-file takes up the same space as before. According to Ashton-Tate, this is a short-coming of CP/M, not of dBASE.

To physically release space, you must make a COPY of your file, after PACK. This is an easy way to release the unused space from your disk. The COPY command is covered in detail, at a later stage.

As you can appreciate, the DELETE, RECALL, and PACK commands form a logical subset of dBASE commands.

INSERT COMMAND

This command, though available, is not of too much direct use in any application. With the use of this command, one may specify to dBASE that a new record is to be INSERTed exactly between, say, existing records 7 and 8.

Now please understand that there is really no need for you to specify that a new, incoming record should be placed exactly after such-and-such existing record. The new record could be simply APPENDed to the end of the data-base, and the data-base could now be either physically sorted or logically indexed to provide you with the desired sequencing effect. The processes of sorting and indexing will be covered in depth, later.

However, if you did want to INSERT a new record at a specific point in the data-base, you would use the following procedure:

1. Select the record in the data-base, say, record #7, after which you want to have the new record.

.7   <cr>

2. .INSERT   <cr>

This opens up a blank structure of the file in use (just like in the APPEND mode). If SET CARRY ON is in effect the mask contains the contents of record #7.

```
RECORD #      00008
EMP:NUM       :                    :
EMP:NAME      :                              :
TOWN          :                         :
ORG           :           :
EXEMPT        : :
YR:OF:HIRE    :                :
SALARY        :                       :
DUMMY         : :
```

This is the mask of the new record to be INSERTed. Enter the data you want, using cursor controls and full-edit features as studied earlier.

3. After the data has been entered, you can only do one of two things:

a. Either save the new record and get out of the INSERT mode (done either with a Ctrl-W, or when you have entered the last character of the last field).
b. Change your mind on this new record, and get out of the INSERT mode (done with a Ctrl-Q.)

Caution: In versions of dBASE prior to 2.4, never use the Ctrl-Q option to change your mind on INSERTing a record, since this option, in these versions, plays some havoc with your data records in the vicinity of the insert. For example, if you were inserting after record #7 and you changed your mind, original record #8 gets deleted and record #9 gets duplicated twice over. If you were using these earlier versions (2.3A or B or C), and if you had to change your mind on the INSERT function, you should enter a Ctrl-U to flag the record as deleted, then Ctrl-W to save it as such! But never use the Ctrl-Q option on these versions. The version under discussion in this book, version 2.41, is OK in this respect.

Regardless of the action taken, you will always get out of the INSERT mode. You can only INSERT one record at a time. In our example, the new record is inserted after the record you are currently on. This new record coming in will now have a record #8, and all succeeding records will have their original record numbers changed!

You may also INSERT before the current record.

```
.7                      <cr>
.INSERT BEFORE          <cr>
```

As always, you are provided with a mask of the structure, and after the new record is saved, record numbers are changed appropriately, to reflect the new record's position in the data-base. In our example, the new record is now record #7.

Again, it should be emphasized that you do not have to use the INSERT feature to position records. New records should be APPENDed, and the sorting/indexing features should be used to obtain the sequencing impact you may be seeking.

APPEND COMMAND

We shall now look at the extended features of this command. The APPEND is very powerful, and should be studied in its entirety.

APPEND FROM <file> [FOR <condition>] [SDF] [DELIM]

With this command, basically, we can take records out of one file and copy them over to another. Let me emphasize one point right at the outset. Deleted records are ignored in the APPEND process!

The FROM file could be either a dBASE file, or it could be a file created under a standard text processor (i.e., a word processing file).

From <file> Parameter

Suppose you have a file called MASTER.DBF (with or without records). You also have another file called TRANS.DBF (with records).

```
.USE MASTER                 <cr>
.APPEND FROM TRANS          <cr>
```

These two commands will take all the records from the TRANS file and APPEND them (copy them over) to the end of the MASTER file. Remember, deleted records will not be copied over. The FROM file is not changed in any way, shape, or form. This implies, obviously, that the structures of the two files should be identical.

What if the structures are similar but not identical? For example:

MASTER	TRANS
EMP:NUM,C,6	ORG,C,3
TOWN,C,12	YR:OF:HIRE,N,4
ORG,C,3	EMP:NUM,C,6
SALARY,N,8,2	SALARY,N,8,2

Here the structures have some similarity, but are not identical. What would happen if we gave the following instructions:

```
.USE MASTER                    <cr>
.APPEND FROM TRANS             <cr>
```

Only those field-names that match are included in the process of APPEND! The other fields are ignored. Also, the matching fields do not have to be in similar positions in both files. A complete reformatting will take place, if necessary!

In our example, since EMP:NUM, ORG and SALARY field-names match, only the data from those fields will get copied over, into the structure of the Master file, for each of the records. The columns identified by the TOWN-field in the Master file will remain blank for each of the new records APPENDed over from the TRANS file. Obviously, records existing in the Master file before the start of the APPEND operation are not affected.

Create another data-base called STUDENTS as follows:

```
EMP:NUM,C,6
EMP:NAME,C,15
SALARY,N,8,2
```

Enter any data you want in this file, but create at least 5 records of data. Then type the following:

```
.USE PERSNL                    <cr>
.APPEND FROM STUDENTS          <cr>
.LIST                          <cr>
```

You will see gaps in the listing of the file PERSNL for the newly-appended records where the field-names that could not be matched (between the PERNSL file and the STUDENTS file) were left without any data coming in from the STUDENTS file.

00001	070707	NINA BHARUCHA	WEBSTER	BSG	.T.	1980	33000.00
00002	7545AD	PETE JOHNSON	brighton	BSG	.T.	1976	27590.00
00003	987178	GLORIA PATEL	FAIRPORT	RMG	.T.	1982	27500.00
00004	232430	MAX LEVENSKY	HENRIETTA	RMG	.F.	1969	27550.00
00005	0989SD	KIM BRANDT	FAIRPORT	RMG	.F.	1977	36000.00
00006	AC9090	TIM MONTAL	ROCHESTER	RBG	.F.	1981	41900.00
00007	08FG09	WILLIAM PATEL	penfield	GSD	.F.	1971	28900.00
00008	091230	JAMES JAMESON	ROCHESTER	GSD	.T.	1977	29800.00
00009	438190	MORRIS KATZ	webster	BSG	.F.	1980	23450.00
00010	087FG0	PAUL BHARUCHA	BRIGHTON	BSG	.T.	1973	29100.00
00011	00707A	PHIL MARTIN	WEBSTER	RMG	.F.	1980	31000.00
00012	8745AD	JOHN PETERSON	BRIGHTON	RBG	.T.	1979	31480.00

00013	070970	JOY HARDY	fairport	RBG	.F.	1979	34200.00
00014	09890A	JAN MOREY	ROCHESTER	GSD	.T.	1967	18190.00
00015	087WRF	JOHN JONES	rochester	GSD	.T.	1970	25100.00
00016	123456	PAUL LANG			.F.	0	23800.00
00017	234567	JOE FERRARO			.F.	0	23000.00
00018	345678	MAX ROBINSON			.F.	0	33500.00
00019	456789	SALLY FALLS			.F.	0	23400.00
00020	567890	ALBERT SPINELLI			.F.	0	22000.00

The above routine highlights a very important use of the APPEND command. Let us say, for example, that you know of an existing dBASE Master file, and you want to use a subset of that information for your own function. All you have to do is to create the structure of the file that you want, ensuring that you use the identical names, types and sizes of the fields as they have been defined in the structure of the Master file.

Suppose the file you have created is called MYFILE.

```
.USE MYFILE                              <cr>
.APPEND FROM MASTER                      <cr>
```

All the field-names that match will have their data pulled over. You have now APPENDed over (copied over) a subset of information from the MASTER file into your file. Take a .LIST to find out that this is true. Later on, in the COPY command, we shall see a much easier way of doing the same thing (i.e., creating a subset of information from a Master file).

You might ask the question, "What if the field-names match but the type and/or length is different?" For example, what would happen if you are trying to APPEND data from a field defined EMP:NUM,C,6 to a field defined EMP:NUM,N,5? The answer is that since the field-names match, the copy over of data will be attempted, but since the types and/or lengths are different, you will end up with *unexpected results.*

At the end of this section on APPEND, we shall cover these what-if type of questions, since the APPEND is an important aspect of dBASE, and you need to appreciate the full impact of the results of APPENDing with nonconforming fields. For now we will emphasize the fact that for any data movement to occur during the APPEND process, the field-names must match. Ideally, even the type and length should match.

For Condition

You may have a condition thrown in, to enhance the utility of the APPEND command. For example:

```
.USE PERSNL                                          <cr>
.APPEND FROM STUDENTS        FOR SALARY > 20000      <cr>
```

Now only those records that satisfy the condition are picked up from the STU-DENTS file, and from those records, only data from the matching field-names is copied over. Obviously, the STUDENTS file structure must contain a field called SALARY.

Please note the following point: Illogical though it may seem, the fields used in the

FOR expression must reside in the structure of both data-bases! Since the SALARY field has been used in the FOR condition, the structures of both "from" and "to" data-bases must contain the SALARY field defined. Hopefully, the definitions will tally exactly.

```
.USE PERSNL    <cr>
.APPEND FROM STUDENTS FOR ORG = 'BSG' .AND. SALARY > 20000
```

Now both SALARY and ORG must be defined in the structures of both data-bases. This is true even if you had an .OR. as the logical operator!

What would happen if we were to attempt an APPEND of totally dissimilar structures? Version 2.41 goes into a lockout! For earlier version, since no field-names match between the sending and the receiving files, no data can be copied over. However, for each record in the "from" file, a blank record is pulled over into the "to" file! Obviously, apart from blowing up the size of your receiving data-base with useless blank records, you will also have wasted quite a bit of processing time.

SDF Parameter

This section is important! This format of the APPEND command helps you transfer data from a *text* file (i.e., a file created under a word processor) into a dBASE format.

```
.USE  PERSNL                          <cr>
.APPEND FROM MYFILE   SDF             <cr>
```

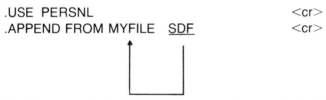

In this command, the SDF is a parameter that stands for Standard Data Format or System Data Format (take your choice). It is the parameter that tells dBASE that the file called MYFILE is a text file, not a dBASE file. The SDF parameter helps to qualify the file named in the command.

dBASE will now look for a file called MYFILE.TXT (as a default for text file), and if it finds it, it will take the records out of that file, character for character, a record at a time, and simply APPEND the data under the data-base structure of PERSNL. In effect, now, the structure of the data-base will define what the newly-appended data fields refer to.

Obviously, it stands to reason that if you are going to build a file under a word processor, and you want that file to finally reside under a dBASE data-base format, you should ensure that the data entered into the word-processor file corresponds exactly to the subsequent, expected format of the dBASE file. If you fail to follow this rule, dBASE will not know the difference, and you could end up getting garbage for your result.

For example, suppose my text-file contained the following record:

My dear so-and-so, How I love you

If you now tried to APPEND this record into the structure of the file called PERSNL, then dBASE will take this record and plug it under the structure of PERSNL, character for character, so that after this APPEND, this record will appear as follows:

My dea	(will be the EMP:NUM, since it was defined as C,6)
r so-and-so, Ho	(will become the EMP:NAME, since it was defined as C,15)
w I love you	(will become the TOWN, since it was defined as C,12)
etc., etc., etc.	

As you can see, dBASE makes a presumption that your text file format conforms exactly with the structure of the data-base that will be receiving the text records, which, of course, is logical enough.

Why is it so important that dBASE should provide you with this capability to communicate with a text file? This facility gives you the ability to communicate with other software. For example, if someone has some data set up under, say, MBASIC or SUPERCALC, and you want to use this data, the MBASIC or SUPERCALC user should be able to create a standard file out of his/her MBASIC or SUPERCALC file, and you can then take this standard file and pull it into the appropriate dBASE format. The standard file so created may or may not be *delimited*. Delimited is explained in the next section.

[To convert MBASIC random files, you will first have to use MBASIC to convert the random file into an MBASIC line-sequential file (with or without delimiters) which can then be pulled off by dBASE into a dBASE format.]

Later, we shall see how we can go in reverse, that is, pull off a standard file (with or without delimiters) from a dBASE file. This will provide the complementary action required for full communication between dBASE and other software, via the SDF format.

Delimited Parameter

This section is important. Study it carefully.

```
.USE PERSNL                        <cr>
.APPEND FROM MYFILE SDF   DELIM    <cr>
```

The delimited parameter specifies that the standard file data is delimited, in one of the following ways:

'-----c-----', '-----c-----', -----n-----, '-----c-----'

The comma and the quote are the delimiters. Here you will notice that each character field is enclosed (delimited) in quotes, and every field is separated (delimited) by a comma. Numeric fields are not enclosed in quotes.

---c-----, -----c-----, -----n-----, -----c-----, -----n-----

Here, every field is delimited with the comma only, without quotes.

"-----c-----", "-----c-----", -----n-----, "-----c-----"

You may even find double-quotes, for the delimiter. The DELIM parameter provides you with the capability of creating a dBASE file out of a standard, *delimited*, text file, regardless of the way the file is delimited. At the end of the APPEND process, the commas and the quotes will have been automatically stripped off, and only real data gets APPENDed into the structures of the receiving data-base.

Why do we need to know about the DELIM parameter? After all, if you were creating your own standard file which was meant to (subsequently) end up under a dBASE format, you would keep it as simple as possible, and avoid keying in so many commas and quotes. You would, of course, stick to the format of the dBASE file into which you want your text file to APPEND, but you could get by without all those commas and quotes. (Or could you?)

This delimited parameter is important because some programming languages (such as versions of BASIC) produce data-files that are delimited with commas and/or quotes. Now, if you were trying to pull in data from a delimited file into dBASE, and if you tell dBASE that the file is SDF (standard), but you forget to tell dBASE that the file is also delimited, can you guess as to what will happen?

Every comma and quote will be pulled into the structure of your data-base, as ordinary data! dBASE would be unable to differentiate before the comma and quote as data, and the comma and quote as delimiters. If the commas and quotes are meant to be delimiters, inform dBASE of that fact!

Try creating your own standard file under a word processor. (This file is to be ultimately APPENDed into a dBASE format.) You will find it a tedious task to keep track of the various columns for the pieces of data (you have to stick to a specific format, remember ?), since you will have to space over exactly so-many columns for the next field of data, etc.

A much easier way would be to enter a comma after every field entered. For example, suppose we had the following 2 records, as text data, in the file called MYFILE.TXT:

23356L,KARL BUCHNER, ROCHESTER,BSG,T,1980
66753A,JOSEPH ARMSTRONG, IRONDEQUOIT,GSD,,1979

Obviously, placing the commas is much easier than trying to keep track of the various columns, for each piece of data. These commas are, of course, the delimiters for the various fields. The data for these fields could be variable in length. You could APPEND this standard file into our PERSNL data-base, with the following instruction:

.APPEND FROM MYFILE SDF DELIM   <cr>

dBASE would interpret each comma to be the end of a field, and the data would come to rest under the structure of the PERSNL file very appropriately. As you can appreciate, the use of the comma as the delimiter makes it easier to create a standard text file which has to conform to a specific data structure.

> **Note:** In the second record (for Armstrong), we did not know the
> EXEMPT data, and so we intended to keep that field blank. Hence, in

order that dBASE would "know" of the "blank field", we placed an extra comma after the "organization" field, since the data is, as we know, positional. Now, the 1979 in that record will fall correctly in the YR:OF:HIRE field, in the PERSNL file structure.

Note: All delimited files are SDF. That is, if you specify the DELIM parameter, you may avoid the SDF parameter. SDF files may, or may not, be delimited.

It is important to realize that regardless of the type of delimited file (with single/double quotes and/or commas) the parameter DELIM ensures a correct APPEND of the actual data, under the required dBASE structure.

Note: The two files used in the APPEND process need not reside on the same disk. Presuming you have not .SET DEFAULT TO B you can always specify:

.USE <master>   [<master> is on the A:drive]
.APPEND FROM B:<trans> [<trans> is on the B:drive]

Appending a Blank Record

One more form of the APPEND command uses the blank parameter.

.USE PERSNL   <cr>
.APPEND BLANK   <cr>

This command will append a blank record to the end of an existing data-base.

.LIST   <cr> [Note record #16]

00001	070707	NINA BHARUCHA	WEBSTER	BSG	.T.	1980	33000.00
00002	7545AD	PETE JOHNSON	brighton	BSG	.T.	1976	27590.00
00003	987178	GLORIA PATEL	FAIRPORT	RMG	.T.	1982	27500.00
00004	232430	MAX LEVENSKY	HENRIETTA	RMG	.F.	1969	27550.00
00005	0989SD	KIM BRANDT	FAIRPORT	RMG	.F.	1977	36000.00
00006	AC9090	TIM MONTAL	ROCHESTER	RBG	.F.	1981	41900.00
00007	08FG09	WILLIAM PATEL	penfield	GSD	.F.	1971	28900.00
00008	091230	JAMES JAMESON	ROCHESTER	GSD	.T.	1977	29800.00
00009	438190	MORRIS KATZ	webster	BSG	.F.	1980	23450.00
00010	087FG0	PAUL BHARUCHA	BRIGHTON	BSG	.T.	1973	29100.00
00011	00707A	PHIL MARTIN	WEBSTER	RMG	.F.	1980	31000.00
00012	8745AD	JOHN PETERSON	BRIGHTON	RBG	.T.	1979	31480.00
00013	070970	JOY HARDY	fairport	RBG	.F.	1979	34200.00
00014	09890A	JAN MOREY	ROCHESTER	GSD	.T.	1967	18190.00
00015	087WRF	JOHN JONES	rochester	GSD	.T.	1970	25100.00
00016					.F.	0	0.00

This form of the APPEND command is not as redundant as it might seem, at first glance. The importance of this form of the command can be highlighted as follows:

Suppose you write a computer program in dBASE (which we will be doing, in the course of this material), which, when invoked, sends up a formatted screen asking the operator to enter a record of information. The format on the screen asks the operator to enter, say, Employee Number, Name, Org and Salary.

When the required pieces of information have been keyed-in, the program now has to undertake the task of creating a new record of data from the information supplied by the operator. So the program will APPEND BLANK to the data-base in use, creating a blank record of information at the end of the data-base, and, more important, getting the record pointer to point to the newly appended record. Now the program can replace the appropriate blank fields of the new record with the information that was keyed in by the operator.

We shall see examples of this later.

Data Movement Outcomes

Now would be an appropriate time to cover the what-if types of questions dealing with data movement. In other words, what is the expected outcome if you were to attempt an APPEND of data between, say, a field defined as EMP:NUM,C,6 and EMP:NUM,N,5? I shall attempt to cover all combinations of cases, as outlined in the table.

One rule of thumb to be followed, for now, is that *the receiving field determines justification*. In general, all numeric data is right justified within its field and all character data is left justified within its field. In conjunction with the rule-of-thumb specified above, this means that if the receiving field is a character field, then that implies left justification, and so the data is picked up left from the sending field and moved in left in the receiving field. Conversely, if the receiving field is a numeric field, then that implies right justification, and so the data is picked up right from the sending field and moved in right in the receiving field. Study the following table.

Note: The ^ symbol signifies a space character.

	FROM field and data		**TO field and result**	
A.	C,6	ABCDEF	C,5	ABCDE
B.	C,6	ABCDEF	C,7	ABCDEF^
C.	N,4	1972	C,3	197
D.	N,4	1972	C,5	1972^
E.	N,4	1972	N,3	0 NUMERIC FIELD OVERFLOW
F.	N,4	1972	N,5	^1972

The above set of examples all follow the rules outlined before, with one exception: a data move of zero takes place and an error message "NUMERIC FIELD OVERFLOW" is issued in case you are attempting data movement from a numeric field into a *smaller* numeric field.

The group of moves classified as character-to-numeric do *not* follow the previous rule-of-thumb. For the character-to-numeric moves, the rule is as follows: data is retrieved, character by character, from the character field, left justified, and the first nonnumeric in that character field stops the data movement. The data comes to rest in the numeric field right justified.

	FROM field and data			TO field and result	
G.	C,3	12A	N,3	^12	
		1A2		^^1	
		A21		^^0	
		123		123	
H.	C,3	12A	N,4	^^12	
		1A2		^^^1	
		A21		^^^0	
		123		^123	
I.	C,3	12A	N,2	12	
		1A2		^1	
		A21		^0	
		123		^0	NUMERIC FIELD OVERFLOW !!

> **Note:** A data move of zero takes place and an error message "NUMERIC FIELD OVERFLOW" is issued in case you are attempting data movement from a character field into a *smaller* numeric field, and the character field contains *valid* data that could all have entered the numeric field had it not been for the size of the numeric field.

For instance, you may have issued an APPEND command to APPEND data into FILE1 from FILE2. While the computer is churning away, suddenly a few messages flash out: "NUMERIC FIELD OVERFLOW". This implies data/structure situations as explained previously, but dBASE does not provide either the names of the fields or the record numbers of the data involved in the process. If you do encounter these messages, back out all your APPENDS, modify the appropriate structures (as is explained in full detail, in this chapter), and proceed with the APPEND again.

What do I mean by back out all your Appends? Normally, when the APPEND command has completed its execution, dBASE flashes a message on the screen indicating the number of records that had been appended at the end of existing data into FILE1 from FILE2. These records would have to be DELETEd from FILE1, and FILE1 then PACKed, to physically back out all the appended records from FILE1.

However, under some situations, you may have issued a prior command to the effect: .SET TALK OFF (this command will be explained later, in the programming portion of this book). Under the effect of the above SET command, there is no message from dBASE regarding the number of records appended from FILE2.

So you should go about it as follows. If all the records from FILE2 had been appended, you can:

```
.USE FILE2        <cr>
.GO BOTT          <cr>
.DISP             <cr>
```

This will display the last record, with the record number, so you now know exactly how many records should be backed out from FILE1.

If only selected records from FILE2 had been appended into FILE1, you should do the following:

```
.USE FILE 2       <cr>
.COUNT FOR <same condition used for the APPEND>   <cr>
```

Now dBASE will indicate on the screen the number of records that fulfilled the condition, and hence how many records you should back out of FILE1. Using either of the above methods you can easily find out how many records from FILE1 need to be backed out.

Now, for the actual process of backing out these records; use the following procedure. Suppose we wanted to back out 100 records.

```
.USE FILE1        <cr>
.GO BOTT          <cr>
.DISP             <cr>
```

The record number of the last record provides us with the total number of records in FILE1. Suppose there were 300 records in FILE1. Obviously, if we have to "back out" the last 100 records out of a total of 300 records, it follows quite logically that we need to back out record numbers 201 through 300. That is, our starting record number is 201 $[(300-100) + 1]$.

```
.201      <cr>
```

This will move the record pointer to record number 201. The file in use, of course, is FILE1.

```
.DELE NEXT 100              <cr>
.PACK                       <cr>
```

This process will back-out all unrequired appended records. Of course, the moral of the story is: Never APPEND with nonconforming (dissimilar) structures.

COPY COMMAND

This is one of the most powerful commands in dBASE. With this command, you could do one or more of the following:

□ Make a backup copy of any data-base, structure and data.
□ Copy over only the structure.
□ Copy over only the data, in the form of a text file.
□ Copy over selected records.
□ Copy over only a limited structure, with or without data.
□ Create a delimited file, for use with other software.

By now, the generic form of the command should tell you all about the capability of the command.

.COPY TO <file> [scope] [FIELD <list>] [FOR <condition>]
        [SDF] [STRUCTURE] [DELIM [WITH
        <delimiter>]]

We shall study each one of these parameters. After each command has been executed, you may want to check out the results for your own curiosity. Use the usual DISP STRU and LIST commands for this purpose. Also remember that deleted records will not be copied over!

To <file> Parameter

This parameter creates another distinct and separate data-base called BACK-UP.DBF, which is identical in structure and data to the file called PERSNL.

.USE PERSNL   <cr>
.COPY TO BACKUP   <cr>

Here we have a quick way of making a complete backup copy of any dBASE data-base Master file. In fact, before the start of our EDITING session, we had used this command to preserve our PERSNL file in the PRESERVE.DBF data-base.

> **Note:** By itself, the COPY command will not COPY over deleted records. If you want to copy over a Master file that has deleted records, and if you want the deleted records retained in their deleted status on the backup file, you will first have to save the deleted records in another data-base of the same structure as the Master. This process is fully explored in the section entitled "Saving Deleted Records in Another Data-Base."
> **Note:** If a file called BACKUP.DBF had existed before the start of the command, it is zapped out, and a new BACKUP data-base is created. No errors or warning messages are issued! Therefore, en-sure that you do not have any typos, before you <cr>!

Next Parameter

The USE command places dBASE in control over the first record of the PERSNL file. Hence the copy command will copy over the entire structure, but only the first ten data-records of the file will be copied over to the BACKUP data-base with the following command. The NEXT 10 is, of course, the *scope* of the operation.

```
.USE PERSNL                        <cr>
.COPY TO BACKUP  NEXT 10           <cr>
```

Field Parameter

This parameter will create a file called BACKUP.DBF comprising all of the data records from PERSNL, but the record structure of these records will only comprise of the fields that are listed after the FIELD statement exactly as they have been defined in the structure of the PERNSL file.

```
.USER PERSNL                                      <cr>
.COPY TO BACKUP FIELD EMP:NUM,EMP:NAME, ORG  <cr>
```

This routine highlights one of the most important uses of the COPY command. It enables you to create a subset of information from a Master file. By simply including the FIELDS parameter, you can specify which fields you want copied over from the Master file, *and in what order!*

The FOR Condition

You can specify a condition under which you want the copy to proceed.

```
.USE PERSNL        <cr>
.COPY TO BACKUP FOR TOWN = 'ROCHESTER'  <cr>
```

Now only records that satisfy the FOR condition will be copied over. The fields used in the FOR condition must, of course, be defined in the structure of the "from" file. As always, the condition can be as simple or as complex as you want it to be. The special functions mentioned earlier can also be used. In this example, the BACKUP file will have the same structure as the PERSNL file, but the data records will be limited to records with TOWN = 'ROCHESTER'.

> **Note:** Deleted records cannot be copied over! Even if you execute the following commands, the deleted records will not copy.

```
.USE PERSNL                        <cr>
.COPY TO BACKUP FOR *              <cr>
```

This sequence will result in zero records being copied over. Note, however, that the structure will be copied over. That is, a file called BACKUP.DBF will be created with structure only, and the structure will be identical to that of the PERSNL file.

You can, of course, specify more than one parameter in the same command. For example:

```
.COPY TO BACKUP FOR TOWN = 'R' FIELDS EMP:NUM,EMP:NAME,ORG
```

This command will create a file called BACKUP.DBF comprised of only 3 fields in its structure, and containing data copied from the Master file for TOWN = 'R' only.

SDF Parameter

I have purposely used the same name BACKUP in the following example to clarify exactly what this command will do.

```
.USE PERSNL                    <cr>
.COPY TO BACKUP  SDF           <cr>
```

The parameter SDF informs dBASE that the file called BACKUP is not to be created as a dBASE file, but as a text file (if you remember, Standard Data Format). The creation of a text file by dBASE results in the last qualifier of .TXT being given to the file.

You could also have done the following:

```
.COPY TO BACKUP.FIL   SDF    <cr>
```

This will create a Text file called BACKUP.FIL. In the absence of a secondary name, a text file will be given the qualifier of .TXT by dBASE.

By using the SDF parameter you can go from a dBASE format to a text format. This is how you can pass your dBASE data over for processing under other software! This is complementary to the APPEND command, which lets us create a dBASE file from an SDF file.

Please remember that a text file has no formalized structure, except as may be inferred by the user of that file. Also, the transition to a text format permits you to include data from a dBASE file as part of a word-processed document.

Structure Parameter

The STRU parameter informs dBASE that you want to copy over only the structure of a file without any of the data.

```
.USE PERSNL                    <cr>
.COPY TO BACKUP  STRU          <cr>
```

Why would you want to copy over only the structure of any file? It is possible that you want to create another data-base having a similar, but not exactly identical, structure as that of the PERSNL file. It is so much easier to MODIFY STRU of an existing data-base for a few changes, than it is to key-in a new structure all over again, especially if you have many fields to define in the new structure.

If the STRU parameter appears in the COPY command, dBASE will copy over the structure, only, without data! (The SDF parameter is an exception. It is explained at the end of this narrative.)

```
.COPY TO BACKUP STRU FIELDS EMP:NUM,TOWN,ORG  <cr>
```

This statement will copy over, in the same BACKUP.DBF, the STRU only, of the defined fields only. No data is copied over.

Delimited [with <delimiter>] Parameter

The last, but by no means the least, of the parameters of the COPY command is the DELIMITED [WITH <delimiter>] parameter. As you can guess, this parameter will help us create Standard Format (text) files which are also delimited.

```
.USE PERSNL        <cr>
.COPY TO MYFILE    SDF      DELIM      <cr>
```

As before, this command will produce a file called MYFILE.TXT, which will be a text file, and it will be delimited. The DELIM parameter by itself will produce the following type of delimited file: [c = "character", n = "numeric"].

'-----c-----', '-----c-----', -----n-----, '------c-----', -----n-----

The file has single quotes and commas, but *no quotes around numeric fields*.

```
.COPY TO MYFILE    SDF    DELIM WITH '   <cr>
```

This statement will produce a standard, delimited file identical to the previous one.

```
.COPY TO MYFILE SDF     DELIM   WITH "          <cr>
```

This statement has the same format as for the previous results, but with double-quotes.

```
.COPY TO MYFILE SDF DELIM WITH, <cr>
```

Here you are specifying the comma only, to the exclusion of any kind of quotes.

-----c-----, -----c-----, ------n----, ------c-----, -----n-----

In other words, you will always get the comma, if you ask for a delimited file. But you may or may not want the quotes. The COPY command, therefore, can provide you with several formats, for delimited files.

In all the previous examples, the parameter SDF was redundant, since, if you remember, the parameter DELIM implies a standard file. Remember: a DELIM file is always a text (SDF) file; a text file may or may not be a DELIM file.

> **Note:** STRU and SDF are the two parameters that should not be used together. This is because a standard file has no structure so your request for a structure only for an SDF file would be illogical. If both SDF and STRU parameters appear in a command, then regardless of their order in the command, dBASE takes a default and provides us with an SDF file!

The SDF and DELIM parameters help you create text files which can be manipulated by other software products, such as MBASIC, SUPERCALC, etc.

REPLACE COMMAND

This command is a very powerful remote edit feature. That is, with the use of just this one command, you can make massive changes to the data-base. By now, the format and the parameters should be self-explanatory:

REPLACE [scope] <field-name> WITH <expression>;
<field-name> WITH <expression>;
[FOR <condition>]

> **Note:** The REPLACE command only changes the contents of field variables. The REPLACE command also ignores deleted records!

As always, if [scope] is not supplied, the command will act on the current record pointed at. If [scope] is not supplied, but a FOR condition exists, the default for scope is ALL.

```
.USE PERSNL                                          <cr>
.REPLACE TOWN WITH 'PERINTON' FOR ORG = 'BSG'        <cr>
.LIST                                                <cr>
```

Since a scope is missing, but a FOR condition exists, all the records that satisfy the condition will be changed. Changed records have been highlighted.

00001	**070707**	**NINA BHARUCHA**	**PERINTON**	**BSG**	**.T.**	**1980**	**33000.00**
00002	**7545AD**	**PETE JOHNSON**	**PERINTON**	**BSG**	**.T.**	**1976**	**27590.00**
00003	987178	GLORIA PATEL	FAIRPORT	RMG	.T.	1982	27500.00
00004	232430	MAX LEVENSKY	HENRIETTA	RMG	.F.	1969	27550.00
00005	0989SD	KIM BRANDT	FAIRPORT	RMG	.F.	1977	36000.00
00006	AC9090	TIM MONTAL	ROCHESTER	RBG	.F.	1981	41900.00
00007	08FG09	WILLIAM PATEL	penfield	GSD	.F.	1971	28900.00
00008	091230	JAMES JAMESON	ROCHESTER	GSD	.T.	1977	29800.00
00009	**438190**	**MORRIS KATZ**	**PERINTON**	**BSG**	**.F.**	**1980**	**23450.00**
00010	**087FG0**	**PAUL BHARUCHA**	**PERINTON**	**BSG**	**.T.**	**1973**	**29100.00**
00011	00707A	PHIL MARTIN	WEBSTER	RMG	.F.	1980	31000.00
00012	8745AD	JOHN PETERSON	BRIGHTON	RBG	.T.	1979	31480.00
00013	070970	JOY HARDY	fairport	RBG	.F.	1979	34200.00
00014	09890A	JAN MOREY	ROCHESTER	GSD	.T.	1967	18190.00
00015	087WRF	JOHN JONES	rochester	GSD	.T.	1970	25100.00

```
.REPLACE   EXEMPT WITH T, ORG WITH 'GSD';            <cr>
           FOR SALARY > 25000                        <cr>
.LIST
```

Changed records have been highlighted.

00001	070707	NINA BHARUCHA	WEBSTER	BSG	.T.	1980	36300.00
00002	7545AD	PETE JOHNSON	brighton	BSG	.F.	1976	30349.00
00003	987178	GLORIA PATEL	FAIRPORT	RMG	.T.	1982	27500.00
00004	232430	MAX LEVENSKY	HENRIETTA	RMG	.F.	1969	27550.00
00005	0989SD	KIM BRANDT	FAIRPORT	RMG	.F.	1977	36000.00
00006	AC9090	TIM MONTAL	ROCHESTER	RBG	.F.	1981	41900.00
00007	08FG09	WILLIAM PATEL	penfield	GSD	.F.	1971	28900.00
00008	091230	JAMES JAMESON	ROCHESTER	GSD	.T.	1977	29800.00
00009	438190	MORRIS KATZ	webster	BSG	.F.	1980	25795.00
00010	087FGO	PAUL BHARUCHA	BRIGHTON	BSG	.T.	1973	32020.00
00011	00707A	PHIL MARTIN	WEBSTER	RMG	.F.	1980	31000.00
00012	9745AD	JOHN PETERSON	BRIGHTON	RBG	.T.	1979	31480.00
00013	070970	JOY HARDY	fairport	RBG	.F.	1979	34200.00
00014	09890A	JAN MOREY	ROCHESTER	GSD	.T.	1967	18190.00
00015	087WRF	JOHN JONES	rochester	GSD	.T.	1970	25100.00

Since it is possible for you to alter the contents of your data-base rather radically through the use of this instruction, you would be well-advised to use the following precaution, before you issue this command.

```
.USE PERSNL                         <cr>
.COPY TO BACKUP                     <cr>
.REPLACE ALL . . .                  <cr>
```

After the REPLACE has completed, check your replacements out, and if good, you can always delete the BACKUP file.

```
[DELETE FILE BACKUP      <cr>]
```

However, in case a typo caused a mess in your PERSNL data-base, the BACKUP file would be your way out of the mess.

```
[.USE BACKUP            <cr>
.COPY TO PERSNL        <cr> Existing PERSNL file is deleted.
.USE PERSNL            <cr>
```

Please be sure to take this precaution and create a backup file prior to the issue of the REPLACE ALL command. To illustrate the power of this command, suppose that you had an INVENTORY Master file, and you decided that it was time to raise unit-costs by, say, 10%. The following REPLACE command makes this task very simple:

```
.USE INVNTRY                    <cr>
.COPY TO BACKUP                 <cr> Keep a backup!
.REPLACE ALL UNIT:COST WITH UNIT:COST * 1.1  <cr>
```

Note: The * symbol signifies multiplication.

All unit-costs are now replaced by amounts that are 10% higher. After you have checked out the replacements, you can delete the backup file.

In our PERSNL file example, to demonstrate this command, you may, perhaps, decide to give the employees in a certain organization a raise of, say, 10%.

```
.USE PERSNL                          <cr>
.COPY TO BACKUP                      <cr>     A precaution.
.REPLACE ALL SALARY WITH SALARY * 1.1;     <cr>
              FOR ORG = 'BSG'              <cr>
```

Only the records with ORG = 'BSG' will have their salary fields changed. Check out the changes, then delete the BACKUP file, to release space.

You can use the REPLACE command to change all suspended lowercase data to uppercase, if required. The following example will convert all lowercase data in the town-field to uppercase.

```
.REPLACE ALL TOWN WITH !(TOWN)   cr
```

The following statement would do the same thing for the organization field data.

```
.REPLACE ALL ORG WITH !(ORG)   cr
```

data-base, decide that you did, after all, want to recover some/all of the PACKed records, and that your PACK decision was a hasty one.

SAVE DELETED RECORDS IN ANOTHER DATA-BASE

At the time we were covering the DELETE, RECALL, and PACK subset of commands, we had mentioned that before you actually PACKed in your data-base, you may want to save all deleted records in another data-base having the same structure as the Master file. This was advisable on account of the fact that you may, after you PACK in your data-base, decide that you did, after all, want to recover some/all of the PACKed records, and that your PACK decision was a hasty one.

We shall now look at the mechanics of copying deleted records in another data-base, before the PACK process. We could not get to this stage without first studying the COPY and REPLACE commands, and hence we take it up at this stage of the game.

Using the Dummy Field

This is where the DUMMY field that you created in the structure of the PERSNL file will play its second important role. Obviously, the following procedure will work only if you had a maximum of 31 real fields of data defined in the structure, with at least one field being defined as the DUMMY field.

> **Note:** If the following command would work, that would be the
> end of this procedure, but unfortunately it does not quite do the trick.

```
.USE PERSNL                     <cr>    Presume that some records are deleted.
.COPY TO SAFETY FOR * <cr>
```

Here we are attempting to create a file called SAFETY.DBF, which is supposed to contain only the deleted records from the PERSNL file. But if you recall, the COPY command ignores deleted records, and so zero records will be copied over. Obviously, we have to come up with a way to fool dBASE into saving deleted records in another data-base of identical structure as the PERSNL file.

Suppose, for now, that our DUMMY field had been defined as DUMMY,C,1. It does not really matter what the definition is, but for now we shall go with C,1. The following string of commands will do the trick. It is important that you take a dry run of this routine on paper using fictitious records to see how it all fits together.

Let us suppose that out of a total of 5 records in our PERSNL file, records #3 and #5 have been deleted. At the end of this routine, we should have saved records #3 and #5 in another data-base, and also PACKed in the PERSNL file.

```
.USE PERSNL                                                     <cr>
.REPLACE ALL DUMMY WITH '1' FOR .NOT. *                         <cr>
[records #1,2,4 all have a '1' in the DUMMY field]

.RECALL ALL                                                     <cr>
[all the * flags are removed, from the PERSNL records]
.COPY TO KEEPEM FOR DUMMY # '1'                                 <cr>
[creates a data-base called KEEPEM.DBF, with the same structure as PERSNL,
and which contains records #3 and 5]
.DELETE FOR DUMMY # '1'                                         <cr>
[replaces the *-flags against records #3 and 5]
.PACK                                                           <cr>
[physically removes records #3 and 5]
.REPLACE ALL DUMMY WITH ' '                                     <cr>
[cleans-up the dummy field, for the next time around]
```

At the end of this routine, you will have managed to save all deleted records in another data-base of the same structure as the original data-base. Note that since the KEEPEM data-base is independent of the PERSNL data-base, the records in that data-base will have their record numbers starting with 1,2,3,4 . . . . ., and those records will obviously not be flagged as deleted. As far as the KEEPEM file is concerned, these records are good, valid records. It is your documentation that will specify the exact nature and use of the KEEPEM file.

Again, it would help if you ran through these instructions on paper, using a few imaginary deleted records.

Without the Use of the Dummy Field

Now we shall study a way of saving deleted records in another data-base even if we did not have the advantage of the dummy-field used earlier. To save deleted records out of a file in which you do not have a dummy field defined, you would have to go about it in a lengthy, round-about manner. In the instructions that follow, ALTE stands for ALTER-NATE.

.SET RAW ON

This ensures that on subsequent DISP or LIST commands, the usual one column of space does not appear between fields as it always does.

.USE PERSNL
.SET ALTE TO TEMP

This defines a file called TEMP.TXT (a text file).

.SET ALTE ON

This activates the TEMP file. From now on, anything that appears on the screen will be recorded in the TEXT file, as standard records of data.

The file in use is still PERSNL.

.LIST FOR * OFF

This command itself gets recorded in the TEMP file. Now, as the deleted records get listed out on the screen, they get entered in the TEXT file, as standard text. The format of this text file is identical to that of PERSNL.

.SET ALTE OFF

This command itself gets recorded in the TEMP file. This command now deacti-vates the alternate file.

.SET ALTE TO

This command closes the Alternate file.

.SET RAW OFF

The file in use is still PERSNL. At this point in time, we have managed to save all our deleted records in a text (SDF) file called TEMP.TXT. Also, the text file has some garbage records at the top and bottom of the text file. The file in use is still PERSNL.

COPY TO KEEPEM STRU

This creates another data-base called KEEPEM.DBF, of identical structure as the file PERSNL.

.USE KEEPEM
.APPEND FROM TEMP SDF

At this point, we will have a data-base called KEEPEM, of identical structure as PERSNL, but containing only the deleted records out of the PERSNL file. However, please note that these records are not flagged as deleted! They are good, valid records in the KEEPEM.DBF data-base. Also, this KEEPEM file contains some garbage records as mentioned earlier.

Now delete the garbage records from the TOP and BOTTOM of the KEEPEM file, and then PACK in the KEEPEM file. The file TEMP.TXT can now be deleted, to release space.

This procedure has now helped us to create another data-base called KEEPEM.DBF containing only the deleted records from the PERSNL file. We did this without the facility of any dummy-field in the structure of the PERSNL file. The KEEPEM.DBF file structure is identical to that of PERSNL. The PERSNL file still has some of its records flagged as deleted.

Now we can safely PACK-in the PERSNL file.

.USE PERSNL   <cr>
.PACK   <cr>

If in future we decide that we want the KEEPEM records back again, we can always APPEND them.

.USE PERSNL   <cr>
.APPEND FROM KEEPEM   <cr>

MODIFY COMMAND

This command is used for four purposes, depending on the parameter that follows the command. It can be used

☐ To change structures of existing data-bases, from any point of view: add a new field; delete an existing field; change the name of the field; change the type of the field; change the length of the field.

☐ To inform dBASE that you wish to work on the development of a Computer Program—existing or new.

☐ To modify the contents of Report Format files.

☐ To modify the contents of Screen Format files.

At the moment, we shall concentrate on the first use. The other topics will be covered at the appropriate places in this book.

If you recall, I began Section 2 with the study of the CREATE command, followed with a detailed discussion of the steps that would have to be undertaken in order to MODIFY the structure you had created. In that discussion, I included a caution to you to the extent that I was advocating a particular method of approach for modifying structures only because our data-base was devoid of any data-records.

Now, of course, our data-base has records in it, and we want to modify the structure of the PERSNL file to some extent. Whatever you had studied earlier in the MODIFY command will hold good. The only change this time is, as you may have guessed, in the creation of a back-up file, for preserving our data.

> **Caution:** If your data-base currently has some deleted records in it, then please note that attempting to modify the structure will result in the loss of these deleted records. So before you go ahead with the following procedure to modify any structures, please ensure that you have managed to save all your deleted records in another data-base of the same structure as your Master file. The process of doing this has been detailed in the previous section.
>
> **Note:** In our discussions for modifying structures, we will always stress the fact that you should not modify the field-type. The reason for this should be apparent, since your attempt to APPEND data from one field into another of a different type could produce rather unpleasant results. We have discussed, quite at length, what would happen under such situations. If necessary, please refer to the section entitled "Data Movement Outcomes", under the APPEND command discussion.

Adding/Deleting Fields in the Structure OR Changing Field Lengths

This option of the modify command can add or delete fields in the structure or it can change field lengths. Do not change the field-names. Begin with the following commands:

```
.USE PERSNL                    <cr>
.COPY TO BACKUP                <cr>
```

At the end of the above command, we have a BACKUP.DBF data-base, identical to PERSNL in structure and data. The file in use is still PERSNL.

```
.MODI STRU                     <cr>
```

MODIFY ERASES ALL DATA RECORDS . . . PROCEED? (Y/N)

```
Y      <cr>
```

At this point in time, we will see the structure of the file on the screen in the full-screen edit mode.

Make the changes you want, as far as adding/deleting fields is concerned. Use Ctrl-N (for adding) and Ctrl-T (for deleting) for this purpose. Make no changes to existing field-names! You may, if you like, make changes to field lengths or field types, but please understand that this may have some adverse effects on the data, when you have to bring the data back in. The exact mechanics of the cursor controls and the various dBASE software controls have been explored in great depth under "Modifying Structures" as part of the CREATE command discussion. Refer back, if you have to.

When you are through modifying, what do you suppose will happen if you enter a Ctrl-Q? As you know, a Ctrl-Q is how you change your mind on modification of the structure. However, you had answered Y to dBASE's statement that modification erases data, and did you still want to proceed. Under the situation, you would conclude that a Ctrl-Q at this stage is too late to save your data. However, that is not the case! The actual data-loss occurs only when you enter a Ctrl-W and confirm the new structure. If you back out with a Ctrl-Q, you will find the old structure and data are all intact. (Try this out, if you like. Enter a Ctrl-Q, then DISP STRU, then LIST.)

Suppose, for now, that you make the following changes to the structure of the PERSNL data-base:

1. Enter a new field: CLASS,C,1 ahead of the yr:of:hire field.
2. Delete the field called EXEMPT.
3. Enter a Ctrl-W, to save the new structure.

At this stage, the file in USE is still PERSNL, and you have just modified its structure by adding/deleting entire fields. Now display the structure.

.DISP STRU   <cr>

STRUCTURE FOR FILE: A:PERSNL .DBF
NUMBER OF RECORDS: 00000
DATE OF LAST UPDATE: 00/00/00
PRIMARY USE DATA- BASE

FLD	NAME	TYPE	WIDTH	DEC	
001	EMP:NUM	C	006		
002	EMP:NAME	C	015		
003	TOWN	C	012		
004	ORG	C	003		
005	CLASS	C	001		This is the new field we had defined.
006	YR:OF:HIRE	N	004		
007	SALARY	N	008	002	
008	DUMMY	C	001		
** TOTAL **				00051	

.LIST   <cr>

Notice that nothing lists out, since the previous modification has deleted all data-records. However, we still have our BACKUP file, which contains the data intact. The file currently in use is still PERSNL. Now APPEND the backup file.

.APPEND FROM BACKUP   <cr>

If you recall, the way the APPEND command works is that data from matching field-names is APPENDed over. Since we had deleted the field called EXEMPT, we can forget retrieving any data for that field in the APPEND process. Also, our new field called CLASS will contain blanks in its format for all the records, since it does not exist on the BACKUP file. But we will have managed to salvage all the data for those remaining field-names that still match. Let us list out the result. (The CLASS field was defined between the ORG and YR:OF:HIRE fields).

.LIST   <cr>

00001	070707	NINA BHARUCHA	WEBSTER	BSG	1980	36300.00
00002	7545AD	PETE JOHNSON	brighton	BSG	1976	30349.00
00003	987178	GLORIA PATEL	FAIRPORT	RMG	1982	27500.00
00004	232430	MAX LEVENSKY	HENRIETTA	RMG	1969	27550.00
00005	0989SD	KIM BRANDT	FAIRPORT	RMG	1977	36000.00
00006	AC9090	TIM MONTAL	ROCHESTER	RBG	1981	41900.00
00007	08FG09	WILLIAM PATEL	penfield	GSD	1971	28900.00
00008	091230	JAMES JAMESON	ROCHESTER	GSD	1977	29800.00
00009	438190	MORRIS KATZ	webster	BSG	1980	25795.00
00010	087FG0	PAUL BHARUCHA	BRIGHTON	BSG	1973	32010.00
00011	00707A	PHIL MARTIN	WEBSTER	RMG	1980	31000.00
00012	8745AD	JOHN PETERSON	BRIGHTON	RBG	1979	31480.00
00013	070970	JOY HARDY	fairport	RBG	1979	34200.00
00014	09890A	JAN MOREY	ROCHESTER	GSD	1967	18190.00
00015	087WRF	JOHN JONES	rochester	GSD	1970	

Obviously, this process works on account of the fact that we can APPEND data back into the new structure from the BACKUP file. The APPEND process works since we have not changed our field-names. At the end of the modify process, the BACKUP.DBF file can be deleted to release space.

Now an immediate question arises: How does one change field-names in the structure of any file?

Changing Field-Names in the Structure

This option of the modify command changes field-names. Do not change add/delete fields or change field lengths.

.USE PERSNL   <cr>
.COPY TO BACKUP SDF   <cr>

At the completion of these commands, we have a BACKUP.TXT standard file with data from the PERSNL.DBF data-base but in standard format. The file in use is still PERSNL.

.MOFIDY STRU   <cr>

MODIFY ERASES ALL DATA RECORDS . . . PROCEED? (Y/N)

Y   <cr>

Make any changes you want as far as changing field-names. Do not add or delete any fields now! Do not change any field lengths or types, now! The exact mechanics of the cursor controls and the various dBASE software controls have been explored in great depth under "Modifying Structures," as part of the CREATE command discussion. Refer back, if you have to.

Suppose, for now, that you make the following changes to the structure of the PERSNL data-base:

1. Change the name of the EMP:NUM field to read EMPNUM.
2. Change the name of the EMP:NAME field to read EMPNAME.
3. Enter a Ctrl-W to save the new structure.

At this stage, the file in use is still PERSNL, and you have just modified its structure, by changing field-names.

.APPEND FROM BACKUP SDF   <cr>

This command will help us put all our data back in. If you like, at this point DISP STRU then LIST. The reason for the success of this operation is, of course, the fact that when dBASE is APPENDing data from a standard file, it simply pulls in the standard record under the structure of the dBASE file blindly, character-by-character. Hence you could change field-names in the structure of the data-base file, and dBASE would not know the difference. Hence, also, that during this phase of the operation, you could not add or delete entire fields, or change field-lengths, else characters from the standard record would now be APPENDed into the wrong fields in the structure of the data-base. At the end of the modify process, the BACKUP.TXT file can be deleted to release space.

If you had a situation where you wanted to add/delete entire fields and change some field-names around, you would have to go through two independent modification steps, as detailed above. The order of execution of the steps is immaterial.

Changing Field-Names and Field Lengths in the Structure

In this option, both field-names and field lengths can be changed, but entire fields can not be added or deleted. We have seen in the previous discussion that in order to change field-names, you will have to create a standard file as your backup file. In this case, we want to change field lengths, too, but if you recall, a change in length will mean that the subsequent Append of data from the standard file back into the dBASE structure will cause the wrong characters of data to fall under the wrong fields in the structure.

We have to make a slight change in our approach, therefore, and when we create the backup file, not only will it have to be a standard file, but it will also have to be a delimited file.

```
.USE PERSNL                                              <cr>
.COPY TO BACKUP SDF DELIM                                <cr>
```

If you recall, the DELIM parameter by itself provides data in the following format:

'-----c-----', '-----c-----', -----n-----, '-----c-----', -----n-----

Commas delimit every field, and single-quotes are placed around the character fields. No quotes appear around numeric fields. Now, proceed as before to modify the structure. After the structure has been modified with the field-name changes and the field-length changes (no adding/deleting entire fields), append the data back into the structure from the standard, delimited file with the following command:

```
.APPEND FROM BACKUP   SDF   DELIM                        <cr>
```

Now although field-lengths may have been changed, dBASE will interpret every comma in the SDF file to be the end of a field of data, and the data will come to rest in the structure of the PERSNL file very appropriately. Obviously, when you change field-lengths, the subsequent append of data back in from the backup file may not work quite as well as you may expect. For example, if you have reduced the length of a character field, then on the Append from the backup file, data will be truncated to the reduced size of the modified field. So be aware of such side effects.

The following table helps to summarize the various options we have seen:

Changes To		Type of
field-NAME	field-LENGTH	BACKUP-file
yes	yes	SDF DELIM, only
yes	no	SDF, or SDF DELIM
no	yes	DBF, or SDF DELIM
add/delete entire fields, and		
no	yes	DBF only

Recovering Deleted Records after Structure Modification

In the preceding pages, we learned how to save all our deleted records in another data-base (the KEEPEM file) of identical structure as the Master, and how to then go about modifying the structure of the Master from several points of view. Now, since the modification process involves the use of the COPY command, at the end of the modification, all deleted records will automatically have been ignored and lost. Now we have to bring in these deleted records back again, from the KEEPEM file, into our modified Master file, to restore the Master file back to its original status.

.USE PERSNL	\<cr\>	This file's structure has been modified.
.GO BOTT	\<cr\>	
.DISP	\<cr\>	This will provide you with the record number of the last record in the modified Master file. Let us suppose that this record number is 115.

Now APPEND the deleted records back into the Master, from the appropriate file in which they had been saved.

.APPEND FROM KEEPEM   \<cr\>

Obviously, the first of these appended records will have a record number of 116.

.116	\<cr\>	This will position the pointer to record number 116.
.DELETE NEXT 9999	\<cr\>	This will flag all records from 116 onwards as deleted.

At the end of this procedure, we will have managed to regain all the deleted records in our Master file whose structure has been modified. The only obvious difference is that all the deleted records will appear clumped at the bottom of the file. That is far better than losing them altogether, and the process of Indexing (which does not ignore deleted records) can be used to obtain our desired sequence. As you may appreciate, the process of modification of structures involves much more than meets the eye at first glance.

At this point in our study of dBASE, you should be able to CREATE structures, APPEND data into the structures, DISPLAY the data in many ways, EDIT/BROWSE the data at will, and MODIFY STRUCTURES around enough to be able to fully guarantee the integrity of your dBASE data-bases.

Deleting All Records Instantly

How would you quickly remove all the records from a dBASE Master file? For instance, if you wanted to follow the standard process:

.DELETE ALL	\<cr\>
.PACK	\<cr\>

This process could take quite an appreciable amount of time depending on the number of records in the Master file. The PACK process involves an internal COPY that dBASE goes through. That is, the PACK is not instantaneous. You could try any one of the following routines to obtain the results you want:

A. This method is a straightforward approach.

1.	.USE "MASTER"	\<cr\>	
2.	.COPY TO BACKUP STRU	\<cr\>	
3.	.USE	\<cr\>	Closes the file currently in use.

4.   .DELETE FILE MASTER   \<cr\>
5.   .RENAME BACKUP TO "MASTER"   \<cr\>

B. This will prove to be a faster solution than the one just outlined.

1.   .USE "MASTER"   \<cr\>
2.   .MODI STRU   \<cr\>

MODIFY ERASES ALL DATA RECORDS . . . PROCEED? (Y/N)

3.   Y   \<cr\>

4. When the structure appears on the screen, enter a Ctrl-W to save the new structure, in effect, making sure that all the data records are instantly lost! The actual structure, of course, remains the same as it was before.

JOIN COMMAND

Suppose you have an INVENTORY Master file, with the following structure:

PART:NUM   DESC   UNIT:COST   ONHAND

Suppose, further, that you have another file containing ORDERS for those part:numbers, and its structure contains:

PART:NUM   CUST:NAME   ONORDER

PART:NUM, of course, is the common factor in these two structures, and we want to use this commonality to produce another file with the following structure:

PART:NUM   CUST:NAME   ONORDER   UNIT:COST

That is, we want to be able to pick up and group together, all individual customer orders for the various part numbers.

The JOIN command is used to add the data from two data-bases, based on certain selection criteria that you provide, to produce a third data-base. One of these input files is to be designated by you as a primary file, (the INVENTORY Master file) and the other input as the secondary file (the ORDERS Master file). The third file, of course, is the output of the primary and secondary, as a result of the JOIN.

The way the JOIN command works is very simple. dBASE will latch on to the first primary record, and compare it, in turn, with each of the secondary records, trying to find a match based on your selection criteria. Each time it finds a match, it produces an output record (in the third data-base), the structure of which is also defined by what is or is not provided in the JOIN command. This process is continued until all secondary records are compared. Now dBASE latches on to the second primary record, and repeats the same comparison, again with each of the records in the secondary data-base, trying to find matches based on your criteria. As before, each time it finds a match, you have a record output into the new data-base.

This process is continued until each primary record is matched against each of the secondary records.

Default Output File Structure

If you are not explicit about what you want as the structure of the new, output file, dBASE provides you with a default structure which is the concatenation (a stringing together) of the structures of the primary and secondary data-bases, in that order. If identical field-names exist in both structures, then the fields from the primary file are the ones selected for the structure of the output file, with their duplicates in the secondary file being ignored.

For example, in our previous structures of the INVENTORY file as primary and the ORDERS file as secondary, if we do not provide explicit parameters for the structure of the new output file, its structure will be as follows:

PART:NUM   DESC   UNIT:COST   ONHAND   CUST:NAME   ONORDER

This structure is a concatenation (a stringing together) of the structures of the primary file followed by the secondary file. Notice, therefore, that in this case you will have one field called PART:NUM in the structure of the output file, and this is the one from the primary file. However, you do not have to live with this default provided by dBASE. You can pick and choose the structure you want to see in the output file. (The mechanics of this will be covered later.)

> **Note:** If your primary and secondary data-bases are too large, this process takes a long time, and in the end, may not complete. For example, if you have 100 records in your primary and 1000 records in your secondary, and your joining criteria were so loosely defined that every match was a hit, then dBASE will attempt to create 100,000 records in the output data-base. We know that the limiting value for the number of records in any one data-base is 65,535 records. So apart from taking forever, it will finally abort.

Issuing the JOIN Command

Before you provide the actual instructions for the JOIN command, you have to go through the following 5 commands:

```
.SELECT PRIMARY
.USE    INVENTRY
```

These two instructions effectively identify the INVENTRY file as the primary file.

```
.SELECT SECONDARY
.USE    ORDERS
```

These two instructions effectively identify the ORDERS file as the secondary file.

.SELECT PRIMARY   You have to end up on this instruction.

Having designated the primary and secondary files, you may now issue the JOIN command.

.JOIN TO NEWFILE FOR PART:NUM = S.PART:NUM   <cr>

Here, you want to create an output file called NEWFILE.DBF, for the condition that dBASE can find a match on the PART:NUM fields. However, since you have not provided any format for the file structure, dBASE will create, by default, a format that is the concatenation of the formats of the primary and the secondary files, as described earlier.

Your selection criterion is that the PART:NUM from the primary file should be equal to that from the secondary file. The S. indicates the secondary. Where there is no prefix indication, it implies primary, simply because that was the instruction you had ended up on, before the issue of the JOIN command.

If NEWFILE.DBF existed before the start of the command, no warnings or errors are indicated, and a new NEWFILE.DBF is created. The old one is wiped out!

> **Note:** If the concatenation tends to produce more than 32-fields in the output file, dBASE simply limits the output file to 32-fields in the structure, with the overflow fields (from the secondary file) being ignored. If the concatenation tends to produce more than 1000 characters in the structure, dBASE appears to provide the entire structure, leading you to believe you have discovered a way to produce a file larger than 1000 characters. But other than the DISP STRU command against such a file, please don't try to run any command (such as LIST), else dBASE will play some graphics with your screen like you have never seen before.

Specifying Output File Structure

You can, of course, specify the exact format of the output file, that you would like to see.

.JOIN TO NEWFILE FOR PART:NUM=S.PART:NUM;
FIELDS PART:NUM,S.CUST:NAME,S.ONORDER,UNIT:COST

The S. specifies the field as the one defined in the secondary file. The type and length of the fields coming over are, of course, exactly as they were originally defined in the primary and secondary files.

> **Note:** Do not leave any spaces in the subparameters, when you mention the FIELDS parameter. This results in a syntax error!
>
> **Note:** Having executed the JOIN command once, if you want to JOIN the primary and secondary files again, for either the same or another condition, you will have to repeat the SELECT commands again. That is, you will have to redesignate the primary and secondary files.

Failure to adhere to this suggestion will provide you with haywire results in the output file!

As another example of the use of the JOIN command, let us say that we want to keep track of which items of inventory are insufficient to meet pending orders. The following sequence will do the trick.

```
.SELE PRIM
.USE INVENTRY
.SELE SECO
.USE ORDERS
.SELE PRIM

JOIN TO BACKLOG FOR PART:NUM=S.PART:NUM .AND. ONHAND <
S.ONORDER;
      FIELDS PART:NUM,S.CUST:NAME,S.ONORDER, UNIT:COST
```

SUMMARY

In the last few chapters, we have learned several powerful ways of changing the structures and/or the data of our data-bases. Since the editing features help you maintain the integrity of your data, it is important that they should be understood well. Always remember to keep backup copies of your data-bases.

We are through with our EDITING features, but before we get out of the EDITING mode completely, our PERSNL file could use some remodelling, as we have been experimenting with it to quite an extent. This is very easily done, since, if you remember, at the start of the EDITING section, we had taken a backup copy of PERSNL, in the name PRESERVE. We now simply use this file, to restore the PERSNL file:

```
.USE PRESERVE            <cr>
.COPY TO PERSNL          <cr>
```

The existing PERSNL file is copied over. This leaves you, once again, with both files, PERSNL and PRESERVE.

```
.USE PERSNL              <cr>
```

Now you may proceed with the PERSNL file, if need be. You must realize, of course, that dBASE is a very powerful software package that requires substantial hands-on experience if you are to make maximum use of the possibilities offered by dBASE.

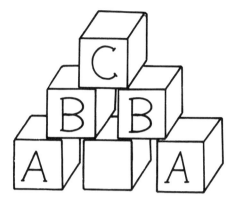

6. Sequencing Process

We will now learn how to prepare our data-base to the point of being able to pull off reports from the data-base. We are, of course, referring to the processes of *physically sorting* or *logically indexing* our data-base.

SORTing and INDEXing refer to the resequencing of the records of the data-base so that these records are presented to any command or program in an expected order. For instance, if you expect to take town-wise totals on the records of your PERSNL file, the records must be pre-arranged in the order of the TOWN-field. Either the records are physically moved around (the SORT operation) before the start of the command or program, or the records must appear to have been moved around (the INDEX operation) before the start of the command or program.

> **Note:** For either the SORT or the INDEX process, if two or more records contain the same data in the key-field(s) being used for the sequencing process, these records will appear in the sorted/indexed versions in the same order as they appear in the original file.

> **Note:** Of the two processes, INDEXING is, by far, superior to SORTING, in terms of overall speed, power, and utility value. However, situations may arise where a SORT is preferred to INDEXing. These situations have been detailed at the appropriate places in this section.

PHYSICAL SORTING

Sorting involves the *physical resequencing* of the records in a data-base. Perhaps you may want the records sequenced so as to be able to produce a report. At the end of the sort process, you will have created another data-base, identical in structure and size to the original file, but with the records physically rearranged in the required sequence. The sort process is quite a slow process.

Sort on Any Character Field

Use the file called PERSNL and sort it on the TOWN-field to produce another data-base called TSORT.DBF.

```
.USE PERSNL                    <cr>
.SORT ON TOWN TO TSORT         <cr>
```

Since TSORT.DBF is a file distinct and separate from PERSNL, note that the record numbers in the TSORT file are in order of 1,2,3,4,5..., etc. TSORT.DBF is the sorted version of the PERSNL file.

```
.USE TSORT      <cr>
.LIST           <cr>
```

00001	087FG0	PAUL BHARUCHA	BRIGHTON	BSG	.T.	1973	29100.00
00002	8745AD	JOHN PETERSON	BRIGHTON	RBG	.T.	1979	31480.00
00003	987178	GLORIA PATEL	FAIRPORT	RMG	.T.	1982	27500.00
00004	0989SD	KIM BRANDT	FAIRPORT	RMG	.F.	1977	36000.00
00005	232430	MAX LEVENSKY	HENRIETTA	RMG	.F.	1969	27550.00
00006	AC9090	TIM MONTAL	ROCHESTER	RBG	.F.	1981	41900.00
00007	091230	JAMES JAMESON	ROCHESTER	GSD	.T.	1977	29800.00
00008	09890A	JAN MOREY	ROCHESTER	GSD	.T.	1967	18190.00
00009	070707	NINA BHARUCHA	WEBSTER	BSG	.T.	1980	33000.00
00010	00707A	PHIL MARTIN	WEBSTER	RMG	.F.	1980	31000.00
00011	7545AD	PETE JOHNSON	brighton	BSG	.T.	1976	27590.00
00012	070970	JOY HARDY	fairport	RBG	.F.	1979	34200.00
00013	08FG09	WILLIAM PATEL	penfield	GSD	.F.	1971	28900.00
00014	087WRF	JOHN JONES	rochester	GSD	.T.	1970	25100.00
00015	438190	MORRIS KATZ	webster	BSG	.F.	1980	23450.00

Notice that the records are sequenced by the TOWN-field. Obviously, since the sorted version of the PERSNL file is exactly as large as the PERSNL file itself, it stands to reason that you must have at least as much space on the disk to contain the sorted version as is occupied by the PERSNL file.

> **Note:** The SORT command ignores deleted records! That is, deleted records will not appear in the sorted version of a file.

You could, of course, always have the Master file and the sorted version of the Master file on two separate disk-drives. Suppose you had not .SET DEFAULT TO B:

```
.USE PERSNL        The PERSNL file is on the A: drive
.SORT ON TOWN TO B:TSORT
```

110

This statement would produce the sorted version on the B: drive.

Notice the order in which the upper and lowercases were sorted. All uppercases appeared ahead of all lowercases in regular ascending order, and within each group of upper and lowercase, the ascending sort is also evident.

Sort Character Field in Descending Sequence

You can sort in DESCENDING sequence, if you like.

```
.USE PERSNL                          <cr>
.SORT ON TOWN TO TSORT      DESC     <cr>
.USE TSORT                           <cr>
.LIST                                <cr>
```

00001	438190	MORRIS KATZ	webster	BSG	.F.	1980	23450.00
00002	087WRF	JOHN JONES	rochester	GSD	.T.	1970	25100.00
00003	08FG09	WILLIAM PATEL	penfield	GSD	.F.	1971	28900.00
00004	070970	JOY HARDY	fairport	RBG	.F.	1979	34200.00
00005	7545AD	PETE JOHNSON	brighton	BSG	.T.	1976	27590.00
00006	070707	NINA BHARUCHA	WEBSTER	BSG	.T.	1980	33000.00
00007	00707A	PHIL MARTIN	WEBSTER	RMG	.F.	1980	31000.00
00008	AC9090	TIM MONTAL	ROCHESTER	RBG	.F.	1981	41900.00
00009	091230	JAMES JAMESON	ROCHESTER	GSD	.T.	1977	29800.00
00010	09890A	JAN MOREY	ROCHESTER	GSD	.T.	1967	18190.00
00011	232430	MAX LEVENSKY	HENRIETTA	RMG	.F.	1969	27550.00
00012	987178	GLORIA PATEL	FAIRPORT	RMG	.T.	1982	27500.00
00013	0989SD	KIM BRANDT	FAIRPORT	RMG	.F.	1977	36000.00
00014	087FG0	PAUL BHARUCHA	BRIGHTON	BSG	.T.	1973	29100.00
00015	8745AD	JOHN PETERSON	BRIGHTON	RBG	.T.	1979	31480.00

Now, of course, since the order of the sort is reversed, all uppercases appear after all the lowercases.

Sort on Any Numeric Field

You can sort on a numeric field, as easily as on a character field.

```
.USE PERSNL                          <cr>
.SORT ON YR:OF:HIRE TO YRSORT        <cr>
.USE YRSORT                          <cr>
.LIST                                <cr>
```

00001	09890A	JAN MOREY	ROCHESTER	GSD	.T.	1967	18190.00
00002	232430	MAX LEVENSKY	HENRIETTA	RMG	.F.	1969	27550.00
00003	087WRF	JOHN JONES	rochester	GSD	.T.	1970	25100.00
00004	08FG09	WILLIAM PATEL	penfield	GSD	.F.	1971	28900.00
00005	087FG0	PAUL BHARUCHA	BRIGHTON	BSG	.T.	1973	29100.00
00006	7545AD	PETE JOHNSON	brighton	BSG	.T.	1976	27590.00

00007	0989SD	KIM BRANDT	FAIRPORT	RMG	.T.	1977	36000.00
00008	091230	JAMES JAMESON	ROCHESTER	GSD	.F.	1977	29800.00
00009	8745AD	JOHN PETERSON	BRIGHTON	RBG	.F.	1979	31480.00
00010	070970	JOY HARDY	fairport	RBG	.T.	1979	34200.00
00011	070707	NINA BHARUCHA	WEBSTER	BSG	.F.	1980	33000.00
00012	438190	MORRIS KATZ	webster	BSG	.F.	1980	23450.00
00013	00707A	PHIL MARTIN	WEBSTER	RMG	.T.	1980	31000.00
00014	AC9090	TIM MONTAL	ROCHESTER	RBG	.F.	1981	41900.00
00015	987178	GLORIA PATEL	FAIRPORT	RMG	.T.	1982	27500.00

The records are now sequenced by the YR:OF:HIRE field.

Sort Numeric Field in Descending Sequence

As you might expect, a numeric sort can also be done in a descending sequence.

```
.USE PERSNL      <cr>
.SORT ON YR:OF:HIRE TO YRSORT      DESC      <cr>
.USE YRSORT      <cr>
.LIST
```

00001	098178	GLORIA PATEL	FIARPORT	RMG	.T.	1982	27500.00
00002	AC9090	TIM MONTAL	ROCHESTER	RBG	.F.	1981	41900.00
00003	070707	NINA BHARUCHA	WEBSTER	BSG	.T.	1980	33000.00
00004	438190	MORRIS KATZ	webster	BSG	.F.	1980	23450.00
00005	00707A	PHIL MARTIN	WEBSTER	RMG	.F.	1980	31000.00
00006	8745AD	JOHN PETERSON	BRIGHTON	RBG	.T.	1979	31480.00
00007	070970	JOY HARDY	fairport	RBG	.F.	1979	34200.00
00008	0989SD	KIM BRANDT	FAIRPORT	RMG	.F.	1977	36000.00
00009	091230	JAMES JAMESON	ROCHESTER	GSD	.T.	1977	29800.00
00010	7545AD	PETE JOHNSON	brighton	BSG	.T.	1976	27590.00
00011	087FG0	PAUL BHARUCHA	BRIGHTON	BSG	.T.	1973	29100.00
00012	08FG09	WILLIAM PATEL	penfield	GSD	.F.	1971	28900.00
00013	087WRF	JOHN JONES	rochester	GSD	.T.	1970	25100.00
00014	232430	MAX LEVENSKY	HENRIETTA	RMG	.F.	1969	27550.00
00015	09890A	JAN MOREY	ROCHESTER	GSD	.T.	1967	18190.00

Note: You cannot sort on a substring of a field. You have to sort on the entire field.

Sort on More Than One Field

In dBASE, you can only sort on one field at a time. So if you did want the output to appear sorted on, say, the TOWN-field, and within that, by the YR:OF:HIRE field, then you would have to perform two iterations to arrive at the sorted version you want.

Say we want to sort on TOWN, and within that, on YR:OF:HIRE. That is, the TOWN-field is logically higher than the YR:OF:HIRE field. We will first sort on one of the fields and then use that sorted version to sort on the other field and obtain the final sorted version we want. The question is, which field do we sort on first? The rule of data processing is "SORT on the logically lowest field first, and then proceed backward.

```
.USE PERSNL                              <cr>
.SORT ON YR:OF:HIRE TO YRSORT            <cr>
.USE YRSORT                              <cr>
.SORT ON TOWN TO TSORT                   <cr>
```

The file called TSORT.DBF is now the final sorted version that we should use, for further processing. The intermediate file called YRSORT.DBF should be deleted, to release space.

```
.USE TSORT    <cr>
.LIST         <cr>
```

00001	087FG0	PAUL BHARUCHA	BRIGHTON	BSG	.T.	1973	29100.00
00002	8745AD	JOHN PETERSON	BRIGHTON	RBG	.T.	1979	31480.00
00003	0989SD	KIM BRANDT	FAIRPORT	RMG	.F.	1977	36000.00
00004	098178	GLORIA PATEL	FIARPORT	RMG	.T.	1982	27500.00
00005	232430	MAX LEVENSKY	HENRIETTA	RMG	.F.	1969	27550.00
00006	09890A	JAN MOREY	ROCHESTER	GSD	.T.	1967	18190.00
00007	091230	JAMES JAMESON	ROCHESTER	GSD	.T.	1977	29800.00
00008	AC9090	TIM MONTAL	ROCHESTER	RBG	.F.	1981	41900.00
00009	070707	NINA BHARUCHA	WEBSTER	BSG	.T.	1980	33000.00
00010	00707A	PHIL MARTIN	WEBSTER	RMG	.F.	1980	31000.00
00011	7545AD	PETE JOHNSON	brighton	BSG	.T.	1976	27590.00
00012	070970	JOY HARDY	fairport	RBG	.F.	1979	34200.00
00013	08FG09	WILLIAM PATEL	penfield	GSD	.F.	1971	28900.00
00014	087WRF	JOHN JONES	rochester	GSD	.T.	1970	25100.00
00015	438190	MORRIS KATZ	webster	BSG	.F.	1980	23450.00

Notice that for the same TOWN, the records are sequenced by the YR:OF:HIRE field.

Sort on Three Fields

Suppose we wanted to sort on three fields: by TOWN, and within that by ORG, and within that by YR:OF:HIRE: Again, following our rule of data-processing, we would use the following sequence:

```
.USE PERSNL                              <cr>
.SORT ON YR:OF:HIRE TO YRSORT            <cr>
.USE YRSORT                              <cr>
.SORT ON ORG TO OSORT                    <cr>
.USE OSORT                               <cr>
.SORT ON TOWN TO TSORT                   <cr>
```

TSORT.DBF is our final sorted version, for further processing. The intermediate files should be deleted to release space.

```
.USE TSORT              <cr>
.LIST                   <cr>
```

00001	087FG0	PAUL BHARUCHA	BRIGHTON	BSG	.T.	1973	29100.00
00002	8745AD	JOHN PETERSON	BRIGHTON	RBG	.T.	1979	31480.00
00003	0989SD	KIM BRANDT	FAIRPORT	RMG	.F.	1977	36000.00
00004	987178	GLORIA PATEL	FAIRPORT	RMG	.T.	1982	27500.00
00005	232430	MAX LEVENSKY	HENRIETTA	RMG	.F.	1969	27550.00
00006	09890A	JAN MOREY	ROCHESTER	GSD	.T.	1967	18190.00
00007	091230	JAMES JAMESON	ROCHESTER	GSD	.T.	1977	29800.00
00008	AC9090	TIM MONTAL	ROCHESTER	RBG	.F.	1981	41900.00
00009	070707	NINA BHARUCHA	WEBSTER	BSG	.T.	1980	33000.00
00010	00707A	PHIL MARTIN	WEBSTER	RMG	.F.	1980	31000.00
00011	7545AD	PETE JOHNSON	brighton	BSG	.T.	1976	27590.00
00012	070970	JOY HARDY	fairport	RBG	.F.	1979	34200.00
00013	08FG09	WILLIAM PATEL	penfield	GSD	.F.	1971	28900.00
00014	087WRF	JOHN JONES	rochester	GSD	.T.	1970	25100.00
00015	438190	MORRIS KATZ	webster	BSG	.F.	1980	23450.00

Sort on a Combination Ascending/Descending

We will sort on three fields this time in a combination of ascending and descending sequences. That is, we want to create a * sorted version as follows: TOWN by descending, within which ORG by ascending, within which YR:OF:HIRE by descending.

```
.USE PERSNL                              <cr>
.SORT ON YR:OF:HIRE TO YRSORT DESC       <cr>
.USE YRSORT                              <cr>
.SORT ON ORG TO OSORT                    <cr>
.USE OSORT                               <cr>
.SORT ON TOWN TO TSORT DESC              <cr>
.USE TSORT                               <cr>
.LIST                                    <cr>
```

00001	438190	MORRIS KATZ	webster	BSG	.F.	1980	23450.00
00002	087WRF	JOHN JONES	rochester	GSD	.T.	1970	25100.00
00003	08FG09	WILLIAM PATEL	penfield	GSD	.F.	1971	28900.00
00004	070970	JOY HARDY	fairport	RBG	.F.	1979	34200.00
00005	7545AD	PETE JOHNSON	brighton	BSG	.T.	1976	27590.00
00006	070707	NINA BHARUCHA	WEBSTER	BSG	.T.	1980	33000.00
00007	00808A	PHIL MARTIN	WEBSTER	RMG	.F.	1980	31000.00
00008	091230	JAMES JAMESON	ROCHESTER	GSD	.T.	1977	29800.00
00009	09890A	JAN MOREY	ROCHESTER	GSD	.T.	1967	18190.00
00010	AC9090	TIM MONTAL	ROCHESTER	RBG	.F.	1981	41900.00

00011	232430	MAX LEVENSKY	HENRIETTA	RMG	.F.	1969	27550.00
00012	987178	GLORIA PATEL	FAIRPORT	RMG	.T.	1982	27500.00
00013	0989SD	KIM BRANDT	FAIRPORT	RMG	.F.	1977	36000.00
00014	087FG0	PAUL BHARUCHA	BRIGHTON	BSG	.T.	1973	29100.00
00015	8745AD	JOHN PETERSON	BRIGHTON	RBG	.T.	1979	31480.00

Note: Each time you produce a sorted file, you are occupying space on the disk equal in size to the original Master file. This can be quite restrictive if you are sorting on multiple fields. So to conserve on space, you may produce the latest sorted version to overlap an earlier sorted version.

Conserving Space

For example, in our previous command, we could have done the following:

```
.USE PERSNL                             <cr>
.SORT ON YR:OF:HIRE TO YRSORT DESC      <cr>
.USE YRSORT                             <cr>
.SORT ON ORG TO PERSNL                  <cr>
.USE PERSNL                             <cr>
.SORT ON TOWN TO YRSORT      DESC       <cr>
```

Now, of course, the file called YRSORT.DBF is the final sorted version we want. By overlapping between the PERSNL file and the YRSORT file, we can manage to go through many iterations, if necessary, without the risk of running out of disk space.

Remember, you cannot sort on a substring of a field. You have to take the entire field, as is. For example, .SORT ON $(TOWN,2,3) TO TSORT is invalid!

Disadvantages of Sorting

By now, of course, the disadvantages of the sort process must have become quite apparent.

The sorting proceeds slowly, and is therefore time-consuming. If you have to sort on multiple fields, each iteration has to be done separately, and again the problems of speed and time and disk capacity come into play. Altogether, then, the SORT command is not too desirable, and if you can avoid it through the use of the INDEX command, you should do so. The SORT does, however, provide you with a sort in descending sequence, if you want.

Possibly the biggest disadvantage with the SORT process is that changes or alterations to the Master file are not automatically reflected in the sorted versions of the Master, these being distinct and separate data-bases, and this creates problems of data inconsistency and redundancy!

LOGICAL INDEXING

You will find this segment of our discussion very interesting and informative, and it should be studied closely. Indexing is an inherent part of the dBASE scenario. In the process of INDEXing, you inform dBASE of your intention to create an *index file* on one or more of the fields of the Master file you are working with. (In our case, PERSNL.DBF.)

Indexing on a Character Field

Use the following statements to perform logical indexing on PERSNL.

```
USE PERSNL                              <cr>
.INDEX ON  TOWN  TO  TINDX              <cr>
```

This results in the creation of a separate file called an index file, whose name is, in this case, TINDX.NDX. You may provide any primary name you want.

> **Note:** This index file is just that, an *index* file! It is not a dBASE data-base. It only contains *pointers* to the actual records in the PERSNL file.

For example, suppose our data-base contained the following 5 records, with only the TOWN data shown.

Master file records	Index file pointers
1 ---PITTSFORD-----	3 BRIGHTON
2 ---WEBSTER-------	5 PENFIELD
3 ---BRIGHTON------	1 PITTSFORD
4 ---ROCHESTER-----	4 ROCHESTER
5 ---PENFIELD------	2 WEBSTER

Based on the data in the Master file and on the fact that an index on TOWN is created, the index pointers specify that the logical order of the record numbers, based on ascending sequences, should be: 3, 5, 1, 4, 2.

Please note that deleted records *will* be indexed!

> **Caution:** Never provide the same name for the index, as provided for the Master file. For example, if your Master file is named PERSNL, the index should not be named PERSNL. While you may argue that the secondary names of .DBF and .NDX should provide for two distinct and separate files, dBASE cannot handle this situation, and within a short time of your providing this environment, your Master file contains garbage in place of data!

The index file is nowhere near the size of the Master (PERSNL.DBF) file, and it merely contains pointers into the original PERSNL data-base. The pointers establish the *logical positioning* of the individual records in the Master file. That is, by default, the index is an *ascending index*.

Please note that the original data-base is untouched! The index pointers merely stipulate what the logical order of the records should be, based on the ascending values currently in the key field you have indexed on.

> **Note:** At the time the index is created, it is automatically brought into play with the Master file. Now any subsequent command will act on the records of the Master file *in the logical order of the index!*

.LIST   \<cr>

00010	087FG0	PAUL BHARUCHA	BRIGHTON	BSG	.T.	1973	29100.00
00012	8745AD	JOHN PETERSON	BRIGHTON	RBG	.T.	1979	31480.00
00003	987178	GLORIA PATEL	FAIRPORT	RMG	.T.	1982	27500.00
00005	0989SD	KIM BRANDT	FAiRPORT	RMG	.F.	1977	36000.00
00004	232430	MAX LEVENSKY	HENRIETTA	RMG	.F.	1969	27550.00
00006	AC9090	TIM MONTAL	ROCHESTER	RBG	.F.	1981	41900.00
00008	091230	JAMES JAMESON	ROCHESTER	GSD	.T.	1977	29800.00
00014	09890A	JAN MOREY	ROCHESTER	GSD	.T.	1967	18190.00
00001	070707	NINA BHARUCHA	WEBSTER	BSG	.T.	1980	33000.00
00011	00707A	PHIL MARTIN	WEBSTER	RMG	.F.	1980	31000.00
00002	7545AD	PETE JOHNSON	brighton	BSG	.T.	1976	27590.00
00013	070970	JOY HARDY	fairport	RBG	.F.	1979	34200.00
00007	08FG09	WILLIAM PATEL	penfield	GSD	.F.	1971	28900.00
00015	087WRF	JOHN JONES	rochester	GSD	.T.	1970	25100.00
00009	438190	MORRIS KATZ	webster	BSG	.F.	1980	23450.00

Notice that the records have been listed in the ascending order of the TOWN-fields. Notice also that the record numbers are not in proper sequence 1,2,3...., since the record numbers listed out are the numbers from the original records in the PERSNL file, and the records have merely been pulled out in the sequence of the index. Let me emphasize that the creation of an index does not alter the Master file in any way. However, once created, the index now plays a role in subsequent commands, in that the records are processed by the commands *in the logical order of the index.*

Indexing on a Numeric Field

Indexing a numeric field is done in exactly the same way that a character field is indexed.

.USE PERSNL   \<cr>
.INDEX ON YR:OF:HIRE TO   YRINDX   \<cr>
.LIST   \<cr>

00014	09890A	JAN MOREY	ROCHESTER	GSD	.T.	1967	18190.00
00004	232430	MAX LEVENSKY	HENRIETTA	RMG	.F.	1969	27550.00
00015	087WRF	JOHN JONES	rochester	GSD	.T.	1970	25100.00
00007	08FG09	WILLIAM PATEL	penfield	GSD	.F.	1971	28900.00
00010	087FG0	PAUL BHARUCHA	BRIGHTON	BSG	.T.	1973	29100.00
00002	7545AD	PETE JOHNSON	brighton	BSG	.T.	1976	27590.00
00005	0989SD	KIM BRANDT	FAIRPORT	RMG	.F.	1977	36000.00
00008	091230	JAMES JAMESON	ROCHESTER	GSD	.T.	1977	29800.00
00012	8745AD	JOHN PETERSON	BRIGHTON	RBG	.T.	1979	31480.00
00013	070970	JOY HARDY	fairport	RBG	.F.	1979	34200.00
00001	070707	NINA BHARUCHA	WEBSTER	BSG	.T.	1980	33000.00
00009	438190	MORRIS KATZ	webster	BSG	.F.	1980	23450.00
00011	00707A	PHIL MARTIN	WEBSTER	RMG	.F.	1980	31000.00

| 00006 | AC9090 | TIM MONTAL | ROCHESTER | RBG | .F. | 1981 | 41900.00 |
| 00003 | 987178 | GLORIA PATEL | FAIRPORT | RMG | .T. | 1982 | 27500.00 |

The records are now listed in ascending order of the YR:OF:HIRE field.

Indexing without Regard to Upper/Lowercase

You can index on a field without regard to upper/lowercase in the data.

```
.USE PERSNL
.INDEX ON ! (TOWN) TO ANYINDX
.LIST
```

00002	7545AD	PETE JOHNSON	brighton	BSG	.T.	1976	30349.00
00010	087FG0	PAUL BHARUCHA	BRIGHTON	BSG	.T.	1973	32010.00
00012	8745AD	JOHN PETERSON	BRIGHTON	RBG	.T.	1979	31480.00
00003	987178	GLORIA PATEL	FAIRPORT	RMG	.T.	1982	27500.00
00005	0989SD	KIM BRANDT	FAIRPORT	RMG	.F.	1977	36000.00
00013	070970	JOY HARDY	fairport	RBG	.F.	1979	34200.00
00004	232430	MAX LEVENSKY	HENRIETTA	RMG	.F.	1969	27550.00
00007	08FG09	WILLIAM PATEL	penfield	GSD	.F.	1971	28900.00
00006	AC9090	TIM MONTAL	ROCHESTER	RBG	.F.	1981	41900.00
00008	091230	JAMES JAMESON	ROCHESTER	GSD	.T.	1977	29800.00
00014	09890A	JAN MOREY	ROCHESTER	GSD	.T.	1967	18190.00
00015	087WRF	JOHN JONES	rochester	GSD	.T.	1970	25100.00
00001	070707	NINA BHARUCHA	WEBSTER	BSG	.T.	1980	36300.00
00009	438190	MORRIS WATZ	webster	BSG	.F.	1980	25795.00
00011	00707A	PHIL MARTIN	WEBSTER	RMG	.F.	1980	31000.00

You may want to use this feature when you are not too sure of how the data may have been created, and you do not want the records segregated merely on account of an upper/lowercase difference.

Removing Index File Influence

You can disassociate an existing index from a Master file simply by USING the Master file.

```
.USE PERSNL                        <cr>
.LIST                              <cr>
```

00001	070707	NINA BHARUCHA	WEBSTER	BSG	.T.	1980	33000.00
00002	7545AD	PETE JOHNSON	brighton	BSG	.T.	1976	27590.00
00003	987178	GLORIA PATEL	FAIRPORT	RMG	.T.	1982	27500.00
00004	232430	MAX LEVENSKY	HENRIETTA	RMG	.F.	1969	27550.00
00005	0989SD	KIM BRANDT	FAIRPORT	RMG	.F.	1977	36000.00
00006	AC9090	TIM MONTAL	ROCHESTER	RBG	.F.	1981	41900.00
00007	08FG09	WILLIAM PATEL	penfield	GSD	.F.	1971	28900.00

00008	091230	JAMES JAMESON	ROCHESTER	GSD	.T.	1977	29800.00
00009	438190	MORRIS WATZ	webster	BSG	.F.	1980	23450.00
00010	087FG0	PAUL BHARUCHA	BRIGHTON	BSG	.T.	1973	29100.00
00011	00707A	PHIL MARTIN	WEBSTER	RMG	.F.	1980	31000.00
00012	8745AD	JOHN PETERSON	BRIGHTON	RBG	.T.	1979	31480.00
00013	070970	JOY HARDY	fairport	RBG	.F.	1979	34200.00
00014	09890Λ	JAN MOREY	ROCHESTER	GSD	.T.	1967	18190.00
00015	087WRF	JOHN JONES	rochester	GSD	.T.	1970	25100.00

Notice that the original records from the PERSNL file, in their original record number sequence, are listed out. The USE command effectively removed the influence of the index file. Understand, also, that the TINDX(.NDX) and YRINDX(.NDX) files created earlier *still exist* on the disk, but we have just negated their influence on the Master file.

Restoring Index File Influence

You may, of course, create an index file today, and want to bring it into play with a Master file, tomorrow. To reassociate/reconnect an *existing* index file with a Master type the following:

```
.USE PERSNL  INDEX    TINDX              <cr>
.LIST                                    <cr>
```

00010	087FG0	PAUL BHARUCHA	BRIGHTON	BSG	.T.	1973	29100.00
00012	8745AD	JOHN PETERSON	BRIGHTON	RBG	.T.	1979	31480.00
00003	987178	GLORIA PATEL	FAIRPORT	RMG	.T.	1982	27500.00
00005	0989SD	KIM BRANDT	FAIRPORT	RMG	.F.	1977	36000.00
00004	232430	MAX LEVENSKY	HENRIETTA	RMG	.F.	1969	27550.00
00006	AC9090	TIM MONTAL	ROCHESTER	RBG	.F.	1981	41900.00
00008	091230	JAMES JAMESON	ROCHESTER	GSD	.T.	1977	29800.00
00014	09890A	JAN MOREY	ROCHESTER	GSD	.T.	1967	18190.00
00001	070707	NINA BHARUCHA	WEBSTER	BSG	.T.	1980	33000.00
00011	00707A	PHIL MARTIN	WEBSTER	RMG	.F.	1980	31000.00
00002	7545AD	PETE JOHNSON	brighton	BSG	.T.	1976	27590.00
00013	070970	JOY HARDY	fairport	RBG	.F.	1979	34200.00
00007	08FG09	WILLIAM PATEL	penfield	GSD	.F.	1971	28900.00
00015	087WRF	JOHN JONES	rochester	GSD	.T.	1970	25100.00
00009	438190	MORRIS KATZ	webster	BSG	.F.	1980	23450.00

Notice that the records are, once again, listed in the order of the index, since we reestablished the index with the PERSNL file.

Indexing on a Substring

You may also index on substrings of a field! For example:

```
.INDEX ON $(TOWN,1,2,) TO TINDX
```

This could be used to group together all towns beginning with the same two characters: eg. ROCHESTER and ROXY. Since the substring function only applies to a character string, to index on a substring of a numeric field, the numeric field should be specified as a STRing function.

.INDEX ON $(STR(YR:OF:HIRE,4),3,1)   TO YRINDX

This statement produces an index on the 3rd character of the YR:OF:HIRE field.

Indexing on Multiple Fields

You can index on more than one field at a time through the use of just one index statement. Suppose we want to index on TOWN, and within that field, on the ORG field. The statement would be as follows:

```
.USE PERSNL                        <cr>
.INDEX ON TOWN + ORG TO TOINDX     <cr>
.LIST                              <cr>
```

00010	087FG0	PAUL BHARUCHA	BRIGHTON	BSG	.T.	1973	29100.00
00012	8745AD	JOHN PETERSON	BRIGHTON	RBG	.T.	1979	31480.00
00003	987178	GLORIA PATEL	FAIRPORT	RMG	.T.	1982	27500.00
00005	0989SD	KIM BRANDT	FAIRPORT	RMG	.F.	1977	36000.00
00004	232430	MAX LEVENSKY	HENRIETTA	RMG	.F.	1969	27550.00
00008	091230	JAMES JAMESON	ROCHESTER	GSD	.T.	1977	29800.00
00014	09890A	JAN MOREY	ROCHESTER	GSD	.T.	1967	18190.00
00006	AC9090	TIM MONTAL	ROCHESTER	RBG	.F.	1981	41900.00
00001	070707	NINA BHARUCHA	WEBSTER	BSG	.T.	1980	33000.00
00011	00707A	PHIL MARTIN	WEBSTER	RMG	.F.	1980	31000.00
00002	7545AD	PETE JOHNSON	brighton	BSG	.T.	1976	27590.00
00013	070970	JOY HARDY	fairport	RBG	.F.	1979	34200.00
00007	08FG09	WILLIAM PATEL	penfield	GSD	.F.	1971	28900.00
00015	087WRF	JOHN JONES	rochester	GSD	.T.	1970	25100.00
00009	438190	MORRIS KATZ	webster	BSG	.F.	1980	23450.00

Notice that for the same TOWN, the records are sequenced by the ORGanization field. This is known as a *hierarchy* of TOWN and ORGANization.

One general observation can be made at this point. The statement is essentially *free-form*. The number of spaces before and after the + sign is immaterial. You may even have no spaces before and after the operator.

.INDEX ON   TOWN+ORG   TO TOINDX

> **Note:** In the case of the INDEXing feature, if you want to index on TOWN and within it, on ORG, you specify the exact hierarchy you want in that order. (This was unlike the SORT process where you had to specify the logically lowest field first.) Also, the spaces before and after the + sign are optional.

To index on the hierarchy TOWN, ORG, and EMP:NAME, specify just that:

```
                    .USE PERSNL                                        <cr>
                    .INDEX ON TOWN + ORG + EMP:NAME TO TONINDX         <cr>
                    .LIST                                              <cr>
```

00010	087FG0	PAUL BHARUCHA	BRIGHTON	BSG	.T.	1973	29100.00
00012	8745AD	JOHN PETERSON	BRIGHTON	RBG	.T.	1979	31480.00
00003	987178	GLORIA PATEL	FAIRPORT	RMG	.T.	1982	27500.00
00005	0989SD	KIM BRANDT	FAIRPORT	RMG	.F.	1977	36000.00
00004	232430	MAX LEVENSKY	HENRIETTA	RMG	.F.	1969	27550.00
00008	091230	JAMES JAMESON	ROCHESTER	GSD	.T.	1977	29800.00
00014	09890A	JAN MOREY	ROCHESTER	GSD	.T.	1967	18190.00
00006	AC9090	TIM MONTAL	ROCHESTER	RBG	.F.	1981	41900.00
00001	070707	NINA BHARUCHA	WEBSTER	BSG	.T.	1980	33000.00
00011	00707A	PHIL MARTIN	WEBSTER	RMG	.F.	1980	31000.00
00002	7545AD	PETE JOHNSON	brighton	BSG	.T.	1976	27590.00
00013	070970	JOY HARDY	fairport	RBG	.F.	1979	34200.00
00007	08FG09	WILLIAM PATEL	penfield	GSD	.F.	1971	28900.00
00015	087WRF	JOHN JONES	rochester	GSD	.T.	1970	25100.00
00009	438190	MORRIS KATZ	webster	BSG	.F.	1980	23450.00

How many fields can you string out, for a multiple index? When you specify multiple fields as we have seen before, you are specifying the key length, for the index. The rule is that the total length of the index-key should not be more than 100 characters. For example: if the key were specified as: TOWN + ORG + EMP:NAME, the key length as obtained from the structure of the PERSNL file is: 12 (for TOWN) + 3(for ORG) + 15 (for EMP:NAME) or a total of 30. This total cannot exceed 100.

Indexing on Multiple Substrings

I mentioned before that you can index on the substring of a field.

        .INDEX ON $(TOWN,1,2) TO TINDX

The above index could be formed to group together all towns beginning with the same two characters: eg. ROCHESTER and ROXY. If the need arises, you can index on multiple substrings.

        .INDEX ON $(TOWN,1,2) + $(ORG,1.1) TO TOINDX

Here we are indexing on the first two characters of TOWN, and within that, on the first character of the ORGanization.

We can extend this concept to index on multiple substrings of the same field! For example, in a specific situation, let us say you have a field called PART:NUM, and this field has a 12-character structure. Let us further suppose that within this 12-character structure, characters 1 through 8 are the actual part-number code, and characters 10 through 12 reflect data pertaining to the part-number revision code. It may be necessary for us to index our file by part-number, and within that field, by the part-revision code. We can obtain such an index using the same concept applied earlier.

.INDEX ON $(PART:NUM,1,8) + $(PART:NUM,10,3) TO PINDX

Hierarchical Indexing on a Combination of Field-Types

Creating an index on one character field works well. Creating an index on one numeric field works well. Creating an index on multiple character fields works well. The problem arises when you are trying to create a *hierarchical index* on multiple fields, *and one or more or all of the fields are numeric.*

In a multiple-field combination for creating a *hierarchical index,* if one or more of the fields to be specified are numeric, the numeric fields will have to be represented as STRing functions! If you recall, to STRing a numeric, use the following format:

[STR(field-name,field-length)]

.USE PERSNL	\<cr\>
.INDEX ON TOWN + *STR(YR:OF:HIRE,4)* TO TINDX	\<cr\>

The formula TOWN + YR:OF:HIRE would be invalid!

.LIST   \<cr\>

00010	087FG0	PAUL BHARUCHA	BRIGHTON	BSG	.T.	1973	29100.00
00012	8745AD	JOHN PETERSON	BRIGHTON	RBG	.T.	1979	31480.00
00005	0989SD	KIM BRANDT	FAIRPORT	RMG	.F.	1977	36000.00
00003	987178	GLORIA PATEL	FAIRPORT	RMG	.T.	1982	27500.00
00004	232430	MAX LEVENSKY	HENRIETTA	RMG	.F.	1969	27550.00
00014	09890A	JAN MOREY	ROCHESTER	GSD	.T.	1967	18190.00
00008	091230	JAMES JAMESON	ROCHESTER	GSD	.T.	1977	29800.00
00006	AC9090	TIM MONTAL	ROCHESTER	RBG	.F.	1981	41900.00
00001	070707	NINA BHARUCHA	WEBSTER	BSG	.T.	1980	33000.00
00011	00707A	PHIL MARTIN	WEBSTER	RMG	.F.	1980	31000.00
00002	7545AD	PETE JOHNSON	brighton	BSG	.T.	1976	27590.00
00013	070970	JOY HARDY	fairport	RBG	.F.	1979	34200.00
00007	08FG09	WILLIAM PATEL	penfield	GSD	.F.	1971	28900.00
00015	087WRF	JOHN JONES	rochester	GSD	.T.	1970	25100.00
00009	438190	MORRIS KATZ	webster	BSG	.F.	1980	23450.00

If you had to index on multiple numeric fields, and if you wanted to specify a hierarchy (field-A within field-B), then each of the numeric fields would have to be specified as STRing functions. For example: To index by YR:OF:HIRE, and within that, by SALARY, you would have to use the following statement:

.USE PERSNL	\<cr\>
.INDEX ON *STR(YR:OF:HIRE,4)* + *STR(SALARY,8,2)* TO YRINDX	\<cr\>
.LIST	\<cr\>

00014	09890A	JAN MOREY	ROCHESTER	GSD	.T.	1967	18190.00
00004	232430	MAX LEVENSKY	HENRIETTA	RMG	.F.	1969	27550.00
00015	087WRF	JOHN JONES	rochester	GSD	.T.	1970	25100.00
00007	08FG09	WILLIAM PATAL	penfield	GSD	.F.	1971	28900.00
00010	087FG0	PAUL BHARUCHA	BRIGHTON	BSG	.T.	1973	29100.00
00002	7545AD	PETE JOHNSON	brighton	BSG	.T.	1976	27590.00
00008	091230	JAMES JAMESON	ROCHESTER	GSD	.T.	1977	29800.00
00005	0989SD	KIM BRANDT	FAIRPORT	RMG	.F.	1977	36000.00
00012	8745AD	JOHN PETERSON	BRIGHTON	RBG	.T.	1979	31480.00
00013	070970	JOY HARDY	fairport	RBG	.F.	1979	34200.00
00009	438190	MORRIS KATZ	webster	BSG	.F.	1980	23450.00
00011	00707A	PHIL MARTIN	WEBSTER	RMG	.F.	1980	31000.00
00001	070707	NINA BHARUCHA	WEBSTER	BSG	.T.	1980	33000.00
00006	AC9090	TIM MONTAL	ROCHESTER	RBG	.F.	1981	41900.00
00003	987178	GLORIA PATEL	FAIRPORT	RMG	.T.	1982	27500.00

Note that the records are indexed by increasing YR:OF:HIRE fields, and for the same YR:OF:HIRE, the records are indexed in increasing order of the SALARY fields. Note also that the STRing option was used since we wanted to bring out a hierarchy: SALARY within YR:OF:HIRE. What do you suppose would have happened if you had specified the previous command without the STRing function? That is, if the command had been entered as follows:

.INDEX ON YR:OF:HIRE + SALARY TO YRINDX   <cr>

dBASE would have provided an index based on a *numerical value* created for each record by adding together the YR:OF:HIRE and SALARY fields. That is, the record having the lowest value as the sum of the YR:OF:HIRE and SALARY would be at the top of the list, and the one with the highest such value at the bottom of the list. Such an index, of course, is garbage!

Indexing on a Sum

As an example of where you may want to use the *sum* (as opposed to a hierarchy) of fields to index upon, suppose you had a data-base built up of test scores for each student, as follows:

NAME,C,20	
MATH,N,2	(math score)
SCIENCE,N,2	(science score)
PHY,N,2	(physics score)
CHEM,N,2	(chemistry score)

Now if you wanted to index on the sum total of two or more of the numeric fields, you could enter:

.INDEX ON MATH + SCIENCE TO MSINDX

This statement would provide you with the lowest through highest scores for the MATH+SCIENCE category.

    INDEX ON   MATH+SCIENCE+PHY+CHEM   TO TOTINDX

This statement would provide you with the lowest through highest grand scores. It is important to realize that STRinging the numeric expressions implies that you want the index to specify a hierarchy, with a major field, some intermediate fields, and a minor field (for example, SALARY within YR:OF:HIRE). Using the numeric field-names directly implies that you want to index on only one field, which is the sum total of the numeric fields used in the command expression (for example, MATH + SCIENCE).

Suppose we want the following hierarchy: We want to be able to list out all scores in the usual ascending sequence of the grand scores, and for the same grand score, we want to list out records in ascending sequence of the MATH scores. While this may seem complex, you know that you will have to STRing the numerics, since a hierarchy is specified, and you know you also have to add the numeric fields together, since total scores are also involved. The above requirement could be solved as follows:

    .INDEX ON STR((MATH+SCIENCE+PHY+CHEM),3) + STR(MATH,2) TO GINDX

A length 3 was used, since the sum of four 2-digit fields cannot exceed 999.
    Note: In a multiple-field index, if there is even one character field involved, then all numeric fields will have to be defined as STR functions!

Advantage of Indexing

The biggest advantage of the indexing feature is that indexes which are currently active for a Master file get automatically updated if the Master file is in any way changed or altered. For example:

    .USE PERSNL   <cr>
    .INDEX ON TOWN TO TINDX   <cr>

After these instructions, the index for town is created, and is active against the PERSNL file.

    .APPEND   <cr>

This, as you know, will open up blank a structure into which you key-in the new records. After the APPEND process is ended, you will find that the newly appended records are in their proper *logical* positions in the *indexed* file! Physically, of course, the newly appended records are at the bottom of the PERSNL file, since the records were APPENDed to the PERSNL file, but the index has been automatically updated to reflect proper logical sequencing for the new records.

Note: This automatic updating would be true even if you changed an existing record's key-field. For example, if you .EDIT 5 <cr> and if you change the TOWN-field to read a value of 'ZZZZZZZZ', then after the EDIT operation is completed, this record will find itself logically repositioned at the bottom of the (uppercase) pile! Physically, of course, it remains in the PERSNL file exactly where it was before the start of the edit command!

General Approach to Indexing

Your general method of procedure should be as follows: Create a dBASE file, then go through the editing features to ensure its integrity, and then create all the indexes you think you will ever need for this file. Now, at the start of each work day, you would invoke the Master file along with the necessary indexes, as follows:

.USE "Master" INDEX I1,I2,I3,I4,I5,I6,I7   <cr>

I1, I2, etc., are the various indexes you had created for this Master file. Now all kinds of updates against the Master file (Append, Edit, Browse, Delete-Pack) will automatically update all indexes.

Note: For versions prior to 2.4, the DELETE-PACK combination will only update the first index-file name (the Master-index), even though you may have actively associated more than one index with a data-base. The other indexes will have to be recreated by you, individually. Version 2.4 will update all actively-associated index-files. Also, regardless of the version used, if too many records were deleted, it would be advisable for you to disassociate all indexes from the data-base, before you issued the PACK command. Lack of this precaution may corrupt your index files. After the PACK command, you may proceed to recreate all indexes again.

At any point in time, up to 7 indexes can be actively associated with the Master file. There may, of course, be any number of index-files on the same disk as the Master file, but only 7 may be actively associated with the master concurrently. If you have all 7 indexes active at one time, the subsequent commands will take much longer to complete (too much system overhead), and ideally, you should not have more than 3 indexes active concurrently.

Precaution: If you are referencing multiple indexes in your command, please do not enter the command line as follows:

.USE "master" INDEX I1 I2 I3 I4 I5

Do not leave any spaces between the index-file names! If you do, dBASE will associate the first index with the data-base and simply ignore the others!

What would happen in the following LIST command?

.USE PERSNL INDEX TINDX,OINDX,YRINDX   <cr>
.LIST   <cr>

Against which index will the LIST command function? Against the first index mentioned. That is, in this case, the records will be listed out in the order of the TOWN-INDEX! Should you alter your data-base, all currently active indexes will be updated, but commands like LIST,EDIT,BROWSE, etc. will *present the records* to you *in the order of the first* index. To repeat, all active indexes will be updated to reflect changes through Edit, Browse, etc.

Indexing Numeric Fields in Descending Sequence

The INDEX command, as it stands, does not support a parameter like DESC, (for descending sequence), but we can fool dBASE into providing us descending sequences for numeric fields. For this purpose, we will use a bit of common sense mathematics.

.INDEX ON   YR:OF:HIRE   TO   YRINDX   <cr>

This will provide the usual ascending sequence we have seen. Study the following statement.

.USE PERSNL   <cr>
.INDEX ON 9999 – YR:OF:HIRE TO YRINDX   <cr>

This format will provide the *descending sequence we want!*

.LIST   <cr>

00003	987178	GLORIA PATEL	FAIRPORT	RMG	.T.	1982	27500.00
00006	AC9090	TIM MONTAL	ROCHESTER	RBG	.F.	1981	41900.00
00001	070707	NINA BHARUCHA	WEBSTER	BSG	.T.	1980	33000.00
00009	438190	MORRIS KATZ	webster	BSG	.F.	1980	23450.00
00011	00707A	PHIL MARTIN	WEBSTER	RMG	.F.	1980	31000.00
00012	8745AD	JOHN PETERSON	BRIGHTON	RBG	.T.	1979	31480.00
00013	070970	JOY HARDY	fairport	RBG	.F.	1979	34200.00
00005	0989SD	KIM BRANDT	FAIRPORT	RMG	.F.	1977	36000.00
00008	091230	JAMES JAMESON	ROCHESTER	GSD	.T.	1977	29800.00
00002	7545AD	PETE JOHNSON	brighton	BSG	.T.	1976	27590.00
00010	087FG0	PAUL BHARUCHA	BRIGHTON	BSG	.T.	1973	29100.00
00007	08FG09	WILLIAM PATEL	penfield	GSD	.F.	1971	28900.00
00015	087WRF	JOHN JONES	rochester	GSD	.T.	1970	25100.00
00004	232430	MAX LEVENSKY	HENRIETTA	RMG	.F.	1969	27550.00
00014	09890A	JAN MOREY	ROCHESTER	GSD	.T.	1967	18190.00

You must subtract the numeric field from the highest possible value containable in that field! To index on the SALARY field in descending sequence use the following statement:

.USE PERSNL   <cr>
.INDEX ON 99999.99 – SALARY TO SALINDEX   <cr>
.LIST   <cr>

00006	AC9090	TIM MONTAL	ROCHESTER	RBG	.F.	1981	41900.00
00005	0989SD	KIM BRANDT	FAIRPORT	RMG	.F.	1977	36000.00
00013	070970	JOY HARDY	fairport	RBG	.F.	1979	34200.00
00001	070707	NINA BHARUCHA	WEBSTER	BSG	.T.	1980	33000.00
00012	8745AD	JOHN PETERSON	BRIGHTON	RBG	.T.	1979	31480.00
00011	00707A	PHIL MARTIN	WEBSTER	RMG	.F.	1980	31000.00
00008	091230	JAMES JAMESON	ROCHESTER	GSD	.T.	1977	29800.00
00010	087FG0	PAUL BHARUCHA	BRIGHTON	BSG	.T.	1973	29100.00
00007	08FG09	WILLIAM PATEL	penfield	GSD	.F.	1971	28900.00
00002	7545AD	PETE JOHNSON	brighton	BSG	.T.	1976	27590.00
00004	232430	MAX LEVENSKY	HENRIETTA	RMG	.F.	1969	27550.00
00003	987178	GLORIA PATEL	FAIRPORT	RMG	.T.	1982	27500.00
00015	087WRF	JOHN JONES	rochester	GSD	.T.	1970	25100.00
00009	438190	MORRIS KATZ	webster	BSG	.F.	1980	23450.00
00014	09890A	JAN MOREY	ROCHESTER	GSD	.T.	1967	18190.00

Note: The correct length of the highest value is important. That is, the YR:OF:HIRE field was defined as N.4 in the structure of the file, so in our command we subtract the YR:OF:HIRE field from 9999. The SALARY field was defined as N,8,2 in the structure of the file, so in our command we subtract the SALARY field from 99999.99

Hierarchial Indexing with a Descending Sequence

To index on TOWN and a descending SALARY sequence (a hierarchy), use the following statement:

Note: Here, you have a combination of types, and so the numeric fields have to converted to their STRing counterparts. Also, you will have to specify the descending version of the SALARY field!

```
.USE PERSNL                    <cr>
.INDEX ON TOWN + STR(99999.99 – SALARY,8,2) TO TINDX           <cr>
.LIST                          <cr>
```

00012	8745AD	JOHN PETERSON	BRIGHTON	RBG	.T.	1979	31480.00
00010	087FG0	PAUL BHARUCHA	BRIGHTON	BSG	.T.	1973	29100.00
00005	0989SD	KIM BRANDT	FAIRPORT	RMG	.F.	1977	36000.00
00003	987178	GLORIA PATEL	FAIRPORT	RMG	.T.	1982	27500.00
00004	232430	MAX LEVENSKY	HENRIETTA	RMG	.F.	1969	27550.00
00006	AC9090	TIM MONTAL	ROCHESTER	RBG	.F.	1981	41900.00
00008	091230	JAMES JAMESON	ROCHESTER	GSD	.T.	1977	29800.00
00014	09890A	JAN MOREY	ROCHESTER	GSD	.T.	1967	18190.00
00001	070707	NINA BHARUCHA	WEBSTER	BSG	.T.	1980	33000.00
00011	00707A	PHIL MARTIN	WEBSTER	RMG	.F.	1980	31000.00
00002	7545AD	PETE JOHNSON	brighton	BSG	.T.	1976	27590.00
00013	070970	JOY HARDY	fairport	RBG	.F.	1979	34200.00

00007	08FG09	WILLIAM PATEL	penfield	GSD	.F.	1971	28900.00
00015	087WRF	JOHN JONES	rochester	GSD	.T.	1970	25100.00
00009	438190	MORRIS KATZ	webster	BSG	.F.	1980	23450.00

Note: In the above multiple index, the TOWN-fields have been sequenced in the usual ascending order. However, for the same TOWNs, notice that the SALARY fields have been presented in descending sequence. For most reporting purposes, a field like the SALARY field is usually required in a descending sequence, presenting the higher salaries ahead of the lower ones.

To index on TOWN and descending YR:OF:HIRE use this statememt:

```
.USE PERSNL              <cr>
.INDEX ON TOWN + STR(9999 – YR:OF:HIRE,4) TO TYRINDX        <cr>
.LIST                    <cr>
```

00012	8745AD	JOHN PETERSON	BRIGHTON	RBG	.T.	1979	31480.00
00010	087FG0	PAUL BHARUCHA	BRIGHTON	BSG	.T.	1973	29100.00
00003	987178	GLORIA PATEL	FAIRPORT	RMG	.T.	1982	27500.00
00005	0989SD	KIM BRANDT	FAIRPORT	RMG	.F.	1977	36000.00
00004	232430	MAX LEVENSKY	HENRIETTA	RMG	.F.	1969	27550.00
00006	AC9090	TIM MONTAL	ROCHESTER	RBG	.F.	1981	41900.00
00008	091230	JAMES JAMESON	ROCHESTER	GSD	.T.	1977	29800.00
00014	09890A	JAN MOREY	ROCHESTER	GSD	.T.	1967	18190.00
00001	070707	NINA BHARUCHA	WEBSTER	BSG	.T.	1980	33000.00
00011	00707A	PHIL MARTIN	WEBSTER	RMG	.F.	1980	31000.00
00002	7545AD	PETE JOHNSON	brighton	BSG	.T.	1976	27590.00
00013	070970	JOY HARDY	fairport	RBG	.F.	1979	34200.00
00007	08FG09	WILLIAM PATEL	penfield	GSD	.F.	1971	28900.00
00015	087WRF	JOHN JONES	rochester	GSD	.T.	1970	25100.00
00009	438190	MORRIS KATZ	webster	BSG	.F.	1980	23450.00

You could have also provided the parameters in the following way:

```
.INDEX ON TOWN + STR((99999.99 – SALARY),8,2) TO TINDX
```

This statement will give an ascending TOWN and descending SALARY sequence.

```
.INDEX ON TOWN + STR((9999 – YR:OF:HIRE),4) TO TINDX
```

This statement provides an ascending TOWN and descending YR:OF:HIRE sequence.

Combination of a Descending Sum and Hierarchy

Let us look at our previously used example of SCORES, and this time let us suppose we want a slightly different type of hierarchy. We want to be able to list out all scores in descending sequence of the grand scores, and for the same grand score, we want to list out records in descending sequence of the MATH scores.

While this may seem complex, you know that you will have to STRing the numerics, since a hierarchy is specified, and you know you also have to add the numeric fields together, since total scores are also involved. When you STRing the numerics, don't forget to use the 9999 option, to get descending sequences. The above requirement could be solved as follows:

.INDEX ON STR(999−(MATH+SCIENCE+PHY+CHEM),3)+STR(99−MATH ,2) TO XYZ

A length 3 was used, since the sum of four 2-digit fields cannot exceed 999.

Status on Active Indexes

If at any point in time you wish to find out which index-files are currently active against the data-base in USE, you can do the following:

.DISP STATUS   <cr>

This command will provide, first, the name of the data-base currently in USE and the name(s) of the index-file(s) currently active against this data-base, with the names of the fields forming the index(es), and the system will WAIT for your response. On entering any key (you would tend to hit the <cr> key), this command then provides a listing of the various SET switches (the SET commands are being covered at appropriate places in the book). In any case, the DISP STAT command could be used to find out which data-base and which index-files are currently active.

Note: If you wish to reindex all currently active indexes, simply enter the following:

.REINDEX   <cr>

Caution on Duplicate Keys

In the case of an indexed file, dBASE always makes an assumption that if a record has been altered, in any way, it should be repositioned in the index. This is O.K. as long as the records have unique key values (such as employee-numbers, or part-numbers) and the key-value has been altered. After all, if a part-number 12345 has been reassigned the value 23456, it should find itself logically repositioned in the index.

However, this automatic repositioning of a record will prove undesirable in situations where you can have several duplicate key-values (such as duplicate ORGanizations or TOWNs), and the records have been changed in any non-key field. For example, let us say we have the following 4 records in a file:

RECORD NUMBER	KEY-FIELD (ORG)	OTHER-FIELDS
000001	BSG	----- ----- -----
000002	BSG	----- ----- -----
000003	BSG	----- ----- -----
000004	GSD	----- ----- -----

Given the above situation, if you were to make changes to any non-key field of record #1, you will find that after the change, record #1 has been repositioned in the index after record #3. The next record available to you is record #4, not record #2!

In many situations it would be required that we should be able to access indexed records sequentially, making changes to them along the way, without losing our position in the order of the index. This point is more fully explored in the programming section of this book.

Disadvantage to Indexing

As you may have come to appreciate, INDEXING is a rather handy feature in dBASE-II, and you should use it to full advantage. However, there is one drawback to the entire scenario of the indexing feature, which is not a problem with the INDEX command or with dBASE, but with the way it works in total.

To clarify this further, suppose we have created a PERSNL file in which one of the fields is the EMP:NUM field. Suppose further, that the following employee numbers have been loaded through APPEND, one for each record: 1, 10, 65, 35, 55, 656, 45, 56, 65, etc. Having created our records, suppose we now create our indexes, and pull off reports, etc. Even in the small example above, we have already created a problem! And the problem is that we have entered duplicate employee number 65 for two different records!

The problem occurs since we are building our data-base first, and then creating the index. But by that time, we may have already entered some duplicate data into key-fields that should not be allowed to have duplicates! Let us emphasize, once again, that this is not a problem created by the indexing feature, but comes about on account of the procedure of doing things. Indexing, in fact, will help us solve the problem.

If you were now to index this data-base on the EMP:NUM field, a listing would ensure that all duplicate records would appear together. This would give you a chance of scanning the list for duplicates, and of making corrections. However, you cannot rely on your sight alone to pick out all duplicates. Please understand that in order to ensure the integrity of your data-base, one recourse would be to write a "quick and dirty" computer program in dBASE, which will scan the indexed list of your records, and pick out duplicates. Also, each time the indexed data-base is updated with new records through APPEND/EDIT commands, you will have to run the program again, since there is no guarantee that the second time around, for the new records, you had not keyed in any invalid (already existing, or duplicate) data in the key-fields.

For those data-bases in which you cannot afford to have any duplicate values in the key-fields (like employee-master, inventory-master, income-tax file, customer-list file, etc.), you may want to prepare a computer program which will scan an indexed list of the data-base, and pull out the duplicates for you. This is one way you can ensure the integrity of your data-base. This program will have to be run as often as records are APPENDed/EDITed into the various Master files. By the time you are through with the study of this book, you will know exactly how to write such a computer program.

The computer program referred to is one way of ensuring the integrity of your data-base. However, you may be saying to yourself that this is all after the fact! That is, the computer program merely helps us to clean up the mess after it has been created.

Is there a way of checking for already-existing keys in a file during the APPEND or EDIT mode? If we could flag duplicate keys as they were being entered/edited, then we would not need to run the quick and dirty program each time, thus streamlining the entire process towards maximum efficiency.

In the Advanced section of this book, we deal exclusively with programming in dBASE, and there you will learn exactly how you can cause the duplicate check to occur during APPEND or EDIT. However, unless you are already advanced in your knowledge of this software and of programming in general, please control the urge to skip ahead. Otherwise you may find yourself in slightly deeper waters than you may prefer at this time.

Mismatching Files and Indexes

By now, perhaps, this what-if question has come to your mind: suppose you have a Master file M1, and an associated index-file I1. Suppose the index was on, say, the TOWN-field. Can you now bring up this I1 index-file in play with another Master file M2? Let us suppose, for now, that Master file M2 also has a field called TOWN defined in its structure.

The answer is both, YES and NO. Physically, it will work, but logically it makes no sense, and in fact, may physically "bomb out" at any point in time. Say that M1 has the following TOWN values, and so M1 and the index I1 will appear as follows:

MASTER FILE		INDEX	
1	------ROCHESTER-----	3	BRIGHTON
2	-----PERINTON------	5	FAIRPORT
3	-----BRIGHTON------	6	GREECE
4	------WEBSTER-------	2	PERINTON
5	-----FAIRPORT------	1	ROCHESTER
6	------GREECE--------	4	WEBSTER

Now let us suppose that you bring the index I1 in play with another Master file M2: Let us also suppose that M2 has only 5 records, in the file.

```
.USE M2    INDEX I1        <cr>
.LIST                      <cr>
```

According to the index I1, record #3 from file M2 will list out first, followed by record #5, and then the LISTing will bomb out with the message, "RECORD OUT OF RANGE," since there is no record #6 in the file M2!

So although physically it can be done, logically it makes no sense to activate the wrong index-file against your Master file. This only serves to highlight the fact that clear documentation is paramount in the efficient execution of your dBASE systems.

COMBINATION OF SORT AND INDEX

Suppose you had the need to obtain the following sequence: by descending TOWN, and within that, by descending SALARY. One way to accomplish this is, of course, by performing 2 iterations using the SORT command.

```
.USE PERSNL                                          <cr>
.SORT ON SALARY TO SALSORT DESC                      <cr>
.USE SALSORT                                         <cr>
.SORT ON TOWN TO TSORT DESC                          <cr>
.USE TSORT                                           <cr>
```

Another way is to use the combination SORT and INDEX. This may prove to be faster.

```
.USE PERSNL                                                   <cr>
.INDEX ON TOWN + STR(99999.99—SALARY,8,2) TO TINDX    <cr>
```

This will provide the usual index by ascending TOWN, and within that, by descending SALARY. We have seen examples of this, before. Now, if this indexed-file were to be SORTED on the TOWN-field in descending sequence, the records should be arranged in the sequence we are seeking. However, on experimenting with this process, I find that, on occasion, some of the records get flipped back to the ascending SALARY sequence, for the same TOWN records. Maybe this is a bug with this aspect of the INDEX feature. So to overcome this problem, after creating the index as stated above, we create a temporary file, as follows:

```
.COPY TO TEMP      <cr>
```

All the indexed records, in the order of ascending TOWN and descending SALARY enter the file called TEMP.

```
.USE TEMP                              <cr>
.SORT ON TOWN TO TSORT DESC            <cr>
```

The file called TSORT.DBF is now the correctly sequenced, final sorted version we are seeking.

SORTING VS INDEXING

Offhand, it would seem that the Indexing feature far outperforms the Sort feature in dBASE. However, there may be situations where you may be better off SORTing than INDEXing.

Indexed files, of course, are most useful when you have to retrieve records at random. However, if all records of an indexed file are to be listed out, dBASE has to proceed in the logical order of the index, record for record, and the physical records will be pulled out as the index demands. This translates into frenzied movement of the disk read-write head across the face of the disk, as the system has to read both, index file and data-base, in effect degrading the overall system performance time. In such a situation, you may prefer to SORT, since the sorted file records are physically in the order you want, and the system will proceed sequentially from one physical record to the next without having to read any logical index, thus providing an overall faster throughput.

Suppose you have made the following observations, with regard to one of the Master files you possess:

Sorting	Indexing
1) Create sort-file 25 minutes.	1) Create index file 5 minutes.
2) Print sorted-file 10 minutes	2) Print indexed-file 20 minutes
35 minutes	25 minutes

These are time spans for a one time deal. That is, you have a file which takes 35 minutes to sort-and-print, and the same file takes 25 minutes to index-and-print. Let us also suppose that you have always been updating your indexes as you were working on your Master files. (We have seen in prior pages exactly how you can do this.) Since you would always have updated indexes, let us disregard the time it would take to create an index, since that would not be necessary.

Let us suppose that our file in question is a mailing-labels file, and we are sending out more than one product sample to the same consumer, and hence our need for printing out the same label file more than once. Using the above figures for our example, if you had to print out the entire indexed file three times in one session, in logical sequence, we can see that it would take $(20 + 20 + 20)$ minutes, or a total of 60 minutes.

Instead of using the indexed file, if we were to sort the file out and print it out three times, we can see that it would take a total of $(25 + 10 + 10 + 10)$ minutes, or a total of 55 minutes. Obviously, you can appreciate that the more times (beyond three) that you have to print out the entire file, the greater the savings in time if you use the SORTed file rather than the INDEXed version.

Hopefully, the above example explains how you may be able to run some quick computations, to help you decide on the SORT or the INDEX question, in your specific situation.

However, as we have seen before, there is one situation wherein you will have to SORT, and that is in case you want to sequence your Master file in descending sequence on a character field. Here the Index feature cannot help you.

FIND COMMAND

This is a very powerful feature of dBASE-II, and is used to find a record having a specific value in a key-field. The required record will be found in about 2 seconds, irrespective of record size or file size!

The FIND command can only execute against an INDEXed file, and hence we take it up at this point in our study of dBASE. For example, let us say that we have indexed a file on the TOWN-field. After the index is created, logically all the towns of, say, ROCHESTER will appear together. To find the very first occurrence of a town of ROCHESTER, we would enter the following:

```
.FIND 'ROCH'        <cr>
```

Note: The value specified, in this case ROCH, may or may not be in quotes, even though TOWN is a character field!

Note: This command only moves a pointer to the found record, but will not automatically display the record. To display the record, and, of course, all the other ROCH records (which are all logically sequenced together), we can enter:

```
.DISP NEXT 10        <cr>
```

This will display 10 records in the logical order of the the index, starting with the current ROCH record, and if there were more ROCH records, they would logically appear together, after the found record.

Each time the FIND command is used, the search begins at the *top* of the *indexed* data-base. If your file was indexed on, say, the YR:OF:HIRE field and you specified the following, can you guess the result:

```
.FIND 19        <cr>
```

This will produce nothing, since, in the case of a numeric field, the value you supply should be algebraically equal to the value contained in a numeric key-field.

Note: Deleted records will be found! That seems logical enough, since the Index command will accept deleted records for Indexing.

Note: Let us go back to the TOWN-index. If you enter .FIND 'R', dBASE will find the first record in the indexed file that has an R in the first location of the TOWN-field. A command like .FIND'RO' will find the first record in the indexed file that has an RO in positions 1 and 2 of the TOWN-field, and so on. That is, the value supplied by you can be generic.

Now let us say that our file has been indexed on TOWN + ORG, and you wanted to find the first record that had a town of 'ROCH' and an organization of 'BSG'. Understand clearly that dBASE must be provided explicit parameters about the TOWN- and organization fields. Since generic values of R, RO, ROC, ROCH, ROCHE, etc., will all find the same record, to find a record with town ROCHESTER and organization BSG would necessitate that you provide the primary key in full! That is, you will have to say:

```
.FIND 'ROCHESTER B'      <cr>        or
.FIND 'ROCHESTER BS'     <cr>        or
.FIND 'ROCHESTER BSG'    <cr>
```

[As before, the values may or may not be supplied in quotes.]

Only the last key value supplied can be generic. All proceeding key-values should be provided in full. This statement is true even if the last key was a numeric key. For instance, if your file was indexed on TOWN + STR (YR:OF:HIRE, 4) and if you wanted to:

```
.FIND 'ROCHESTER 19'          <cr>
```

This will find the first town of ROCHESTER, having a YR:OF:HIRE field beginning with the digits 19. This, of course, ties in with the fact that at the time of creation of the index, the YR:OF:HIRE field was represented as a character string.

Since TOWN is defined in the structure as 12 characters, enough spaces are left at the end of the value ROCHESTER to take care of the first 12 positions of the key-value supplied.

      Note: Let us say that our file has been indexed on the YR:OF:HIRE field, and you wanted to find 1970.

.FIND 1970	\<cr\>	or
.FIND '1970'	\<cr\>	will do the trick.

This command will not work if the file has been indexed in the descending sequence! The indexing feature assumes an ascending sequence, and your fooling around with the 99999 trick in dBASE does not work directly with the FIND command!

However, if you can specify that you want to find 9999 – 1970, you will get the desired result.

.FIND 8029   \<cr\>

This will find the record with YR:OF:HIRE = 1970.

This works the way it does is because when you first specified the creation of the index, you had specified: 9999 – YR:OF:HIRE (for the descending index), and so these *complementary values* had been stored in the index-file. So while you cannot directly find records in a descending-index file, you can always compute and provide the appropriate complementary value yourself and thus find that record.

One last point should be mentioned in the case of an indexed file. The functioning of the LOCATE command against an indexed filed is identical to its functioning against an unindexed file. The only obvious difference is, of course, that in this case, the records are scanned in the order of the index.

RECORD OUT OF RANGE PROBLEM

If you have been using dBASE for some time, you may have encountered an unpleasant problem that crops up once in a while: the "record out of range" situation. The problem is as follows; you have an indexed file, and you have been working at it for some time now, and everything is fine, until one day, the system comes up with the above message. The system is trying to tell you that the next record number (say record number 201), as ordained by the index, is not to be found in the file. That is, the system is telling you that you now have only have a possible maximum of 200 records in your file.

You might suspect the index, and so you may want to try reindexing your Master file again. Sometimes, however, it is not the index that somehow got goofed up, but the Master file that somehow got to be the recipient of an unwelcome *end-of-file* character in record #201! Exactly how these end-of-file markers suddenly crop up in a file is not quite clear (Ashton-Tate technical support newsletters say that the reason could be as vague as a power glitch), but let us understand a possible solution for the problem.

Suppose the system informs you that you now have only 200 records in your file, whereas you know that until yesterday you had more than 500. In other words, there is an end of file marker in record number 201. The following commands will help you recover your file. (Our presumption is that you only have the one extra end of file marker in the file.)

```
.USE <master>                        <cr>
.COPY TO TEMP1 NEXT 200              <cr>
```

You have managed to save the first 200 records in a file called TEMP1, of identical structure to <master>. At this point, the current-record-pointer is positioned at record number 200.

```
.GOTO # + 2                          <cr>
```

With this, you are bypassing record number 201, the one with the end of file character in it. The current record is 202.

```
.COPY NEXT 9999 TO TEMP2             <cr>
```

You are copying all records from record number 202, through to the end of the file, into another temporary file called TEMP2. The file in use is still <master>.

```
.COPY TO TEMP STRU                   <cr>
```

This statement creates only a structure of a file, identical to <master>, with no data.

```
.USE TEMP                            <cr>
.APPEND FROM TEMP1                   <cr>
.APPEND FROM TEMP2                   <cr>
```

You have now managed to salvage all your data records, with the exception, of course, of the one that contained the illegal end of file character. Better to sacrifice the one record, than a few hundred.

```
.DELETE FILE <master>                <cr>
.RENAME TEMP TO <master>             <cr>
```

This routine may not always work, since you may have been blessed with more than one end of file character in your file, and as soon as you execute the command: GOTO # + 2, the system may again come up with the "RECORD OUT OF RANGE" message. In that case, try repeating the GOTO command, with either the +2 displacement, or try with +3, +4, etc.

If you find yourself with many of these illegal characters, you should enlist the aid of someone more into software support, and request him/her to run a utility program to find, and reduce to spaces, all illegal end-of-file characters from your file, except, of course, for the last one. There are several utility-programs on the market which purport to remove these illegal EOF markers, and if you browse through some magazines on personal computing, you will find the names of these packages and their vendors.

A simple rule-of-thumb will reduce the impact of this kind of problem. Always keep backup copies of your Master files.

SUMMARY

Sequencing of records forms an inherent part of any data-processing system, and dBASE provides us with two methods of creating the sequences we want. Of these, Indexing is rather superior to Sorting, and the only place where a Sort would be necessary is when you want to sequence your file in the descending sequence of a character field. Outside of this (remote) requirement, you would probably prefer to stay with the indexing mode.

There are several software products on the market which promise to speed up dBASE's sort and index process, and your perusal of any magazine on personal computing should provide you with the names of the vendors of these products if you feel inclined to try them out.

The ability to sort/index our files now leads us to the next logical step in this book, that of attempting to pull off reports from our dBASE files.

7. Reporting Process

Up until now, our efforts had been concentrated on building a good, workable data-base. We have seen how structures can be built and modified and how data could be entered and subsequently edited in a variety of ways. We have also studied the processes of physically sorting or logically indexing our data so that the records are retrieved in a specifically designed sequence.

Having obtained the skills necessary to be able to guarantee the integrity of our data-base, we shall now look to the aspect of pulling off Reports out of the data-base. After all, the end product of any computerized commercial application is the all-important report which assists management in the decision-making process. In fact, the design of any commercial application to be computerized starts off with a study of the outputs required from the computerized system. And that definitely includes hard-copy (report) outputs.

BUILDING THE REPORT FORMAT FILE

First, we are going to study the dBASE built-in report feature that is going to aid us in obtaining fast, accurate reports. However, as is the case with all prepackaged software, the user will have to live within the limitations of the software. In the case of dBASE's report generator facility, the user will have to be content with the format as presented by dBASE. If you want complete freedom in designing your own report formats, you can always write your own computer program to pull off any report format you want. The study of computer programs in dBASE is presented in Section 3. You will learn, among other things, how to write your own reports in your own formats. For now, however, we shall be studying, in detail, the built-in reporting facility of dBASE.

Report-Format File

Let us suppose that you want a report prepared out of the data you have created, and let us suppose that you are quite clear in your mind about the format of that report. You have visualized the main heading of the report, you know what column headings are required, and you know the fields on which totals are required, etc. Now, all you have to do is *translate the requirements of your conceptual report into words and phrases* that tell dBASE exactly what it is that you want!

That is, you have to build up a file (which, incidentally, will be a text file), containing a few words and phrases in answer to some questions thrown at you by dBASE. This file, since it describes in detail the required format of your conceptual report, is called, appropriately, a *Report Format File*. In the absence of any specific last-qualifier, dBASE will provide a secondary qualifier of .FRM for the format file.

Once a format file is built up, if you initiate the process of report generation from that file, dBASE simply filters your data-records from the data-base, through the words and phrases of the format file, and pulls off the report you want. Conceptually, the process could be shown as follows:

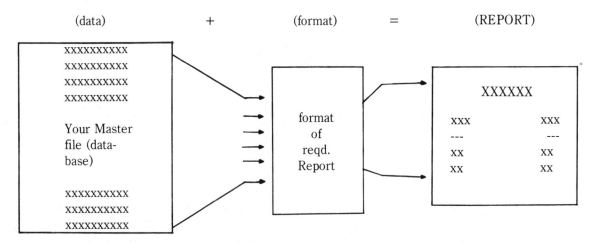

| (data) | + | (format) | = | (REPORT) |

To emphasize, generating any Report simply involves knowing how to produce the report format file (the words and phrases file) using dBASE. As you can imagine, in the study of any report-generating procedure, you can come up with a myriad What If . . . types of questions pertaining to formats and/or totals and/or subtotals and/or doll-up of headings, etc. As a result, you could get quite lost in the various options available, unless you proceed in some logical manner.

On account of the multitude of options to be covered, (and this book will attempt to anticipate most, if not all, of your What If . . . questions), we shall proceed logically.

First I will cover all options pertaining to formats as a separate topic. That is, I shall cover areas relating to main headings, column headings, columns of data on the report, extra headings, obtaining a good spread of the report in a 132-column width, and so on. When we engage in the study of formats, we shall not look at any totals.

Following formats, you will see to generating totals, at which point you will not have anything to do with formats, so as to keep everything in proper perspective. After you are through with the options for totals, you will see to generating subtotals in your report, but again at this point you will not concentrate on formats.

Creating Format Files

When you want to start creating a report format file, you have to inform dBASE of that fact by typing the following:

.USE PERSNL   \<cr>

Some file has to be in use, against which a report format is required.

.REPORT FORMAT RPT1   \<cr>   or

.REPORT FORM RPT1   \<cr>

You have specified to dBASE your intention to create a report format file called RPT1.FRM. At this point, dBASE will start asking you some questions about your proposed report format, and your responses will be stored in the report format file called RPT1.FRM. You can, of course, have any primary name that you want.

Let us study the questions that dBASE will ask you, and study the responses we could provide. Remember, for now, we are studying formats, only, without going into totals or subtotals. The questions asked by dBASE are shown in regular type. Our responses are shown in bold letters. For each of the responses (in bold type), the \<cr> may not have been shown, but is to be presumed present.

USE PERSNL   \<cr>
.REPORT FORM RPT1   \<cr>

ENTER OPTIONS, M=LEFT MARGIN, L=LINES/PAGE, W=PAGE WIDTH **\<cr>**

> **Note:** If you simply \<cr> at this point, you are asking dBASE to assume some default values and proceed. For LEFT MARGIN, the default is column #8. This is the left-most column at which the report will print. Please note that this really translates to the 16th print position from the edge of the paper, since the normal print-position #1 is itself 8 print positions from the edge of the paper. For LINES/ PAGE, the default is 57. For PAGE WIDTH, the default is the screen width (80). The PAGE WIDTH parameter has nothing to do with the width of the report. If this sounds like a contradiction, it really is not, since dBASE only uses this entry to center the main heading. Obviously, therefore, if you want your header centered correctly, you should specify the exact intended width of your proposed report format.

PAGE HEADING? (Y/N)   **Y**
ENTER PAGE HEADING: **REPORT 1**

You could have specified that you did not want any header. However, having answered Y for the header, you will now be required to give a report-header, even if it is a blank.

```
DOUBLE SPACE REPORT? (Y/N)        N
ARE TOTALS REQUIRED? (Y/N)        N
```

Initially, we are studying formats only.

Now dBASE wants us to specify the columns of information we would like to see on the report. We have to specify, for each column, the width of the column, and the contents of the information to go in that column. The 001, 002, . . . simply stand for the first column of information, the second column of information, etc.

```
COL    WIDTH,CONTENTS
001    10,EMP:NUM
ENTER HEADING: EMPNUM
002    20,EMP:NAME
ENTER HEADING: EMP-NAME
003    15,TOWN
ENTER HEADING: TOWN
004         <cr>
```

Use <cr> on a blank line, to wrap up defining the report format. dBASE will then pull off the report.

```
PAGE NO. 00001
07/01/84
                              REPORT 1


   EMPNUM            EMP-NAME              TOWN


   070707        NINA BHARUCHA         WEBSTER
   7545AD        PETE JOHNSON          brighton
   ------        ------------          --------        etc., etc.
```

Observations on Report Formats

1. The main heading is automatically centered across the width we had asked for.

2. The column headings are also automatically centered across the respective column widths we had specified.

3. The page number and literal have been provided by dBASE.

4. The date has been provided to us, since we had entered a date at the time we had loaded dBASE. Bypassing a date-entry at load time would have left the date line blank.

Note: If, at the time of loading dBASE, we had bypassed a date entry, and we now wanted to date all our reports, it is not necessary to

142

quite out of dBASE to enter the date. You can easily do this with the following command

.SET DATE TO mm/dd/yy   \<cr\>
.REPORT FORM xyz . . . .   \<cr\>

The above format of the SET command can be used either to enter a date, or change an existing date.

5. Within a specified width, the data will always enter that width correctly justified. That is, character data will always enter the width left justified, and numeric data will always enter right justified. We cannot change the justification. (More information on this is provided later.)

6. Between columns of data, dBASE automatically provides us with 1 column of space.

7. To send this report to the printer, simply enter:

.REPORT FORM RPT1   TO PRINT

The report format now goes to both, screen and printer.

Note: When you invoke the TO PRINT option, dBASE makes a presumption that your printer is not positioned correctly on a new page for the report, and so it takes an eject and brings up a new page before it prints out the report. To deactivate this primary eject feature, you can turn the eject off.

.SET EJECT OFF
.REPORT FORM RPT1 TO PRINT

Note: This only affects the primary eject at the start of the report print-out. Subsequent page ejects, for a report longer than one page, will take place automatically.

8. To use this same report format, but restrict the output of the report to selected records, you can specify a condition, in the report command:

.REPORT FORM RPT1 [TO PRINT] FOR \<condition\>

Now only records that satisfy the condition will appear in the report, but in the format as designed in the format-file. As always, the condition can be as simple or as complex as you may want to make it.

9. To use this same report format, but restrict the output of the report to selected records, you can specify a scope in the report command.

.REPORT FORM RPT1 [NEXT n] [TO PRINT]

Now only the next N records will appear in the report starting with the current record but in the format as designed in the format file.

10. On sending this report to paper, dBASE will automatically format out the main heading and column headings on pages following page 1. The page numbers also get incremented.

11. On subsequent occasions, to pull of this report again, we simply have to enter: .REPORT FORM RPT1 [TO PRINT] and dBASE will pull off the report again, provided, of course, the correct data base has been brought into USE.

12. Which means, that if you want to make any kind of change to an existing report format, specifying **REPORT FORM RPT1** again, hoping to bring up the questions and answers for changes, does not work since dBASE simply pulls off the report. Making changes to existing report formats will be covered after we are through with all the explanations on Reports.

13. If you want a special heading entered ahead of the entire report, use the SET HEADING TO command to set this heading before invoking the REPORT command. For example:

```
.SET HEADING TO REPORT AS OF JUNE 15, 1984.    <cr>
.REPORT FORM RPT1 [TO PRINT]    [FOR <condition>]
```

```
               REPORT  AS  OF  JUNE  15,  1984.

PAGE  NO.  00001
07/01/84
                                         REPORT  1


      EMPNUM            EMP-NAME                 TOWN

      070707        NINA  BHARUCHA          WEBSTER
      7545AD        PETE  JOHNSON           brighton
      987178        GLORIA  PATEL           FAIRPORT
      232430        MAX  LEVENSKY           HENRIETTA
      ------        ------------            ---------
      ------        ------------            ---------
```

Now this implies, obviously, that although the report was pulled off on July 1, 1984, the data in the report is only valid up through June 15, 1984. It is quite common to see such special headings in reports.

> **Note:** Once the SET HEADING TO command has been invoked, it remains in effect, across any other report formats you may want to pull off. To deactivate this feature, enter:

```
.SET HEADING TO       <cr>
```

Dolling up Column Headings

This section will help you design a more eye appealing report form.

.REPORT FORM RPT2   <cr>

ENTER OPTIONS, M=LEFT MARGIN, L=LINES/PAGE, W=PAGE
WIDTH **<cr>**
PAGE HEADING? (Y/N) **Y**
ENTER PAGE HEADING: **REPORT 2**
DOUBLE SPACE REPORT? (Y/N) **N**
ARE TOTALS REQUIRED? (Y/N) **N**
COL   WIDTH,CONTENTS
001   **10,EMP:NUM**
ENTER HEADING: **<EMP-NUM**
002   **20,EMP:NAME**
ENTER HEADING: **<EMP-NAME**
003   **15,TOWN**
ENTER HEADING: **<TOWN**
004   **<cr>**

Note the < symbol, to show left justification.

```
PAGE NO. 00001
07/01/84


                                    REPORT  2


EMP-NUM       EMP-NAME                TOWN

070707        NINA BHARUCHA           WEBSTER
7545AD        PETE JOHNSON            brighton
987178        GLORIA PATEL            FAIRPORT
232430        MAX LEVENSKY            HENRIETTA
------        -----------             ---------
```

The results of our manipulations are as follows:

1. Now the column headings are properly aligned over the data.

2. Within a specified width, the data will always enter that width correctly justified. That is, character data will always enter the width left justified, and numeric data will always enter right justified. We cannot change the justification, but we can always make the column heading move around, and so obtain the visual impact we want. We use the < symbol for left justification, and the > symbol for right justification, for the column headings. Columns for character data should be left justified, and for numeric data, right justified.

3. If it is imperative for visual impact that the column heading should be moved around just a little, you can always move the column over, through the use of leading or trailing blanks, as shown here:

.REPORT FORM RPT3   **<cr>**

ENTER OPTIONS, M=LEFT MARGIN, L=LINES/PAGE, W=PAGE
WIDTH **<cr>**
PAGE HEADING? (Y/N) **Y**
ENTER PAGE HEADING: **REPORT 3**
DOUBLE SPACE REPORT? (Y/N) **N**
ARE TOTALS REQUIRED? (Y/N) **N**
COL   WIDTH,CONTENTS
001   **10,EMP:NUM**
ENTER HEADING: <   **EMP:NUM**
002   **20,EMP:NAME**
ENTER HEADING: <   **EMP:NAME**
003   **15,TOWN**
ENTER HEADING: <   **TOWN**
004   **<cr>**

Note the spaces before the literals.

```
PAGE  NO.  00001
07/01/84
                                      REPORT  3


    EMP:NUM      EMP:NAME                TOWN

    070707       NINA BHARUCHA           WEBSTER
    7545AD       PETE JOHNSON            brighton
    987178       GLORIA PATEL            FAIRPORT
    232430       MAX LEVENSKY            HENRIETTA
    ------       ------------            ---------
    ------       ------------            ---------
```

You can use the > symbol to right justify the column heading for character data. The
result would appear very lopsided, and such stunts should be avoided.

Let's try another form for the column headings.

.REPORT FORM RPT4   **<cr>**

ENTER OPTIONS, M=LEFT MARGIN, L=LINES/PAGE, W=PAGE
WIDTH **<cr>**
PAGE HEADING? (Y/N) **Y**
ENTER PAGE HEADING: **REPORT 4**
DOUBLE SPACE REPORT? (Y/N) **N**
ARE TOTALS REQUIRED? (Y/N) **N**
COL   WIDTH,CONTENTS

146

```
001     10,EMP:NUM
ENTER HEADING: <EMPLYEE;NUMBER
002     20,EMP:NAME
ENTER HEADING: <EMPLOYEE;NAME
003     15,TOWN
ENTER HEADING: <TOWN;----
004         <cr>
```

```
PAGE NO.  00001
07/01/84
                                            REPORT  4


EMPLOYEE        EMPLOYEE                    TOWN
NUMBER          NAME                        ----

070707          NINA BHARUCHA               WEBSTER
7545AD          PETE JOHNSON                brighton
987178          GLORIA PATEL                FAIRPORT
232430          MAX LEVENSKY                HENRIETTA
------          -------------               ---------
------          -------------               ---------
```

Now each of our column headings has been dolled up to provide two lines. The ; (semicolon) character is used to show that whatever follows is to be provided on the second line. Notice that the character for justification (either the < or the > symbol) should not appear again on the second line when specifying that the column heading should be more than one line. If it is used, the symbol will print out as any other character.

You could extend the procedure shown above, to include more than just 2 lines in the column heading. In this example, we have called for the TOWN-field multiple times, and in each case, the column header has been manipulated in a different way. Note that you can always use multiple ; (semicolons) to produce the "leave a line" effect. Notice that entry #003 and 004 produced the same result.

.REPORT FORM RPT5   <cr>

```
ENTER  OPTIONS,  M=LEFT  MARGIN,  L=LINES/PAGE,  W=PAGE
WIDTH  <cr>
PAGE HEADING? (Y/N) Y
ENTER PAGE HEADING: REPORT 5
DOUBLE SPACE REPORT? (Y/N) N
ARE TOTALS REQUIRED? (Y/N) N
COL     WIDTH,CONTENTS
001     10,EMP:NUM
ENTER HEADING: <EMPLOYEE;NUMBER;------
```

```
002     12,TOWN
ENTER HEADING: <TOWN;----
003     12,TOWN
ENTER HEADING: <TOWN;      ;----
004     12,TOWN
ENTER HEADING: <TOWN;;----
005     12,TOWN
ENTER HEADING: <;TOWN;----
006        <cr>
```

```
PAGE NO. 00001
07/01/84
                                           REPORT 5
```

EMPLOYEE	TOWN	TOWN	TOWN	
NUMBER	----			TOWN
------		----	----	----
070707	WEBSTER	WEBSTER	WEBSTER	WEBSTER
7545AD	brighton	brighton	brighton	brighton
987178	FAIRPORT	FAIRPORT	FAIRPORT	FAIRPORT
232430	HENRIETTA	HENRIETTA	HENRIETTA	HENRIETTA

Dolling Up the Main Heading

We can use the same procedure to obtain more than one line of output in our main report heading.

.REPORT FORM RPT6   **<cr>**

```
ENTER OPTIONS, M=LEFT MARGIN, L=LINES/PAGE, W=PAGE WIDTH
PAGE HEADING? (Y/N) Y
ENTER PAGE HEADING: REPORT 6;====== =
DOUBLE SPACE REPORT? (Y/N) N
ARE TOTALS REQUIRED? (Y/N)
COL     WIDTH,CONTENTS
001     10,EMP:NUM
ENTER HEADING: <EMPLOYEE;NUMBER
002     20,EMP:NAME
ENTER HEADING: <EMPLOYEE;NAME
003     15,TOWN
ENTER HEADING: <TOWN;----
004        <cr>
```

```
PAGE NO. 00001

07/01/84

                                            REPORT 6

                                            ====== =

EMPLOYEE        EMPLOYEE                     TOWN
NUMBER          NAME                         ====

070707          NINA BHARUCHA               WEBSTER
7545AD          PETE JOHNSON                brighton
987178          GLORIA PATEL                FAIRPORT
232430          MAX LEVENSKY                HENRIETTA
------          -------------               ---------
------          -------------               ---------
```

Now we have two lines in our main heading. On the screen, it will appear as if dBASE has included one extra line space, between the two main heading lines. However, this is not the case, and if this report were to be sent to the printer, there will be no extra line space. This line space only appears on the screen.

If we did want extra spaces to appear between the various lines of the main heading, we could do this with the aid of two or more consecutive semicolons:

.REPORT FORM RPT7   **\<cr>**

ENTER OPTIONS, M=LEFT MARGIN, L=LINES/PAGE, W=PAGE WIDTH
PAGE HEADING? (Y/N) **Y**
ENTER PAGE HEADING: **REPORT 7;;====== =**
DOUBLE SPACE REPORT? (Y/N) **N**
ARE TOTALS REQUIRED? (Y/N) **N**
COL   WIDTH,CONTENTS
001   **10,EMP:NUM**
ENTER HEADING: **\<EMPLOYEE;NUMBER**
002   **20,EMP:NAME**
ENTER HEADING: **\<EMPLOYEE;NAME**
003   **15,TOWN**
ENTER HEADING: **\<TOWN;----**
004   **\<cr>**

Now our report format has really called for extra line spaces in-between the lines of the main heading. If we wanted to generate a few extra blank lines between the main heading lines and the column headings, this too could be done with the aid of more semicolons after the main heading definitions.

```
PAGE NO. 00001

07/01/84

                                        REPORT 7

                                        ====== =

EMPLOYEE        EMPLOYEE                TOWN

NUMBER          NAME                    ====

070707          NINA BHARUCHA          WEBSTER
7545AD          PETE JOHNSON           brighton
987178          GLORIA PATEL           FAIRPORT
232430          MAX LEVENSKY           HENRIETTA
------          ------------           ---------
```

.REPORT FORM RPT8   <cr>

ENTER OPTIONS, M=LEFT MARGIN, L=LINES/PAGE, W=PAGE WIDTH
PAGE HEADING? (Y/N) **Y**
ENTER PAGE HEADING: **REPORT 8;====== =;;;**
DOUBLE SPACE REPORT? (Y/N) **N**
ARE TOTALS REQUIRED? (Y/N) **N**
COL   WIDTH,CONTENTS
001   **10,EMP:NUM**
ENTER HEADING: **<EMP:NUM**
ENTER HEADING: **<EMPLOYEE;NUMBER**
002   **20,EMP:NAME**
ENTER HEADING: **<EMPLOYEE;NAME**
003   **15,TOWN**
ENTER HEADING: **<TOWN;----**
004   <cr>

```
PAGE NO. 00001
07/01/84
                                        REPORT 8
                                        ====== =

EMPLOYEE        EMPLOYEE                TOWN
NUMBER          NAME                    ====

070707          NINA BHARUCHA          WEBSTER
7545AD          PETE JOHNSON           brighton
987178          GLORIA PATEL           FAIRPORT
232430          MAX LEVENSKY           HENRIETTA
------          ------------           ---------
------          ------------           ---------
```

Multiple Main Heading Lines

You could have multiple lines in your main report header. During the report format generation phase, simply use the ; to produce the multiple lines as we have seen before without regard to the screen size, or the fact that the line wraps around on the screen! See the example that follows:

REPORT FORM RPT8A   <cr>
ENTER   OPTIONS,   M=LEFT   MARGIN,   L=LINES/PAGE,   W=PAGE WIDTH   <cr>
PAGE HEADING? (Y/N) **Y**

ENTER PAGE HEADING: **REPORT 8A;------ --;REPORT ON EMPLOYEE LO-CATIONS;DATA GENERATED FOR DISTRICT MANAGERS' MEETING**

DOUBLE SPACE REPORT? (Y/N **N**
ARE TOTALS REQUIRED? (Y/N) **N**
COL   WIDTH,CONTENTS
001   **10,EMP:NUM**
ENTER HEADING: <**EMPLOYEE;NUMBERS**
002   **15,EMP:NAME**
ENTER HEADING: <**EMPLOYEE;NAMES**
003   **12,TOWN**
ENTER HEADING: <**TOWN;----**
004   <**cr**>

PAGE NO. 00001
07/01/84

REPORT 8A
------ --

REPORT ON EMPLOYEE LOCATIONS

DATA GENERATED FOR DISTRICT MANAGERS' MEETING

EMPLOYEE NUMBERS	EMPLOYEE NAMES	TOWN ----
070707	NINA BHARUCHA	WEBSTER
7545AD	PETE JOHNSON	brighton
987178	GLORIA PATEL	FAIRPORT
------	-------------	----------
------	-------------	----------

Displaying Record Numbers

As we have seen earlier, you can specify that the report format be generated only for records satisfying a specific condition. Now it would be necessary, in some situations, to be able to come up with the record numbers of those records that satisfied the conditions. To bring the record numbers into play, use the # function.

.REPORT FORM RPT9 FOR TOWN = 'ROCH'   **<cr>**

ENTER OPTION, M=LEFT MARGIN, L=LINES/PAGE, W=PAGE WIDTH **<cr>**
PAGE HEADING? (Y/N) **N**
ENTER PAGE HEADING: **REPORT 9**
DOUBLE SPACE REPORT? (Y/N) **N**
ARE TOTALS REQUIRED? (Y/N) **N**
COL   WIDTH, CONTENTS
001   **6,#**
ENTER HEADING: **RECNUM**
002   **10,EMP:NUM**
ENTER HEADING: **<EMPLOYEE:NUMBERS**
003   **15,EMP:NAME**
ENTER HEADING: **<EMPLOYEE:NAMES**
004   **12,TOWN**
ENTER HEADING: **<TOWN;----**
005

The record number field is considered numeric, so data in column 2 will be right justified.

```
PAGE NO. 00001
07/01/84
                                    REPORT 9

RECNUM EMPLOYEE    EMPLOYEE          TOWN
       NUMBERS     NAMES             ----

     6 AC9090      TIM MONTAL        ROCHESTER
     8 091230      JAMES JAMESON     ROCHESTER
    14 09890A      JAN MOREY         ROCHESTER
```

The function provides the way for obtaining record numbers of records selected in the report process.
> **Note:** What would happen if the column width you have specified for a column of information is smaller than the width of either the column-header or the data? The column-header literal and the data coming in would wrap around within the confines of the column width.

.REPORT FORM RPT10 FOR TOWN = 'ROCH'   **<cr>**

ENTER OPTIONS, M=LEFT MARGIN, L=LINES/PAGE, W=PAGE WIDTH **<cr>**
PAGE HEADING? (Y/N) **Y**

ENTER PAGE HEADING: **REPORT 10**
DOUBLE SPACE REPORT? (Y/N) **N**
ARE TOTALS REQUIRED? (Y/N) **N**
COL   WIDTH, CONTENTS
001   **3,EMP:NUM**
ENTER HEADING: **EMPNUM**
002   **12,TOWN**
ENTER HEADING: **<TOWN**
003   **<cr>**

The EMP:NUM field, as set up for column 1, is not big enough to contain either header or data.

```
PAGE NO. 00001
07/01/84
                                    REPORT 10


EMP TOWN
NUM

AC9 ROCHESTER
090
091 ROCHESTER
230
098 ROCHESTER
90A
```

Notice the wrap around of both header and data, for the EMP:NUM field.
    Note: If your column-header literal is the exact size as the column width, then you don't need the semicolon to specify the second line of the column header. For example:

        5,WIDTH   <cr>
        WIDTH-----   <cr>

    Here our column-header literal is longer than the specified column width. As seen earlier, since the wrap-around to the second line will automatically occur anyway, you don't need the semicolon to specify the second line of the column header. In fact, if you do specify the semicolon, it will only generate an extra line space between the first and the second lines of column header!

Obtaining a Good Spread

Now we shall look to methods of obtaining more than just the one column of space that dBASE provides as default between columns of data in the report. We want to be able to specify our own spread for the various columns, and be able to come out with the exact format we want for a report. Suppose for now, that we want 5 columns of spread between our columns of data.

.REPORT FORM RPT11 FOR TOWN = 'ROCH'   **\<cr\>**

ENTER OPTIONS, M=LEFT MARGIN, L=LINES/PAGE, W=PAGE WIDTH **\<cr\>**
PAGE HEADING? (Y/N) **Y**
ENTER PAGE HEADING: **REPORT 11;CLEAN SPREAD**
DOUBLE SPACE REPORT? (Y/N) **N**
ARE TOTALS REQUIRED? (Y/N) **N**
COL   WIDTH, CONTENTS
001   **10,EMP:NUM**
ENTER HEADING: **\<EMPLOYEE;NUMBERS**
002   **5,' '**   Note this line!
ENTER HEADING:
003   **15,EMP:NAME**
ENTER HEADING: **\<EMPLOYEE;NAMES**
004   **5,' '**   Note!
ENTER HEADING:
005   **12,TOWN**
ENTER HEADING: **\<TOWN;----**
006   **5,' '**   Note!
ENTER HEADING:
007   **3,ORG**
ENTER HEADING: **ORG---**
008   **\<cr\>**

For the second column of data, you are specifying that across a span of 5 columns you want the literal BLANK. That is, you are specifying that you want some blanks as the second column of information. There is, of course, no heading over that blank space, so you simply hit the \<cr\> key to bypass the heading.

```
PAGE NO. 00001
07/01/84
                              REPORT 11

                            CLEAN SPREAD


EMPLOYEE                 EMPLOYEE                 TOWN                    ORG
NUMBERS                  NAMES                    ----                    ---

AC9090                   TIM MONTAL               ROCHESTER               RBG
091230                   JAMES JAMESON            ROCHESTER               GSD
09890A                   JAN MOREY                ROCHESTER               GSD
```

154

Note: So far, we have seen that the column of information asked for on a report format could be either a *field-name* from the file in use, or a *literal,* described in quotes.

In the above example, did we really manage to obtain 5 columns of spaces between our columns of data? If you recall, dBASE treats the column of spaces you asked for as any other column of information. Now since dBASE always provides us with one column of space between columns of data, if you really ask for a column of 5 spaces between FIELD A and FIELD B, you will end up with 7 spaces for that spread (1 column after FIELD A, 5 columns of blanks and 1 column after the 5 columns of blanks). So you will always end up with 2 more spaces than you had bargained for. Keeping this in mind, if you really want 10 spaces between columns of real data fields, you should ask for 8, and so on. In this way, you can obtain the exact spacing you want between columns of real data in a report.

Expressions in Report Formats

In mentioning which fields you want listed out in a report, you are not restricted only to the fields defined in the structure of the file in use. You could even invent some fields of your own!

For example, if you want a listing which provides SALARY, and you also want to show the salary field again, but this time with an increase of 10% in the amount, you could proceed as follows:

REPORT FORM RPT12 FOR TOWN = 'ROCH'   **<cr>**

ENTER OPTIONS, M=LEFT MARGIN, L=LINES/PAGE, W=PAGE WIDTH **<cr>**
PAGE HEADING? (Y/N) **Y**
ENTER PAGE HEADING: **REPORT 12;CLEAN SPREAD**
DOUBLE SPACE REPORT? (Y/N) **N**
ARE TOTALS REQUIRED? (Y/N) **N**
COL   WIDTH, CONTENTS
001   **10,EMP:NUM**
ENTER HEADING: **<EMPLOYEE;NUMBERS**
002   **5,' '**
ENTER HEADING:
003   **8,SALARY**
ENTER HEADING: **<SALARY;------**
004   **5,' '**
ENTER HEADING:
005   **9,SALARY * 1.1**
ENTER HEADING: **>HIGHER;SALARY**
006   **<cr>**

For the fifth column of data, you are specifying that across a span of 9 columns, you want the expression, SALARY * 1.1. You are specifying that you want the salary increased by 10%, in the body of that column. Obviously, this expression is valid only for the duration of the report, and does nothing to the original salary data in the file under USE.

155

```
PAGE NO.  00001
07/01/84
                              REPORT 12

                             CLEAN SPREAD

EMPLOYEE           SALARY          HIGHER
NUMBERS            ------          SALARY

AC9090           41900.00         46090.00
091230           29800.00         32780.00
09890A           18190.00         20009.00
```

At this point we may note that a column of information required on a report could be either:

☐ A field-name from the file under use.
☐ A literal.
☐ An expression.

Further examples of where you may use the power of the expression could be as follows. Suppose you are working with an inventory file, and you have defined in the structure of the file, the following fields (among others): QYT:ON:HAND, and UNIT:-COST.

Now, in the body of the report, if you want to specify the dollar amount of inventory carried in each item, you could specify your expression as follows:

10,QTY:ON:HAND * UNIT:COST

Across a span of 10 columns, you want to see the product of QTY:ON:HAND and UNIT:COST. We shall touch upon this again later.

132 Column Spread

Systems analysts and users generally prepare layouts of expected reports on specially prepared paper called the *printer spacing chart,* which is like graph paper, and each column and line on that paper reflects a physical column and line that the printer can assume, on regular paper. Using this printer spacing chart to prepare an exact format of an expected report facilitates the creation of the report format file in dBASE, since the exact number of columns of space can now be readily counted. Using the formatting features studied so far, you can now prepare a report format spread out to your exact specifications.

Most printers are set for printing out 132 characters per line, at the pitch of 10 characters per linear inch. In such a setting, if your dBASE format file extends to more than 132 characters, then during the printing of the report, all characters beyond the 132nd position will get crunched into the 132nd position on the printer. If that happens, either you reduce the width of your report format (modifying report formats will be covered later), or you can alter the pitch setting on your printer, to more than 10 characters per linear inch. Try a 12-pitch setting, or a 15-pitch setting if your printer allows it. However, please understand that the appropriate print-wheel is recommended for the different pitch settings. Otherwise your report has a highly compressed appearance.

> **Note:** If you forget about the extra 2 columns that dBASE always provides you when you ask for a blank column of spaces, then you will overrun the intended width of the report. Now every character on the report beyond the 132nd position gets crunched into the 132nd position on the printer.

Vertical Formats

The built-in REPORT command can be used to provide us with vertical formats in our reports. For example, let us suppose that we want the following format to be generated:

```
EMPLOYEE-NUMBERS        ORG
EMPLOYEE-NAMES          YRHR
TOWN
SALARY


070707                  BSG
NINA BHARUCHA           1980
WEBSTER
36300.00
```

We can use the special functions of concatenation of character strings to generate such a format.

.REPORT FORM RPT13 FOR TOWN = 'ROCH'   **<cr>**

ENTER OPTIONS, M=LEFT MARGIN, L=LINES/PAGE, W=PAGE WIDTH <cr>
PAGE HEADING? (Y/N) **Y**
ENTER PAGE HEADING: **REPORT 13 – VERTICAL FORMATS**
DOUBLE SPACE REPORT? (Y/N) **N**
ARE TOTALS REQUIRED? (Y/N) **N**
COL   WIDTH,CONTENTS
001   **20,EMP:NUM+';'+EMP:NAME+';'+TOWN+';'+STR(SALARY,8,2)+';;;'**
ENTER HEADING: **<EMPLOYEE-NUMBER;EMPLOYEE-NAME;TOWN;SALARY**
002   **5,' '**
ENTER HEADING:
003   **4,ORG+';'+STR(YR:OF:HIRE,4)**
ENTER HEADING: **<ORG;YRHR**
004

                    REPORT 13 - VERTICAL FORMATS

```
EMPLOYEE-NUMBER              ORG
EMPLOYEE-NAME                YRHR
TOWN
SALARY


070707                      BSG
NINA BHARUCHA                1980
WEBSTER
36300.00


7545AD                      BSG
------------                -----        etc.
```

Some observations can be made. For the first column of information, we have specified that we want to see a concatenated string consisting of EMP:NUM *immediately followed by, though on the next line, EMP:NAME, immediately followed by, though on the next line, TOWN, immediately followed by, though on the next line, SALARY. Notice also that concatenation only applies to string variables, and so the SALARY field had to be specified as a string function.

After specifying the SALARY field as the last of the items of information from any record, notice the ';;;' symbol. That has been used to inform dBASE that we want to keep 2 spaces after each SALARY field has been printed out. That is, we have asked for 2 spaces between records printed out. Three semicolons will produce 2 spaces, four semicolons will produce 3 spaces, and so on.

> **Note:** Since the SALARY field had to be specified as a string function, we would not have been able to provide any totals on the salary field, even if we had wanted to. See "Taking Totals" in the next chapter.

For the second column of information, we asked for 5 blanks. For the third column of information, we have specified a concatenation as follows: ORGanization, immediately followed by, though on the next line, YR:OF:HIRE. We had to specify the STRING function for the YR:OF:HIRE field for the same reason as outlined for the SALARY field.

Obtaining a Ratio

Suppose you want a ratio as one of the columns of data in your report format. Say you have a field called YTD:QTY, and you want to be able to divide this value by the current month picked up from the date provided upon entry into dBASE, and so obtain an average figure for monthly consumption.

If the YTD:QTY item referred to, say, an inventory of shoes, then the figure in that field will be a whole number, that is, not a decimal or fraction. Now if dBASE divides a whole number with another whole number, it will produce a result in whole numbers, only, although the result would normally be required with decimal places.

In general, in dBASE, if you divide a whole number with another whole number, the answer is in whole numbers. If one of the fields is defined with one decimal place, the result comes out to one decimal place. If one of the fields is defined to one decimal position, and the other field is defined to two decimal positions, the result is to two decimal positions, and so on.

In this example, since both fields (YTD:QTY and current month) are defined without decimal positions, the result will come out without decimals, i.e., dBASE will truncate the decimal portion. Now if it were essential for us to come up with the answer accurate to two decimal positions, we have to either change the structure of the file around so that one of the fields is now defined with 2 decimal positions, or, far easier, fool dBASE into thinking it is working with a field defined with 2 decimal positions.

Using the VAL special function described in an earlier section, suppose we have managed to store the current month in a numeric *memory variable* called MONTH. Refer back to the VAL and DATE() functions, if necessary. A memory variable is simply a small section of memory set aside that can contain any data. Each memory variable is assigned a name to permit subsequent access to the variable. The STORE command is used to place data into the memory variable. We will cover more on memory variables and the STORE command, in the advanced (programming) section of this book.

.STORE VAL (DATE()) TO MONTH

Since DATE has the format: MM/DD/YY the VAL function will take only the MM portion, and store it into a numeric memory variable called MONTH. Now in the report, you could ask for the following:

```
------
------
------
6,(YTD:QTY / MONTH)      + 0.00
-----
```

The / defines the division operation. We have also managed to introduce one more parameter (+0.00) in the mathematical expression, which will have no effect on the answer, but it will force dBASE to provide us the answer to 2 decimal places. You can use this trick to obtain the answer to any number of decimal places you require without changing field structures. Just ensure that the width of the field specified is large enough to contain the number of decimal places in the dummy parameter inclusive of the decimal point.

Simultaneous Reporting from Two Data-Bases

So far we have seen how we can format out a good report using one data-base. Now let us enhance the formatting to include two data-bases simultaneously. In our study of the DISPLAY command, we have seen how we may activate two data-bases through the use of the .SELECT PRIM and .SELECT SECO commands. We shall follow the same procedure, here.

```
.SELE PRIM
.USE FILEA
```

These two commands effectively designate FILEA as the primary file.

```
.SELE SECO
.USE FILEB
```

These two commands effectively designate FILEB as the secondary file.

```
.SELE PRIM
```

You should end up on this command.

```
.SET LINKAGE ON
```

Now the two files will behave as one.

```
.REPORT FORM XYZ [TO PRINT]
```

When producing this report format file, simply mention the field-names just as you would have done, had you been using just one data-base. However, in the event that you have identical field-names in the structures of both data-bases (whatever the reason), you will have to prefix the secondary field-names with S. to differentiate the field as the one coming in from the secondary file. In the absence of the prefix qualifier, dBASE will always presume you are referring to the field from the primary file on account of the .SELE PRIM command issued before the .SET LINKAGE ON command.

The same precaution provided in the DISPLAY command holds good here, too. After you have LINKed the two data-bases for the purpose of the report type the following:

```
.SET LINKAGE OFF
```

Taking Totals

We will now see to the method of producing some kinds of totals on numeric fields, in our reports. Out of necessity, therefore, we will have to answer Y to dBASE's question on whether or not we want totals. Note that if you change an answer from N to Y, dBASE goes off on a tangent, and asks some other, pertinent, questions.

> **Note:** You may obtain totals and subtotals from LINKed data-bases as easily as from a single data-base.

.REPORT FORM RPT14 FOR TOWN = 'ROCH' <cr>

ENTER OPTIONS, M=LEFT MARGIN, L=LINES/PAGE, W=PAGE WIDTH <cr>
PAGE HEADING? (Y/N) **Y**
ENTER PAGE HEADING: **REPORT 14;TOTALS**

160

```
DOUBLE SPACE REPORT? (Y/N) N
ARE TOTALS REQUIRED? (Y/N) Y
SUBTOTALS IN REPORT? (Y/N) N
COL     WIDTH, CONTENTS
001     10,EMP:NUM
ENTER HEADING: <EMPLOYEE;NUMBERS
002     15,EMP:NAME
ENTER HEADING: <EMPLOYEE;NAMES
0003    12,TOWN
ENTER HEADING: <TOWN;----
004     8,SALARY
ENTER HEADING: >SALARY;------
ARE TOTALS REQUIRED? (Y/N) Y
```

When you specify Y for totals on any field, you are referring to the running vertical total of that column.

```
PAGE NO.  00001
07/01/84
                                    REPORT 14

                                      TOTALS

EMPLOYEE        EMPLOYEE          TOWN              SALARY
NUMBERS         NAMES             ----              ------

AC9090          TIM MONTAL        ROCHESTER         41900.00
091230          JAMES JAMESON     ROCHESTER         29800.00
09890A          JAN MOREY         ROCHESTER         18190.00
** TOTAL **
                                                    89890.00
```

Record Counts of Selected Records

We shall now get dBASE to provide for us a count of the number of records that appear in a report. There is no direct method of doing this, but we shall fool dBASE into providing us the count we want. We do this with the aid of a dummy request for dBASE to provide us with a numeric 1 against each record listed out. Since the dummy field is numeric, dBASE will ask us if we want totals against this field, to which we respond yes.

.REPORT FORM RPT15 FOR TOWN = 'ROCH'   <cr>

```
ENTER OPTIONS, M=LEFT MARGIN, L=LINES/PAGE, W=PAGE WIDTH <cr>
PAGE HEADING? (Y/N) Y
ENTER PAGE HEADING: REPORT 15;RECORD-COUNTS
DOUBLE SPACE REPORT? (Y/N) N
ARE TOTALS REQUIRED? (Y/N) Y
```

SUBTOTALS IN REPORT? (Y/N) **N**
COL   WIDTH, CONTENTS
001   **10,EMP:NUM**
ENTER HEADING: **<EMPLOYEE;NUMBERS**
002   **15,EMP:NAME**
ENTER HEADING: **<EMPLOYEE;NAMES**
003   **3,ORG**
ENTER HEADING: **ORG**
004   **8,SALARY**
ENTER HEADING: **>SALARY**
ARE TOTALS REQUIRED? (Y/N) **Y**
005   **10,' '**
ENTER HEADING:
006   **3,1**
ENTER HEADING:
ARE TOTALS REQUIRED? (Y/N) **Y**
007   **<cr>**

Note the instruction in line 006. This will provide the total we want.

```
PAGE NO. 00001
07/01/84
                              REPORT 15

                           RECORD-COUNTS

EMPLOYEE       EMPLOYEE          ORG   SALARY
NUMBERS        NAMES

AC9090         TIM MONTAL        RBG 41900.00
091230         JAMES JAMESON     GSD 29800.00
09890A         JAN MOREY         GSD 18190.00
** TOTAL **
                                     89890.00
```

The dummy field should be segregated from the rest of the report format, to avoid any confusion arising from its presence.

In the above report format, for the sixth field in the body of the report, we specified that across a span of 3 columns we would like to see the numeric literal 1. Note that the numeric literal was specified without quotes to keep it a numeric literal. By specifying a width of 3 columns, we have informed dBASE that we do not expect the total number of records satisfying our condition to exceed 999. Obviously, the width you ask for must be able to accommodate the expected number of records satisfying your condition, else garbage is printed out for the total. The dummy field lets you see at a glance on the last page of the report exactly how many records qualified for your specific condition.

Please note very clearly that our dummy-field is a numeric field, and so dBASE asked us if we wanted totals on that field. Had we defined that field as a character field (simply by entering the literal in quotes), dBASE would not have asked us if we wanted to see any totals against that field.

Expressions in a Report Column

We have seen, so far, that the column of information on a report could be either a field-name out of a file in use, or a literal. The literal is either a character literal or a numeric literal. We shall now see how expressions could also form a column of information in the report.

For example, suppose we have an inventory file containing, among other fields, the qty:on:hand and unit:cost. To print out the amount of inventory for each item in the file, we could request the following:

.REPORT FORM RPT16   **<cr>**

ENTER OPTIONS, M=LEFT MARGIN, L=LINES/PAGE, W=PAGE WIDTH **<cr>**
PAGE HEADING? (Y/N) **Y**
ENTER PAGE HEADING **REPORT 17;INVENTORY RPT**
DOUBLE SPACE REPORT? (Y/N) **N**
ARE TOTALS REQUIRED? (Y/N) **Y**
SUBTOTALS IN REPORT? (Y/N) **N**
COL   WIDTH, CONTENTS
001   **10,ITEM:NO**
ENTER HEADING: **<ITEM;NUMBER**
002   **5,QTY:ON:HAND**
ENTER HEADING: **>Q-O-H**
ARE TOTALS REQUIRED? (Y/N) **N**
003   **8,UNIT:COST**
ENTER HEADING: **>UNIT-CST**
ARE TOTALS REQUIRED? (Y/N) **N**
004   **9,QTY:ON:HAND * UNIT:COST**
ENTER HEADING: **>EXTENDED;COST**
ARE TOTALS REQUIRED? (Y/N) **Y**
005   **<cr>**

Line 004 is an expression, and the * implies multiply.

Totals in Vertical Formats

Can we take totals in our report if we have specified vertical formats? The answer is no, at least for those numeric fields which form a part of a vertical format. The reason, as we have seen before, is that such numeric fields have to be specified as character strings in order to format them vertically, and so dBASE does not ask you if you want totals on those character fields. However, you may have a mixture of columns in your report where column 1 may specify a vertical format and column 2 is a stand-alone, numeric field. Now, of course, there is nothing to prevent you from taking totals on the stand-alone numeric field. An example follows:

.REPORT FORM RPT17   **\<cr\>**

ENTER OPTIONS, M=LEFT MARGIN, L=LINES/PAGE, W=PAGE WIDTH **\<cr\>**
PAGE HEADING? (Y/N) **Y**
ENTER PAGE HEADING **REPORT 17 - VERTICAL FORMATS, WITH TOTALS**
DOUBLE SPACE REPORT? (Y/N) **N**
ARE TOTALS REQUIRED? (Y/N) **Y**
SUBTOTALS IN REPORT? (Y/N) **N**
COL   WIDTH, CONTENTS
001   **10,EMP:NUM+';'EMP:NAME+';'TOWN+';'STR(SALARY,8,2)+';;;'**
ENTER HEADING: **\<EMPLOYEE-NUMBERS;EMPLOYEE-NAMES;TOWN;SALARY**
002   **5,' '**
ENTER HEADING:
003   **8,SALARY**
ENTER HEADING: **\>SALARY**
ARE TOTALS REQUIRED? (Y/N) **Y**
004   **\<cr\>**


```
PAGE NO. 00001
07/01/84
                    REPORT  17 - VERTICAL FORMATS, WITH TOTALS


        EMPLOYEE-NUMBERS              SALARY
        EMPLOYEE-NAMES
        TOWN
        SALARY

        070707                       36300.00
        NINA BHARUCHA
        WEBSTER
        36300.00

        7545AD                       30349.00
        PETE JOHNSON
        brighton
        30349.00


        987178                       27500.00
        GLORIA PATEL
        FAIRPORT
        27500.00


        ------              ---------
        ------------
        ---------
        ---------
```
164
```

        ** TOTAL **
                            456074.00
```

Subtotals in Reports

We will now move on into the realm of providing subtotals within our report format.

To dBASE's question about whether we want subtotals, our response now will be yes, and immediately dBASE goes off into a tangent, asking more details about the subtotal requirements.

> **Note:** If you want to take subtotals on, say, the TOWN-field, it stands to reason that the file will have to be either physically sorted or logically indexed in the TOWN-field. Obviously, records with the same towns must appear together for correct subtotals. So we will first go ahead and create an appropriate index, and then go in for the subtotal request.

.INDEX ON TOWN TO TINDX

00015 RECORDS INDEXED

.REPORT FORM RPT18 FOR TOWN = 'W' .OR. TOWN = 'R'

ENTER OPTIONS, M=LEFT MARGIN, L=LINES/PAGE, W=PAGE WIDTH **<cr>**
PAGE HEADING? (Y/N) **Y**
ENTER PAGE HEADING: **REPORT 18;SUB-TOTALS**
DOUBLE SPACE REPORT? (Y/N) **N**
ARE TOTALS REQUIRED? (Y/N) **Y**
SUBTOTALS IN REPORT? (Y/N) **Y**
ENTER SUBTOTALS FIELD: **TOWN**   *
SUMMARY REPORT ONLY? (Y/N) **N**   **
EJECT PAGE AFTER SUBTOTALS? (Y/N) **N**   ***
ENTER SUBTOTAL HEADING:Q **SUB-TOTALS FOR TOWN OF**   ****
COL   WIDTH,CONTENTS
001   **12,TOWN**
ENTER HEADING: **<TOWN;----**
002   **10,EMP:NUM**
ENTER HEADING: **<EMPLOYEE;NUMBER**
003   **15,EMP:NAME**
ENTER HEADING: **<EMPLOYEE;NAME**
004   **8,SALARY**
ENTER HEADING: **>SALARY;------**
ARE TOTALS REQUIRED? (Y/N) **Y**
005   **<cr>**

*This is the field on which you want subtotal breaks to occur.

**If you said Y to this one, you will not see any detail lines in the body of the report. Only the subtotal lines and the final total line will print out.

***Usually you do not want to say Y to this one, since you will be wasting quite a bit of paper. A Y will cause a new page eject after each subtotal line of print.

****If you do not enter anything (simply hitting the <cr>), no literal will print out, but only the appropriate town name would print out. You should enter some kind of subheading, for the benefit of the user of the report.

```
PAGE NO.  00001
07/01/84

                                       REPORT   18

                                       SUB-TOTALS

TOWN            EMPLOYEE    EMPLOYEE              SALARY
----            NUMBER      NAME                 ------

* SUB-TOTALS FOR TOWN OF ROCHESTER
ROCHESTER       AC9090      TIM MONTAL           41900.00
ROCHESTER       091230      JAMES JAMESON        29800.00
ROCHESTER       09890A      JAN MOREY            18190.00
** SUBTOTAL **

                                                 89890.00


* SUB-TOTALS FOR TOWN OF WEBSTER
WEBSTER         070707      NINA BHARUCHA        36300.00
WEBSTER         00707A      PHIL MARTIN          31000.00
** SUBTOTAL **

                                                 67300.00


** TOTAL **

                                                157190.00
```

Grouping Records

We can make use of the subtotal facility of the REPORT command to produce reports in which records with similar data is grouped together. Say we have our PERSNL file indexed on TOWN + ORG. We now produce a report format that requests both, totals and subtotals, even if we want neither totals nor subtotals! However, the field on which to take subtotals is declared to the the TOWN-field.

.REPORT FORM RPT19   <cr>

ENTER OPTIONS, M=LEFT MARGIN, L=LINES/PAGE, W=PAGE WIDTH <cr>
PAGE HEADING? (Y/N) **Y**
ENTER PAGE HEADING: **REPORT 19**
DOUBLE SPACE REPORT? (Y/N) **N**
ARE TOTALS REQUIRED? (Y/N) **Y**
SUBTOTALS IN REPORT? (Y/N) **Y**
ENTER SUBTOTALS FIELD: **TOWN**
SUMMARY REPORT ONLY? (Y/N) **N**

166

```
EJECT PAGE AFTER SUBTOTALS? (Y/N) N
ENTER SUBTOTAL HEADING: RECORDS FOR THE TOWN OF
COL     WIDTH, CONTENTS
001     10,EMP:NUM
ENTER HEADING: <EMPLOYEE;NUMBER
002     20,EMP:NAME
ENTER HEADING: <EMPLOYEE;NAME
003     4,YR:OF:HIRE
ENTER HEADING: YRHR----
ARE TOTALS REQUIRED? (Y/N) N
004     6,EXEMPT
ENTER HEADING: EXEMPT------
005
```

```
PAGE NO.  00001
07/01/84
                                    REPORT 19


EMPLOYEE      EMPLOYEE                  YRHR EXEMPT
NUMBER        NAME                      ---- .------

* RECORDS FOR THE TOWN OF BRIGHTON
087FG0        PAUL BHARUCHA             1973 .T.
8745AD        JOHN PETERSON             1979 .T.


* RECORDS FOR THE TOWN OF FAIRPORT
987178        GLORIA PATEL              1982 .T.
0989SD        KIM BRANDT                1977 .F.

----------------------------------------------
---------------------------------------------- etc., etc.
```

Subtotals at More Than One Level of Control

We can use the same strategy outlined above to obtain subtotals at more than one level of depth. Once again, our file is indexed on TOWN + ORG, and we will produce a report format that requests totals and subtotals, and this time, our subtotals field will be declared to be the concatenation of TOWN+ORG!!

```
.REPORT FORM RPT20                                      <cr>

ENTER OPTIONS, M=LEFT MARGIN, L=LINES/PAGE, W=PAGE WIDTH <cr>
PAGE HEADING? (Y/N) Y
ENTER PAGE HEADING: REPORT 20
DOUBLE SPACE REPORT? (Y/N) N
```

```
ARE TOTALS REQUIRED? (Y/N) Y
SUBTOTALS IN REPORT? (Y/N) Y
ENTER SUBTOTALS FIELD: TOWN+ORG
SUMMARY REPORT ONLY? (Y/N) N
EJECT PAGE AFTER SUBTOTALS? (Y/N) N
ENTER SUBTOTAL HEADING: SUB-TOTAL FOR TOWN & ORG
COL     WIDTH,CONTENTS
001     10,EMP:NUM
ENTER HEADING: <EMPLOYEE;NUMBER
002     20,EMP:NAME
ENTER HEADING: <EMPLOYEE;NAME
003     8,SALARY
ENTER HEADING: >SALARY;------
ARE TOTALS REQUIRED? (Y/N) Y
004             <cr>


PAGE NO. 00001
07/01/84
                                    REPORT 20


EMPLOYEE      EMPLOYEE                 SALARY
NUMBER        NAME                     ------

* SUB-TOTAL FOR TOWN & ORG BRIGHTON     BSG
087FG0      PAUL BHARUCHA       32010.00
** SUBTOTAL **
                                32010.00


* SUB-TOTAL FOR TOWN & ORG BRIGHTON     RBG
8745AD      JOHN PETERSON       31480.00
** SUBTOTAL **
                                31480.00

------------------------------------------------
------------------------------------------------    etc., etc.
```

THE WHILE PARAMETER FOR REPORT FORMATS

If we are using an indexed file to pull off a report, the records are obtained in the order of the index. Now, if for some reason the same report format is to be used, but only for one category of records (say for records for the TOWN of ROCHESTER), then one method of producing such a report would be the following:

```
.USE PERSNL INDEX TINDX     (TOWN index is active)
.REPORT FORM XXXXX FOR TOWN ='ROCHESTER'
```

However, this will force the system to go through an appreciable amount of overhead, since every record in the Master file will have to be accessed via the index, and the record will then have to be checked for TOWN = 'ROCHESTER', and either accepted or rejected, and the cycle then repeated for the next record, etc. This will have to be done for the entire file!

A far better approach is to make use of the fact that in the indexed file, all ROCHESTER records appear together, and we need to have dBASE pull off the records only so long as the key of the index is equal to the value ROCHESTER.

.FIND ROCH   <cr>

This command will place the record pointer on the very first record in the indexed-file which has a TOWN = 'ROCHESTER'. Now enter the following statement:

.REPORT FORM XXXX WHILE TOWN = 'ROCHESTER'   <cr>

This will pull off only those indexed records with key-value = ROCHESTER, and as soon as another key is sensed, the report process will cease. This method will save valuable time in the case of an appreciably large data-base, since it will not necessarily start at the top of the indexed file and does not have to go all the way through to the end of the indexed file.

Incidentally, a side benefit of this method must have come to mind. If your file had no records with TOWN = 'ROCHESTER', the FIND command itself would have returned a NO FIND message, saving you much valuable time in trying to produce a report on nonexistent records!

MAKING CHANGES TO EXISTING REPORT FORMAT FILES

We have covered quite a range of options you can use with the built-in REPORT command in dBASE, and now the one area of interest for the user lies in how you would make modifications to an existing report format file. After all, if you needed to show one or more extra fields in the body of the report, that should not necessitate your having to rewrite the report format all over again.

As you know by now, simply entering .REPORT FORM RPT1, hoping to bring up the questions and answers for RPT1 so you could make changes to the existing report format does not work, since if the report format file exists, dBASE goes ahead and pulls off the report. To inform dBASE of your desire to modify existing report format files, you have to do the following:

.MODIFY COMMAND XXXX.FRM   <cr>

XXXX is the name of the report.

  Note: If at this time you get the message "FILE IS CURRENTLY OPEN," then the report format file needs to be closed before you can alter it. Enter .USE <cr> to close the data-base file in use, and the associated report format file also gets closed. Now you can .MODI COMM XXXX.FRM as noted. Note that if you do have to take this route (depending on the version of dBASE being used), then after modifying the file, before you can pull off the report again, you will have to bring the appropriate data-base file in USE.

Now dBASE erases the screen clean, and shows you the contents of the appropriate report-format file on the screen, in full screen edit mode. And the first thing you realize is that the report format file consists only of your answers that you had provided to dBASE's questions at the time of the format file creation. The questions themselves do not appear on the screen. So if you did want to make changes to the report format, unless you were familiar with the order in which the questions had been asked, it is virtually impossible to make changes to the format file.

For example, suppose we attempt to modify the report format file for one of our previous reports, Report 19.

.MODI COMM RPT19.FRM   <cr>

Let me comment each line that would appear on the screen, so I can provide an explanation of why that line is present. Obviously, these comments are only for our understanding, here.

	(Blank, since we took defaults for left-margin lines-per-page, etc.)
Y	(We wanted a page header)
REPORT 19; SUB-TOTALS	(This is our literal for page header)
N	(We did not want the report double spaced)
Y	(We wanted totals.)
Y	(We wanted subtotals)
TOWN	(The subtotals field)
N	(We did not want a summary report only)
N	(We did not want to eject page on every subtotal break)
SUB-TOTALS FOR TOWN OF	(Our subtotal header)
12,TOWN	(Across a width of 12 columns, we wanted the TOWN data)
<TOWN;----	(Column header)
10,EMP:NUM	(Across a width of 10 columns, we wanted the EMP:NUM data)
<EMPLOYEE;NUMBER	(Column header)
15,EMP:NAME	(Across a width of 15 columns, we wanted the EMP:NAME data)

170

```
<EMPLOYEE;NAME            (Column header)
8,SALARY                  (Across a width of 8
                          columns, we wanted the
                          SALARY data)
>SALARY;------            (Column header)
Y                         (Yes, we wanted totals
                          on SALARY)
                          (Blank, for wrap-up)
```

As you can see, only your responses get recorded as the words and phrases in the format file, and unless you knew exactly what it was that you answered Y (yes) or N (no) to, you will be unable to make any kind of educated change in the report format.

In the previous report format file, if you wanted to introduce a new field, ORG, between the EMP:NAME and SALARY fields, then you would bring the cursor to the line where you request the SALARY data, and enter a Ctrl-N twice, to open up 2 blank lines. In the first blank line you would enter: 3,ORG to specify that, across a width of 3 columns, you want the ORG data. In the second blank line, you would enter something like: ORG to specify the column header. You would have followed this sequence since this is exactly the pieces of information that dBASE would have asked of you, had you entered this field during the original build-up of this report format file.

If you wanted to introduce a blank field between the EMP:NAME and SALARY fields (in order to spread them out) then you would bring the cursor to the line where you request the SALARY data, and enter a Ctrl-N twice to open up 2 blank lines. In the first blank line you would enter something to the effect of 10,' ' to specify that across a width of 10 columns, you want spaces. In the second blank line, you would enter nothing, to specify a blank column-header line. You would have followed this sequence since this is exactly the pieces of information that dBASE would have asked of you, had you entered this field during the original build-up of this report format field.

If you wanted to introduce a new field, say, YR:OF:HIRE, between the EMP:NAME and SALARY fields, then you would bring the cursor to the line where you request the SALARY data, and enter a Ctrl-N three times to open up 3 blank lines. In the first blank line, you would enter 4,YR:OF:HIRE to specify that, across a width of 4 columns, you want the YR:OF:HIRE data. In the second blank line, you would enter something like: YRHR to specify the column header. In the third blank line you would enter the letter N to specify that you did not want any totals on this numeric field. You would have followed this sequence since this is exactly the pieces of information that dBASE would have asked of you, had you entered this field during the original build-up of this report format file.

Note that if you specify up-front that there are no totals required, dBASE will not ask you if subtotals are required, and in this case if you mention a numeric field as one of the columns of data in the report, dBASE does not ask you if totals are required on that numeric field. You realize, of course, that if you wanted to say no to totals, hence no to subtotals, all the questions dBASE raises regarding the subtotals should now also get negated! So you can visualize the number of lines of the above report format that will have to be changed if you wanted to modify the format of Report 19 to now produce the report without any totals whatsoever.

Once again it is worth mentioning that if you are unsure of the way dBASE would have asked you questions on the report format, it is probably advisable to generate a new one, instead of attempting to modify an existing one. If you are fairly confident that you have understood the sequence in which the questions could come up, go ahead and try out some changes in any report format file.

Having made your changes, enter a Ctrl+W to save your changes, and then run the report format again. A Ctrl+Q would negate your changes to the report format file.

I mentioned before that this report format file is a text file. Please understand clearly that you could make the same modifications noted earlier to this report format file, using a standard word-processing program! If you are more conversant with the editing features of a word processor and would rather use that than the edit features available under the Modify mode, in dBASE, feel free to QUIT out of dBASE, enter the word processing program, edit the file called XXXX.FRM, save it, then enter dBASE again to execute the report. However, please note that under the word-processing program, you will still see the same entries you would have seen under dBASE. That is, only your responses to the questions, and not the questions themselves, are available under the word-processor's edit. Also, if you are making changes this way, use the *edit a program* option in the word-processor software, not the *create a document* option, since this latter option produces embedded control characters in the records/lines of the program.

SUMMARY

In this section we learned to produce reports in varied formats, and we are now able to obtain any report spread we want, doll up column headings and main headings substantially, provide for record counts, totals and subtotals, and even produce vertical formats for our reports.

While the built-in reporting feature of dBASE provides great flexibility in creating your own report formats, it is not, as you have obviously noticed, without its own set of restrictions. For instance, you have to live with the fact that the date and page number will always be provided in the top left of the page, not the top right. In those situations where you must have a radically different format of a report, and the built-in reporting facility cannot be of much help, you still have the freedom of writing your own report programs. That is, you can write a computer program in dBASE, and this program will generete any report format you may have in mind. The generation of our own computer programs in dBASE is our next logical step, in this book.

Part 3
Advanced Features

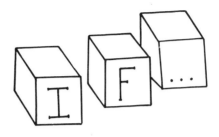

8. Programming in dBASE-II

So far we have studied, in depth, several dBASE commands which can be executed as stand-alone instructions, and which really tend to make an *instant programmer* out of the user. Command such as COPY and APPEND, and functions such as STR and $ (substring) are so powerful that even an experienced programmer would have to put in considerable effort to be able to do what you, the user, can do through the use of just these instructions and functions alone.

However, the scope of dBASE-II lies far beyond the provision of stand-alone instructions for execution. dBASE-II provides you the capability of your being able to put together the very same instructions we have studied all along into modules of instructions. These *modules* can then be initiated for execution, providing you with the ability of executing several instructions concurrently, without any further interaction on your part. This is what forms the basis of *programming*, in any computer language.

This portion of the book is designed to show you how you can write your own computer programs in dBASE, and really bolster up the capability and efficiency of your computerized applications. Out of necessity, of course, we will have to study some more commands and concepts in addition to the ones we have seen so far to be truly effective in writing computer programs in dBASE.

I want to emphasize at this point that programming is an art, not a science. Any number of programmers may come up with any number of variations in the programming solution to a problem, all of them converging on the identical end result. But there are such things as good programs and bad programs, depending on how they are written and documented and on how well they lend themselves to comprehension and modification by other programmers.

I will start off with the simplest of computer programs and increase the complexity gradually until you find yourself generating your own screen formats in support of sophisticated, highly versatile, menu-driven systems. Upon completion of this section you may realistically expect to be able to write and understand complex dBASE-II programs. At this point in time, you should be fairly conversant with the basics of dBASE.

OVERVIEW OF dBASE PROGRAMMING

A computer program is nothing more than a set of *instructions* to a computer that cause it to perform a series of functions. The instructions are, for the most part, sequential in nature. If you can group together a string of computer instructions (in any language), give the group a name, and store the group on a disk, you have created a computer program. A computer program is also referred to as a module.

In dBASE-II, when you are at the dot prompt phase, you are being prompted with a "What Next" type of situation. That is, dBASE expects you to enter a command. If you were to try and collect together a group of dBASE instructions at this stage, as soon as you entered the first instruction, dBASE would take off and execute it. Which means, of course, that at the dot prompt phase, you cannot hope to build your computer program.

To start the process of creating a program, you have to inform dBASE of your intention to build a set of instructions with the following command:

.MODIFY COMMAND   Pgml

> **Note:** Pgml is merely the name of the program. You may come up with any name you want.

This informs dBASE of your intention to create a *command file* (program) called Pgml.CMD.

> **Note:** For 16-bit processors, the name will turn out to be PGM1.PRG. The screen is now erased, there is no dot prompt, and whatever you key in will now remain on the screen under your control until you either SAVE your creation (Ctrl-W), or decide you don't want it, after all (Ctrl-Q).

To invoke the execution of an existing program, you simply request dBASE to do it.

.DO PGM1   <cr>

We will start off with examples of programs, and will build upon the complexity of these programs, as we proceed.

A Sequential Command File

As the name suggests, our first program will be nothing more than a pure sequential series of instructions to the machine. That is, there will be no logic involved. Suppose we enter the following command:

.MODI COMM   PGM1   <cr>

Now when the screen goes blank, let us key in the following string of instructions. Please note that only the instructions are to be keyed in, not the title, nor the comments to the right-hand side. This will be true of any program provided in this book.

ERASE	Clean up the screen.
USE PERSNL	Open the PERSNL file.
INDEX ON TOWN TO TINDX	Create the index.
LIST	Provide an indexed list.
WAIT	Wait for operator response.
ERASE	Clean up the screen.
INDEX ON ORG TO OINDX	Create the index.
LIST	Provide an index list.
WAIT	Wait for operator response.

Having entered the command statements, you will have to enter a Ctrl-W, to save your program. At this stage, dBASE slips back to the dot prompt.

Now that your program is saved, execute it with the DO command.

```
.DO  PGM1                    <cr>
```

As you may appreciate, when the program executes, it will proceed to execute the instructions exactly as they had been specified in the program, and so we can expect the following string of events to take place on program execution: the screen goes blank; the PERSNL file is USEd; dBASE now gives you an INDEX on the TOWN-field; dBASE then gives you a LISTing of the indexed file; and then dBASE WAITs, for you!

The WAIT command is important, and is widely used in programming with dBASE. The effect of this command is that a literal WAITING appears on the screen, providing you the opportunity to study the LISTing that just preceded the WAIT. Please note that if at this stage you don't do anything, dBASE will wait for you indefinitely! In reality, dBASE is waiting for you to enter *any key* (you would tend to <cr> and it will then take off to execute the next group of instructions after the WAIT.

In this example, if you do a <cr> in response to the WAITING statement, to go ahead, dBASE will now proceed to: clean up the screen again; INDEX the same file, this time on the ORG field; provide an indexed LISTing by ORGanization; and again WAIT for your response. At this stage, if you <cr>, dBASE simply slips back to the dot prompt, asking you "What Next?", because there are no more instructions in the program.

And that, basically, is the overview of creating and running any dBASE program. Obviously, our example was one of a very trivial program, which had no logic embedded in it. We will increase the complexity of our programs gradually.

Using the mechanics outlined above, let us suppose we have keyed in the following sequential program:

```
USE PERSNL
SORT ON TOWN TO TSORT
SORT ON ORG TO OSORT
SORT ON EMP:NUM TO ESORT
```

```
*
USE TSORT
REPORT FORM RPT1 TO PRINT
*
USE OSORT
REPORT FORM RPT2 TO PRINT
*
USE ESORT
REPORT FORM RPT3 TO PRINT
*
USE                                    will close the file in use.

DELETE FILE TSORT
DELETE FILE OSORT
DELETE FILE ESORT
```

When this program is made to execute, we can see from the commands provided that the following events will take place: the PERSNL file will be USEd; then 3 sorted files will be created out of that file, one each for a TOWN-sort, ORG-sort and EMP:NUM-sort. Now the program will proceed to use the TOWN-sort file, and produce a report out of that file; it will then do the same with the other two sorted files. At the end of producing the reports, the program will proceed to close the file last in use, and then delete the sorted files to release space. After which, of course, it will drop back to the dot prompt.

> **Note:** This book was prepared based on the CP/M operating system, and as such all the program files will have a second qualifier of .CMD. If you are working with MSDOS or PCDOS (16-bit versions), please make mental substitutions of .PRG, throughout.

General Comments on dBASE Programs

1. After you have typed in your program instructions, you can either Ctrl-W to save your program, or Ctrl-Q to change your mind on saving the creation. If you Ctrl-Q, you will have a second chance to clarify your intention.

2. If you have to make changes to an existing program, use the same set up:

```
.MODI COMM     Pgml
```

If Pgml.CMD exists, the first screen will show the contents of the program. To scroll back and forth into the body of an existing program, use Ctrl-C or the return-key (for forward) or Ctrl-R or the up-arrow key (for backward). As before. Ctrl-W will save all your changes, and Ctrl-Q will negate the changes.

3. Note that the command file (program file) is a text file, and if you feel more comfortable using the text-editor of a word-processor program to build and change your program files, feel free to do so. Of course, to subsequently execute these program files, you will have to go back into dBASE.

4. The converse is also true. Having created your program file in dBASE, you may print out the entire program itself, using any word-processor program.

5. If you want a print-out of a short program (which can all fit on one screen), use Ctrl+HELP or the appropriate conbination for your computer system to obtain a screen image.

6. To break up the lines of program code, for visual benefit, you may use the * as the first character on a line of code. That indicates a comment statement, and may either contain nothing else on the line, or could easily be used for explanations of what the next few or the preceding few lines of code were expected to do in the program. A comment statement is simply ignored and bypassed, during execution, but such statements are crucial for an explanation of the logic of the program and are to be encouraged.

7. There are times when you want to create a program (PGM2) which is similar to another existing program (PGM1). Obviously, it would make life so much easier for you if you could make a copy of the existing program, in the new program-name, rather than having to key-in the new program from scratch.

In order to make a copy of a program file, you could do as follows:

a. Create a dummy file, containing only one field, of length 80 characters: Fl,C,80
b. .USE DUMMY
   .APPEND FROM PGM1.CMD   SDF

> **Note:** The program file is a text file. At the end of the previous APPEND, the DUMMY data-base contains the program records out of PGM1.CMD. Within the structure of the Dummy file, of course, these records are viewed as a dBASE data-base.

c. .COPY TO PGM2.CMD   SDF

The COPY command will create another file called PGM2.CMD, as a text file.
d. The file in use is still DUMMY, and so you should:

.DELETE ALL   <cr>
.PACK   <cr>

In this way a clean DUMMY file is obtained for the next time around when you may want to make a copy of another program. The above process—appending from a program text, then copying into another text file—provides the method of quickly creating new programs, by using copies of existing programs. Now, of course, the required changes for PGM2 should be made in the usual way.

For the reason just outlined, you may want to keep the structure of an empty data-base containing only one field of record-length 80 characters handy.

A Decision Command File

Let me introduce an elementary piece of LOGIC into our computer program so that, instead of just following commands sequentially, the program can make minor/major decisions during execution. I shall proceed with the minor type, first. The purpose of this program is to:

1. Ask the operator for a town name, and wait for a response.
2. Accept the response entered by the operator.
3. Read the first record out of our PERSNL file.
4. Check to see if the town name (from that record) matches the response of the operator.
5. Indicate the outcome of the comparison with either a "Good Match" or "Too Bad, Try Again" type of message on the screen.

In order to be able to create this program, we shall have to study a new command called ACCEPT.

ACCEPT "Please enter a town name" TO MTOWN

On execution, this instruction will cause the literal (following the ACCEPT command) to appear on the screen, and wait for the operator's response. Now when the operator keys-in a response and uses the return key, the response entered will be accepted and placed into a character memory variable called MTOWN. (The literal can be defined either with single quotes or with double quotes.) If no response is made, but the operator enters <cr>, the character blank is generated into the memory variable.

> **Note:** A *memory variable* is a piece of memory set aside, containing some data. You may name it whatever you like. The size of the memory variable created will vary, depending on the contents of the variable. The maximum length of a memory variable name is 10 characters. If you define a name of more than 10 characters, only the first 10 are accepted.
> **Note:** You must differentiate between the name of the memory variable and the contents of that memory variable.
> **Note:** Since the ACCEPT verb is used, the memory variable created is automatically of the character type. That is, if *quotes* are used in entering the response, the quotes will be accepted as part of the data! If digits are entered, these numbers will be stored as character data!

Now let's write the program described above.

ERASE   Clean up the screen.
ACCEPT "Please enter a town name" TO MTOWN

> **Note:** This will cause the literal to appear on the screen, the system will automatically wait for the operator's response, and whatever response is entered through the <cr>, that response will be accepted and stored in the character memory variable called MTOWN.

USE PERSNL   Open the file to be used, and
                                     control the first record.
IF !(TOWN) = !(MTOWN)   If the content of the TOWN-

180

@ 15,10 say "Good"

field from the record in use is equal to the content of the memory variable MTOWN, then put out this comment starting at line 16 column 11 on the screen.

ELSE
@ 15, 10 say "Too Bad, Try Again"

Note: The screen configuration is 24 lines by 80 columns. However, the lines are numbered from 0 through 23, and the columns are numbered from 0 through 79.

The @15,10 command identifies the screen coordinates as the 16th line and the 11th column on the screen. This is the position where a literal has to start, or the contents of memory variable have to be displayed. Avoid the use of 0,0 since this line and column are required by dBASE for its internal use.

The use of the uppercase function suggests that you may not be too sure of how the data was created in the Master file (upper/lowercase, etc.), and you cannot, of course, rely on the operator's response being all in uppercase either. For this reason I use the uppercase function in all areas where variable operator inputs are accepted.

Replace the previous logic statement with the one that follows. Try it out to see the variation in the screen replies.

```
---------
---------
---------
If !(TOWN) = !(MTOWN)
  @ 10,15 say "GOOD MATCH"
ELSE
  @ 10,15 SAY "THE TOWN WAS NOT"
  @ 10, 35 SAY MTOWN            where the operator's response
                                was saved
  @ 12,15 SAY "IT WAS"
  @ 12,35 SAY TOWN              from the record in use
```

For now, we will use the standard form of the @--SAY command. The various other possibilities will be introduced later.

A Repetition Command File

We will now enhance the complexity of the logic of this program. We want to increase the scope of this program to:

1. Put out the message, as usual.
2. Accept the response.
3. Compare the response with the field from the first record.

4. Repeat the comparison for each record of the file, and provide "Good" or "Bad" messages for each comparison.

The following sequence is one way of writing the program:

```
ERASE

ACCEPT   "Please enter a town name"  TO   MTOWN
```

> **Note:** This will cause the literal to appear on the screen, the system will automatically wait for the operator's response, and whatever is the response entered through the <cr>, that response will be accepted and stored in the character memory variable called MTOWN.

ERASE	
USE PERSNL	Open the file to be used, and control the first record.
DO WHILE .NOT. EOF	Start a logical loop: "For as long as it is not the end-of-file, do the following."
IF !(TOWN) = !(MTOWN)	If the content of the Town-field from tthe record in use is equal to the content of the memory variable MTOWN, then put out this comment starting at line 16 column 11.
`@ 15,10 say "Good"`	
ELSE	
`@ 15,10 say "Too Bad, Try Again"`	
ENDIF	Regardless of the outcome of the IF statement, go to the next instruction so operator can see the outcome of the comparison.
WAIT	
`@ 15,10`	Specifying nothing will erase the previous literal, at that position.
SKIP	Pass control to the next record.
ENDDO	End of DO; backup to IF.

ERASE   Program control will reach here, at end-of-file.

```
@ 15,10 SAY "How's that, folks ?"
```

> **Note:** Double quotes are required since the literal itself has single quotes embedded in it.

Observations

1. Having accepted all the required operator inputs, it would be good practice to ERASE the screen, before proceeding to pull off any type of display or report.

2. You have to initiate the start of a logical loop through the command: DO WHILE .NOT. EOF (There are other ways, too, to start loops, and we shall see these later.) Each DO WHILE is accompanied by an ENDDO statement. The DO WHILE statement says that as long as the condition in the DO WHILE is satisfied, all the statements following the DO WHILE, through the statement just before the ENDDO, should be continuously executed. This is one way of pumping several records (one record at a time) through the same logic of several instructions.

3. The statement after the DO WHILE is the IF statement. Since the previous USE command has passed control to record #1 of the PERSNL file, the first time the IF statement is executed, it will check the operator's response against the TOWN-field from record #1, and come out with a good or bad message.

4. The ENDIF statement is very important. It breaks the logic of the IF statement. The ENDIF statement says something to the effect of, "this is it!". Regardless of the outcome of the IF statement, control should pass to the instruction after the ENDIF. If you forget to place ENDIF statements or if you misplace them in the logic of your program, the output results will not be worth a dime.

5. After the comparison resulting in either good or bad, (regardless of the outcome), we want the program to pause and wait for us to see the outcome of the comparison with record #1. Having checked out the result, we now <cr> to go ahead with the next instruction in the program. (Basically, we want to repeat the comparison for the second record.) However, before we pass control to the next record, we want to erase the good or bad literal from the screen, else in the case of unequally long literals, a GOOD followed by a BAD will result in the BADD literal on the screen since they are sent to the same location on the screen.

6. Having seen the outcome of the comparison for the first record, and having then cleaned up the literal, we now pass control to the next record through the SKIP command.

7. We want to send this next record through the same logic of the instructions: Go through the comparison, come up with good or bad, let the operator check the result, erase the literal, pass control to the next record, and so on. That is where the ENDDO statement plays a role. We said before that a DO WHILE and an ENDDO are always in pairs, and the program control will continuously execute all instructions that lie between these two instructions for as long as the condition in the DO WHILE is satisfied. If you forget to place an ENDDO statement to complement the DO WHILE, there is nothing to inform program control as to when you want to loop back, and in that case only record #1

would get processed through your entire program.

8. After the last data record from the PERSNL file has been processed, that is, at end-of-file, the condition specified in the DO WHILE statement is no longer true, and hence control breaks off out of the loop and passes to the instruction after the ENDDO statement in the program. At that point, you can provide any clean-up instructions you may want.

9. It is crucial to understand that the USE statement should be outside of the DO WHILE loop. If your USE statement is within the loop itself, then although the SKIP statement passes control to record #2, as soon as the ENDDO statement sends control back to repeat the loop, the USE statement would place the record pointer back to record #1. Which means that record number 1 will always be processed, and you will never encounter the end-of-file, and since the looping effect is dependent on the end-of-file to stop looping, you will have landed yourself into an infinite loop, with record #1 being sent through the mill each time.

10. To cancel (interrupt) the execution of any program, use the ESC key.

11. The statements within the DO WHILE—ENDDO combination have been indented only for ease of readability. With indentation, one can identify the start and end of the looping instructions very quickly. The instructions within the IF—ENDIF combination have also been indented for ease of comprehension of logic, and, as we shall see later, for helping to ensure that each IF is matched up with an ENDIF statement. Without the indentation, execution will proceed correctly, but the programmer is more likely to mismatch the IFs and the ENDIFs, or the DO WHILEs and the ENDDOs.

A PRACTICAL PROGRAM

From here on, our programs will begin to have a more practical appearance. Also, subsequent programs will not be followed by detailed explanation for each step unless we encounter a command that is new, or plays a new role in that program.

Let's write a program to do the following:

1. Ask the operator for an ORG name.
2. Accept the response.
3. Read the file called PERSNL.
4. For those records that match the operator's response, display EMP:NUM, EMP:NAME, SALARY.

We will be using the following shell, in the program:

```
If <some condition is satisified>
   DISP  EMP:NUM  EMP:NAME  SALARY
ENDIF
```

The program could be written as follows:

```
ERASE
ACCEPT  "Please enter an ORGANIZATION name" TO MORG
```

```
ERASE
USE PERSNL
DO WHILE .NOT. EOF
    IF !(ORG)=!(MORG)
        DISP EMP:NUM   EMP:NAME   SALARY
    ENDIF
    SKIP
ENDDO
WAIT
ERASE
@ 15,10 SAY "HOW'S THAT, FOLKS !"
```

> **Note:** We needed to have a WAIT command after the end-of-file was encountered, so as to be able to view the records that were selected for display by the program. Without this WAIT command, the screen would have been ERASEd as soon as the end-of-file was encountered without providing the operator a chance to study the output.

When you execute this program, you will notice that dBASE provides record numbers, and also clutters up the output with record numbers of those records that did not match (dBASE's way of being helpful). To get dBASE to stop being so helpful in putting out the additional comments (in effect, to stop talking to you) you have to use the instruction: SET TALK OFF. This is one of the many housekeeping instructions available.

```
ERASE
SET TALK OFF
ACCEPT   "Please enter an ORGANIZATION name" to MORG
ERASE
*
*
USE PERSNL
DO WHILE .NOT. EOF
    IF !(ORG)=!(MORG)
        DISP EMP:NUM   EMP:NAME   SALARY
    ENDIF
    SKIP
ENDDO
WAIT
ERASE
@ 15,10 SAY "HOW'S THAT, FOLKS !"
```

To send the output of this program to the printer, try SET PRINT ON in the housekeeping section. This is equivalent to a Ctrl-P in dBASE. Remember to have another SET PRINT OFF as the last instruction in your program, else the printer will remain with the Ctrl-P feature active.

Note: SET PRINT ON has no effect on @----SAY commands. It only affects DISPLAY commands, in that the output of the DISPLAYS would then go to the printer.

Hopefully, you realize that this kind of program is quite useful, in that it is totally generic. Nothing is hard-coded, and depending on the responses provided by the operator, different outputs can be obtained.

Note: on the Set Command: There are several switches that can be set using the SET command, and when dBASE is first invoked, it is loaded with a default of either ON or OFF, for any particular switch. The status of these switches can be obtained through the DISP STATUS command. This command will provide, first, the name of the data-base currently in USE and the name(s) of the index-file(s) currently active against the data-base in USE, and the system will WAIT for your response, after which it will show you the current status (ON or OFF) of all the switches. The full list of these switches may be obtained from the dBASE manual. We will cover some of them in the course of this material.

Extending the Logic with More Variables

You can extend the logic of this program to include more variables. The program can be written to request the operator to respond with a town name and an organization name. Now only those records meeting both criteria can be selected for display.

```
SET TALK OFF
ERASE
*
ACCEPT "Please enter a town-name"     TO     MTOWN
ERASE
*
ACCEPT "Now please enter an organization-name"   TO    MORG
ERASE
*
USE PERSNL
DO WHILE .NOT. EOF
   IF  !(TOWN)  =  !(MTOWN)  .AND.  !(ORG) = !(MORG)
       DISP EMP:NUM, EMP:NAME, SALARY
   ENDIF

   SKIP

ENDDO
WAIT
ERASE
@ 10,15 SAY "HOW'S THAT, FOLKS ?"
```

186

This type of program is known as an interactive program. That is, a program which interacts with the operator in its execution. Such programs request low-volume operator inputs at various times during execution, and the logic of such programs is designed to produce specific outputs during execution depending on the response from the operator.

From another perspective, the word *interactive* merely means "in dialogue mode"; that is, a dialogue is maintained between the program and the user, with the program intermittently asking for operator inputs and the operator providing parameters and/or yes/no type responses, to which the program reacts as per the logic of its instructions.

Accepting Numeric Input

Write a program based on the following criteria:

1. Use the file called PERSNL.
2. Accept two responses from the operator: Town, and Year/Hire Caution: YR:OF:HIRE is defined as a numeric field.
3. Read through PERSNL and from those records that match on town but whose year:of:hire is less than the operator's response, display EMP:NAME, ORG and YR:OF:HIRE
4. If you like, try the SET PRINT ON/OFF feature.

> **Note:** Instead of ACCEPT, where the value accepted is always of the character type, you may try the command INPUT. For example: INPUT "Please enter any character/s you wish" to MCHAR

During the execution of this command, the memory variable created could be of either character or numeric type. The type of memory variable created depends on the response entered by the operator. For example, if the operator enters 1234 or 12.34 the memory variable is automatically of the numeric type and will contain the value keyed-in by the operator. If the operator enters a value with leading spaces, the spaces are ignored, and the numeric value will be retained. If the operator enters something like 2 5 then the value 2 will be retained, and everything after the first space will be ignored. If the operator enters 2AM then only 2 will be retained as the input. If the data is entered as 2A3B then, again, only 2 is retained as the input. The entry AB23C will result in a syntax error! That is, the INPUT statement anticipates numeric data!

If the operator enters "ABCD" or "1234" or '12.34' the memory variable is automatically of the character type and will contain exactly what the operator has keyed in. Obviously, the quote (single or double) makes or breaks the type called character.

If the operator enters ABCD or AB23C etc, dBASE will flag this entry as an error, and will request the operator to re-enter the data.

The program that we specified earlier could be coded as follows:

```
SET TALK OFF
ERASE
*
ACCEPT "Please enter a town-name"        TO     MTOWN
ERASE
*
INPUT "Now please enter the year-of-hire"   TO    MYR
ERASE
*
USE PERSNL
DO WHILE .NOT. EOF
   IF   !(TOWN)  =  !(MTOWN)  .AND.  YR:OF:HIRE < MYR
      DISP EMP:NAME    ORG    YR:OF:HIRE
   ENDIF
   SKIP
ENDDO
WAIT
ERASE
@ 10,15 SAY "HOW'S THAT, FOLKS ?"
```

Providing a Record Count

The above program can be extended to also provide a count of the number of records that actually meet the selection criteria. Look at the following instruction.

```
STORE 1 + Counter TO Counter
```

This is dBASE's way of saying "Add 1 to Counter."
Note: You will first have to define the memory variable, before you can add values into it. In the housekeeping section, provide another instruction: STORE 0 TO COUNTER. This instruction will define and initialize a numeric memory variable called counter.

```
[    SET TALK OFF
     STORE 0 TO COUNTER
     ------
     ------
     ------
     IF <the required condition is satisfied>
        DISP ..............
        STORE  COUNTER+1  TO  COUNTER
        ------
        ------      ]
     ENDIF
```

At the end of this program, provide instructions to display the contents of the memory variable, as follows:

```
SET TALK OFF
STORE Ø TO COUNTER

ERASE
*
ACCEPT "Please enter a town-name"   TO      MTOWN
ERASE
*
INPUT "Now please enter the year-of-hire"   TO    MYR
ERASE
*
USE PERSNL

DO WHILE .NOT. EOF

    IF  !(TOWN)  =  !(MTOWN)   .AND.  YR:OF:HIRE < MYR

        DISP EMP:NAME    ORG    YR:OF:HIRE
        STORE COUNTER+1  TO  COUNTER

    ENDIF

    SKIP
ENDDO
WAIT
ERASE
@ 10,15 SAY "NUMBER OF MATCHING RECORDS"
@ 10,45 SAY COUNTER
```

Providing Averages

The previous program can be extended to provide averages. For example:

```
IF  <the required condition is satisfied>

    STORE  1 + RECCNT    TO    RECCNT

    STORE  SALARY + SAL:COUNT    TO   SAL:COUNT

    . . . . . . . . . . . . . . .
    . . . . . . . . . . . . . .
ENDIF
```

At the end, to obtain the average, insert this statement:

STORE   SAL:COUNT/RECCNT   TO   AVERAGE

(then DISPLAY the mem-var. called AVERAGE)

Will this work? The answer is yes, since SAL:COUNT is defined with 2 decimal places. As a result, the average will also be provided to 2 decimal places. However, if you were working with the following two fields: MALE:CNT which contains a total of male children (and which, therefore, is a whole number, without decimals) and RECCNT as defined above, then MALE:CNT/RECCNT would produce only the whole-number as the result, with the decimal places being truncated.

Under the above situation, to obtain the answer to two decimal places, you would have to specify the following:

.STORE (MALE:CNT/ RECCNT + 0.00 TO AVERAGE

While the answer is not affected, this trick ensures that the results are obtained to 2 decimal places.

> **Note:** For any expression, the result will be provided to the number of decimal places as specified in that operand which has the most decimal places defined in its structure.

The previous program could be written as follows:

```
SET TALK OFF                    Don't talk to me.
STORE Ø TO RECCNT               Defines a memory variable,
                                RECCNT, and initializes it to
                                zero.
STORE Ø TO SAL:COUNT            Defines a memory variable,
                                SAL:COUNT and initializes it
                                to zero.
STORE Ø TO AVERAGE              Defines a memory variable,
                                AVERAGE and initializes it to
                                zero.
ERASE
*
ACCEPT "Please enter a town-name"    TO    MTOWN
ERASE
*
INPUT "Now please enter the year-of-hire"    TO    MYR
ERASE
*
USE PERSNL
DO WHILE .NOT. EOF
    IF  !(TOWN)  =  !(MTOWN)  .AND.  YR:OF:HIRE < MYR
        DISP EMP:NAME    YR:OF:HIRE    SALARY
```

190

```
              STORE RECCNT+1  TO  RECCNT
              STORE SAL:COUNT+SALARY TO SAL:COUNT
        ENDIF
        SKIP
     ENDDO
     WAIT
     ERASE
     STORE  SAL:COUNT / RECCNT  TO AVERAGE

     @ 10,15 SAY "NUMBER OF MATCHING RECORDS"
     @ 10,45 SAY RECCNT
     @ 12,15 SAY "TOTAL OF SALARY"
     @ 12,45 SAY SAL:COUNT
     @ 14,15 SAY "AVERAGE SALARY"
     @ 14,45 SAY AVERAGE
```

Note: Exact spacing and formats will be covered later, as we proceed along these lines.

CALLED PROGRAMS

Just as you invoke the execution of a program by asking dBASE to: DO Pgm you can invoke the execution of another program from within the first one in the same way.

```
Program-A.                              | Program-B. ("Accepts.CMD")
---------                               | ---------
SET TALK OFF                            |
ERASE                                   |
DO Accepts ------>-----><-----><-->     | ACCEPT "Please enter a
                                        | town  name"
                                        | TO MTOWN
                                        |
ERASE          <-----<-----<-----<-|  |
USE PERSNL                          |  |
DO WHILE .NOT. EOF                  |  | ERASE
   IF !(TOWN) = !(MTOWN);           |  | ACCEPT "Now please
      .AND.  !(ORG) = !(MORG)       |  |           enter an org.
      DISP                          |  |           name" TO MORG
   ENDIF                            |<--RETURN
   SKIP                             |
ENDDO                               |
                                    |
```

Program-A is our *calling* program, that is, at some logical point in its execution, it transfers control to the program called ACCEPTS (.CMD). This *subprogram* (or submodule, or just plain module) will now be responsible for obtaining all the inputs required from the operator. At the end of the execution of the submodule, control is automatically transferred to the instruction after the DO instruction that passed control to the submodule. At that point, we want to erase the screen of all entries and inputs from the operator, and start pulling off records that match the operator's requirement. Obviously, both PGMA and PGMB must be ready before this little system will function, and PGMA will have to be invoked (DO PGMA) to get the ball rolling.

It should be noted that memory variables could be created in any program, and once created, are available to any other program to which control is transferred.

Note: The RETURN statement at the end of the called module is not mandatory. Program control is transferred back to the main module even in the absence of the RETURN statement.

Note: Instead of ACCEPT, where the value accepted is always of the character type, you may try the command INPUT.

INPUT "Please enter any character/s you wish" to MCHAR

During the execution of this command, the memory variable created could be of either character or numeric type. The type of memory variable created depends on the response entered by the operator. Refer to the earlier section on Accepting Numeric Input.

NESTED IF STATEMENTS

You can have an IF statement nested within another IF statement. For example:

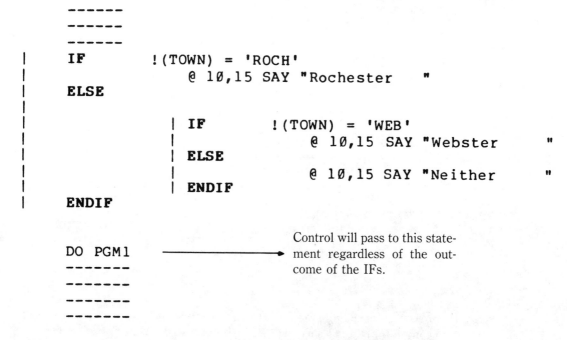

```
------
------
------
| IF        !(TOWN) = 'ROCH'
|               @ 10,15 SAY "Rochester    "
| ELSE
|
|           | IF        !(TOWN) = 'WEB'
|           |               @ 10,15 SAY "Webster       "
|           | ELSE
|           |               @ 10,15 SAY "Neither       "
|           | ENDIF
| ENDIF

  DO PGM1      ──────────────→
  ------
  ------
  ------
  ------
```

Control will pass to this statement regardless of the outcome of the IFs.

Note: In the above example, we are checking each record for either the town of ROCHESTER or the town of WEBSTER, and accordingly are putting out the appropriate literal for the town name. In the event of neither ROCH nor WEB, we are stating so, too.

Note: You must always have a matching ENDIF statement for any IF statement. Just so that you may not miss out on this crucial requirement for successful nesting of IF statements, you would be well-advised always to indent your nested IF statements, as shown in the example. *Indentation* refers to the practice of starting a line of code away from the very left-most column (column 1), so that you are able to match the IF ... ELSE ... ENDIF statements. (The matching refers to the logical matching of these statements, not to their physical alignment in one straight line.)

Note: There is nothing to prevent you from starting every line of code in your program from column 1, and the program will execute correctly, provided you have been able to complement each IF with its matching ENDIF. The indentation approach makes this matching so much easier. It also makes the program much more comprehensible, not only to others who may have to read your program, but also to yourself, if you have to pick it up at some later stage. You would be surprised how easy it is to forget the detailed working of your own program within a week of your having written it—especially if you are taking care of several programs simultaneously.

THE CASE APPROACH

Instead of using the nested IF approach, you may use the CASE approach in creating the logic of your program.

```
-----
DO CASE
          CASE       !(TOWN) = 'ROCH'   .AND.   !(ORG) = 'BSG'
-----
----- any dBASE commands you want executed, for records which
----- fulfill the above condition.
-----
-----
          CASE       !(TOWN) = 'ROCH'   .AND.   !(ORG) = 'GSD'
-----
-----
----- any dBASE commands you want executed, for records which
----- fulfill the above condition.
-----
-----
ENDCASE
-----
```

During execution, if any of the cases is true, the appropriate set of instructions is executed and then control is passed to the instruction after the ENDCASE statement. Which means, of course, that if a record qualified for more than one case, only the first case commands are executed, after which control drops out of the case study.

You may use the CASE approach instead of nested IFs to obtain the same end-result as the nested-IF statements:

```
DO CASE
        CASE     !(TOWN) = 'ROCH'
                @ 10,15 SAY "ROCHESTER     "
        CASE     !(TOWN) = 'WEB'
                @ 10,15 SAY "WEBSTER       "
        CASE     !(TOWN) # 'ROCH'    .OR.    !(TOWN) # 'WEB'
                @ 10,15 SAY "NEITHER       "
ENDCASE
```

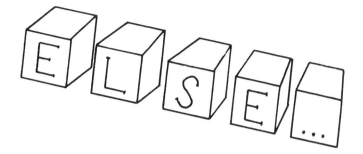

9. Writing Your Own Report Program

I f you have understood the preceding topics, we can now go ahead and attempt to write a report. This time, we shall write our own program to generate the report instead of using the built-in reporting feature of dBASE.

It is important to note that while the ability to write your own report-programs in dBASE frees you from the built-in REPORT command restraints, you may come to realize after you have read through the next few paragraphs, that the built-in REPORT command is not bad at all and makes reporting far easier than attempting to write your own report-programs.

In any case, the following few paragraphs will demonstrate how you could manipulate report formats to obtain just about any format you have in mind. You could then extend this logic to more complex reports.

REPORT PROGRAM EXPLANATION

This program will operate as follows:

1. Obtain operator inputs for Town and Organization.
2. Put out column headings on the screen.
3. Read every record out of PERSNL.
4. If records match the required Town and Organization; keep count of the number of such records that qualify, display emp:num, emp:name, yr:of:hire, and salary; ensure that each line follows the previous one (no overlap); and keep track of salary total.

At the end of the file, the program should print out the total obtained for the salary, and also print out the average.

```
ERASE

DO          Accepts              This subprogram will obtain
                                 operator inputs.
ERASE

DO          Hdr                  This subprogram will put out
                                 main headings and column
                                 headings on the screen.

STORE 0 TO MSALARY               Define a memory variable for
                                 salary.

STORE 0 TO RECORDCNT             Define a memory variable for
                                 record count.

USE PERSNL                       Read first record of PERSNL.

SET FORMAT TO PRINT              The output of the @ ..SAYs
                                 goes to the printer.
```

Note: The statement SET PRINT ON (that is, the Ctrl-P option while in dBASE) will only send the output of the DISPLAY statements onto the printer. In this report program, we will be responsible for formatting every requirement of this report ourselves, through the @ ..SAY commands, and so we need the instruction: SET FORMAT TO PRINT. This statement will send the output of the @ ...SAY

```
DO WHILE  .NOT.  EOF             For as long as it is not EOF.

  IF !(TOWN) = !(MTOWN)  .AND.  !(ORG) = !(MORG)

    @ LINECNT,10 SAY EMP:NUM         Left justified data.
    @ LINECNT,25 SAY EMP:NAME        Left justified data.
    @ LINECNT,38 SAY YR:OF:HIRE      Right justified data.
    @ LINECNT,43 SAY SALARY          Right justified data.
```

Note: The line number at which each record from the file should be made to print out should, of course, be made a variable, since it has to be incremented for each record to be printed out. Hence the use of the variable called LINECNT. You may name the variable anything you want. This variable has been initialized in the submodule called "HDR".

Note: If you see the subprogram called HDR, the 'EMP-NUMBER' column header has been specified as extending from col-

196

umn 10 through column 19. The EMP:NUM data should be made to go in left justified under that column, that is, it should be made to start at column 10. Hence the column 10 requirement for the EMP:NUM data. Similarly, for the other items of data printed out.

```
STORE RECORDCNT+1  TO RECORDCNT
STORE MSALARY + SALARY   TO   MSALARY
STORE LINECNT+1 TO LINECNT
```

Note: You want to add 1 to record count, keep a running total of salary, and increment the line count by 1 (for the next record) only if the current record under scrutiny qualifies the condition specified in the IF statement. And so these statements are all within the IF statement.

```
IF    LINECNT  >  55
```
The suggested line number for the end-of-page.

```
         DO  Hdr
     ENDIF
   ENDIF
   SKIP
ENDDO
```
If end-of-page DO headings, again.

Note: Notice the correct pairing off of the IF and ENDIF statements.

At EOF, program control passes to the next statement and prints totals and average.

```
STORE LINECNT+3 TO LINENT
@ LINECNT,10 SAY "SALARY TOTAL:"
@ LINECNT,25 SAY MSALARY
```

Note: The "SALARY TOTAL:" literally extends from column 10 through column 22. So the MSALARY memory variable should begin at column 23 or beyond. Also, we must remember that numeric fields are accepted up to 10 digits of accuracy, and so the memory variable called MSALARY is 10 digits wide. Hence the actual salary data appearing in the report will appear rather far removed from the literal, since it will be right justified in the 10-digit wide memory variable. More information on positioning and the use of masks follows shortly.

```
STORE LINECNT+1 TO LINECNT

@ LINECNT,10 SAY "TOTAL RECORDS"
@ LINECNT,25 SAY RECORDCNT

STORE LINECNT+1 TO LINECNT
```

```
@ LINECNT,10 SAY "AVERAGE SALARY:"
@ LINECNT,25 SAY (MSALARY/RECORDCNT)
```

Note: MSALARY was initially defined as a memory variable without decimals. However, we have subsequently been adding the SALARY fields into MSALARY, and SALARY is defined with 2 decimals. Now MSALARY also has the 2 decimals defined in its structure. As a result, to obtain the average, we did not find it necessary to specify: @LINECNT,25 SAY (MSALARY/RECORDNCT)+0.00.

Note: Memory variable "LINECNT" should be incremented only if the record matches the required condition, and hence the increment has to be within the logic of the IF statement.

Accepts Program

The Accepts program is called by our report program.

```
Accept "Please enter a town name"    to     mtown
Erase
Accept "Now please enter an organization name"  to   morg
Erase
Return
```

Header Program

The Hdr program is also called by our program.

```
EJECT

@ 2,28 SAY "REPORT AS OF JUNE 15, 1984"
@ 2,70 say DATE()
```

Note: The EJECT statement positions the printer to a new page. If you had forgotten to enter a data when you first initiated dBASE, you can always execute the special SET command:

.SET DATE TO mm/dd/yy   <cr>

Having set a date, to subsequently pull it out in the report, refer to the special date-function: DATE().

```
@ 3,28 say "-------------------------------"
@ 5,10 say "EMP-NUMBER"              Extends from 10 - 19.
@ 5,25 say "EMP-NAME"                Extends from 25 - 32.
@ 5,35 say "YR/HIRE"                 Extends from 35 - 41.
@ 5,45 say "SALARY"                  Extends from 45 - 50.
```

Store 8 to linecnt   Reset linecnt.
Return

You have noticed, of course, that even a simple report program can get to be quite a task. The complexity of such programs increases rapidly if subtotals at more than one level are involved. You would conclude, very correctly, that the built-in report generator feature of dBASE is, after all, quite handy.

POSITIONING AND THE USE OF MASKS

Suppose you entered the following two lines of code in a program:

```
@10,15 SAY 'TOTAL DOLLAR-AMOUNT = '
@10,41 SAY DOLLARS
```

The literal 'TOTAL DOLLAR-AMOUNT = ' itself spans the columns 15 through 36, so of course the memory variable called DOLLARS should begin beyond column 36, and in this case we have chosen column 41. If the actual data in DOLLARS was the value 100, would this value actually appear starting in column 41? The answer is no, since the memory variable itself is 10 digits wide, and the 100 is right justified within that width, and so the value 100 would actually appear in columns 48 through 50.

For various reasons, you may prefer to have the actual amount (however small or large it may be) to start exactly at the column you had specified in your code; in this case, we want the 100 to appear starting in column 41. You can accomplish this through the use of MASKS.

A *mask* can be looked upon as a shell which specifies how your data (in this case, numeric data) should be presented as output. Suppose you had modified your above two lines of code slightly, as follows:

```
@10,15 SAY 'TOTAL DOLLAR-AMOUNT = '
@10,41 SAY  DOLLARS USING '999.99'
```

The mask of '999.99' specifies that a digit out of DOLLARS would replace any 9 in the mask. So if DOLLARS contained the value 100, then since the mask starts in column 41, the output starting in column 41 would appear as 100.00. Now your literal and numeric data are in close proximity, as intended. The following table summarizes the results obtained out of different combinations of data and masks:

Date	Using <mask>	Result
1	999.99	1.00
12	999.99	12.00
1	.99	.00
12.34	99999	12
12.34	9,999.99	12.34
12.34	***9.99	**12.34

199

Date	Using <mask>	Result
12.34	*,**9.99	***12.34
12.34	**,*99.99	****12.34
12.34	***99.99	***12.34
12.34	$999.99	$ 12.34
12.34	***.**	*12.**
12.34	$$$.$$	12.$$
12.34	*,***.**	***12.**
−123.45	9999.99	−123.45
−123.45	999.99	123.45
−123.45	$999.99	−123.45
−123.45	$$999.99	$−123.45
123.45	−999.99	−123.45

Note: The mask should be at least as large as the expected number of digits to be accommodated.

The system aligns the decimal point in the data (actual or implied) with the decimal point provided in the mask, if any.

The mask will start at the column location specified by you, and should not, of course, overlay any columns containing literals or other data-masks.

The minus sign in a data-field behaves just like any other digit.

The above table would also be true in the case of numeric results obtained through computation, rather than from an existing field or memory variable.

@ 10,41 say (TOT:DOLLAR / REC:COUNT) +0.00 USING '999.99'

This statement would produce similar results as shown in our table, and the actual resultant value would be shown beginning in column 41.

The aid of masks will help to enhance your outputs, either in your own report programs, or when designing screen layouts (to be covered later).

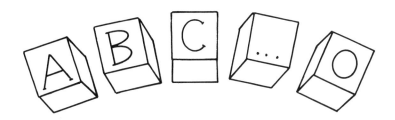

10. Writing A Menu Driven System

So far we have written stand-alone programs that are not part of a system. We can now go on to program a more functional menu-driven system. Let me explain the way a menu system works.

When the menu program is invoked, it first throws up a *menu* on the screen, providing the operator several functional alternatives. The operator makes a choice of any one function to perform. That choice results in the execution of a program *called* by the menu program. At the end of the chosen function, the menu screen comes up again, asking the operator for another choice of function, and this process goes on until the operator chooses that option which will cause dBASE to exit out of the menu loop.

In our pursuit of menu-driven systems, we shall make use of another data-base, called the Inventory data-base. The format of our fictional inventory file will be as follows, for the duration of the next few pages:

PART,C,6	COST,N,8,2	SELLPRICE,N,8,2	
ONHAND,N,3	ONORDER,N,3	USAGE,N,2	LEAD,N,2

Most of the fields are self-explanatory; the USAGE refers to the estimated daily usage/consumption of the item, and the LEAD refers to the lead time in days that is required between ordering new supplies and receiving them in stock.

MENU SHELL

There are basically two ways to generate menus with dBASE. We will first study the method that works on all versions of dBASE, (the General approach) and then we can look at the method that may prove easier to use if you had version 2.4 or beyond. The general approach, of course, works with version 2.4 or higher.

General Approach

A new command needs to be introduced. The ? command is a type of print command. When the ? command is interpreted, whatever you have keyed in quotes gets thrown back on the screen exactly as you had keyed it in. Now this is provided you had SET PRINT OFF (which is the default). If you had SET PRINT ON then the output of the ? command also goes to the printer.

An example of a menu-shell follows:

CLEAR	Close all files, clear out all memory variables, etc.
SET TALK OFF	You may want this.
STORE ' ' TO ERRMSG	
DO WHILE T	Note this instruction.

T is a built-in function which means TRUE. DO WHILE T attempts to DO <something> WHILE TRUE. Since T (TRUE) will always be TRUE, this type of DO WHILE specifies the beginning of an infinite loop.

```
ERASE

?  "                    INVENTORY CONTROL MENU"
?  "                    ----------------------"
?
?
?  "     A    -   Report of items with ONHAND below a stated level"
?
?  "     B    -   Report of items in danger of a stock-runout"
?
?  "     C    -   Full inventory report."
?
?  "     D    -   Add more data into the Inventory data-base"
?  "     E    -   Add more data        with duplicates-check"
?
?  "     F    -   Edit existing data - Sequentially"
?  "     G    -   Edit Sequentially    with duplicates-check"
?
?  "     H    -   Edit existing data - Random, by record-numbers"
?  "     I    -   Edit Random on rec-numbers, with duplicates-check"
?
?  "     J    -   Edit Random  based on the KEY-value"
?  "     K    -   Edit Random on KEY   with duplicates-check"
```

```
?
?   "    L    -    Delete records at Random, by KEY-value"
?
?   "    M    -    Scan records Sequentially"
?   "    N    -    Scan records at Random, by KEY-value"
?   "    O    -    Remove duplicate records from master file"
?   "    P    -    Exit from this menu"
?
? ERRMSG
```

As outlined before, the ? command puts whatever has been written in quotes after it on the screen exactly as has been specified in the program. That is, to format the menu requires nothing more than laying out the menu exactly as you want to see it with the ? commands. To provide for vertical spacing in the menu, use the ? command without any other parameter after it. Note that the literal in the ? command should be preceded and succeeded by the same type of quote, either single or double. Note also, that you can use memory variables (such as ERRMSG) whose contents can be displayed through the ? command.

WAIT   TO   ACTION   Note this instruction.

This statement causes a wait with the word WAITING appearing at the bottom of the menu. The single character that the operator enters in response to the request automatically releases the wait. This character is then placed into a character memory variable called ACTION. The program should now go ahead and check the entry made by the operator, that is, check the contents of ACTION.

It should be noted that you may name the memory variable anything you like. You could have said WAIT TO ETERNITY and then a character memory variable called ETERNITY would have been created. The program would then have to check the contents of the variable called ETERNITY.

Since we cannot presume that the operator will always enter UPPERcase letters in response to the menu, we will have to accept either upper or lowercase letters. Hence the use of the UPPER-case function, in the next few statements.

Our program will now check the entry placed in the memory variable called ACTION. In essence, we have to check to see if any entry between the letters A through P has been made, and if so, either transfer control to the appropriate program, or cancel the execution of the menu program, as the case may be.

Checking the Results of Operator Action

We will first look at the lengthy, but easier to understand approach to testing the contents of ACTION, and at a later, more appropriate, time we shall study one command that can produce the same result.

```
IF !(ACTION) = 'A'          PGMA has been programmed to do what
    DO PGMA                 option A suggests.
```

203

```
ENDIF
IF !(ACTION) = 'B'
   DO PGMB
ENDIF
IF !(ACTION) = 'C'
   DO PGMC
ENDIF
IF !(ACTION) = 'D'
   DO PGMD
ENDIF
IF !(ACTION) = 'E'
   DO PGME
ENDIF
IF !(ACTION) = 'F'
   DO PGMF
ENDIF
IF !(ACTION) = 'G'
   DO PGMG
ENDIF
IF !(ACTION) = 'H'
   DO PGMH
ENDIF
IF !(ACTION) = 'I'
   DO PGMI
ENDIF
IF !(ACTION) = 'J'
   DO PGMJ
ENDIF
IF !(ACTION) = 'K'
   DO PGMK
ENDIF
IF !(ACTION) = 'L'
   DO PGML
ENDIF
IF !(ACTION) = 'M'
   DO PGMM
ENDIF
IF !(ACTION) = 'N'
   DO PGMN
ENDIF
IF !(ACTION) = 'O'
   DO PGMO
ENDIF
IF !(ACTION) = 'P'
   RETURN
ENDIF
IF ACTION < 'A'  .OR.  !(ACTION) > 'P'
   STORE 'INVALID OPTION SELECTED !!'  TO   ERRMSG
ELSE
   STORE ' ' TO ERRMSG
ENDIF

ENDDO
```

Similarly for the other programs, PGMB, PGMC, etc.

This causes program executon to halt.

This is the end of the loop.

Since the loop has been set up as an infinite loop, the set of commands within the loop will execute indefinitely. That is, after the execution of any function chosen by the operator, the program control will again force the screen to the ERASEd, and the menu screen to come up. The only way out of this loop is if the operator enters a P.

Note also, that if the operator makes a choice other than what has been requested in the menu screen (which is quite likely), then the only IF statement that will fall true is the one where we check for an operator entry less than the letter A (numbers would qualify) or for an entry greater than the letter P, in which case an error message is placed into the memory variable called ERRMSG (if you notice, the menu provides for displaying ERRMSG onto the screen), and once again the menu screen comes up, this time with the error message displayed. So really, the only way out of this menu loop is through the use of the exit option as provided by the menu.

You may have noticed that in our menu program we are providing for a lengthy error message, and yet in the same program, we use only one blank to blank out the ERRMSG memory variable. If we use memory variables to store different types of messages, we don't have to define it with an exact length. When our memory variable has to be blanked-out, it hardly matters to us whether it is a one character blank or a hundred character blank; hence the use of only one blank, to clean-up the ERRMSG memory variable. You may, subsequently, store a lengthy message into the same memory variable that had been initialized with just one space.

Memory variables need to have predefined lengths only when they will be used for replacing values in data-fields of any file in use. Now their lengths must tally with those of the data-fields they will be replacing. (More on this, later.)

Let us suppose that the operator makes a valid choice of parameter, and one of the programs gets executed. At the end of the execution, program control would automatically pass to the next IF statement in the menu program. Now, of course, none of the remaining IF statements would be satisfied, and the last IF statement would ensure that ERRMSG is set to blank, before the menu screen is shown once again, with the words WAITING appearing at the bottom of the menu.

We have seen, then, that the creation of a menu program is really very simple. All it takes is a few ? commands containing the appropriate literals you would like to see in the menu, and then the program only needs to test the entry made by the operator and initiate the execution of the appropriate subprogram.

> **Note:** This menu example is, obviously, an overkill, since in any real world situation, you would not have such an extravagant combination of functions, for any system. You would pick and choose the options you would want to provide for your user. However, since our objective here is to highlight the power of the programming option in dBASE, we have elected to present all of the above programs.

> **Note:** When the menu program is initiated, it first CLEARs all memory variables, to start with a clean-slate. Since memory variables are accessible across modules, it is very essential that none of the submodules should have the CLEAR command in them, else the memory variable called ACTION would no longer exist after the execution of the very first submodule, and as soon as program control is transferred back to the next IF statement in the menu program, your system would crash, for lack of the memory variable called ACTION. This is true only on account of the way we have written the IF statements in our program. We have several, individual IF statements

checking the result of ACTION. IF we had written a nested IF statement, or had taken the CASE approach in checking out the results n
ACTION, the above paragraph would not hold true.

TEXT Approach

Let us see a slightly different method of building a menu that may prove faster for you.
The option we will be studying is not valid for dBASE versions prior to 2.4.

```
CLEAR
SET TALK OFF
STORE ' ' TO ERRMSG
DO WHILE T
    ERASE
    TEXT
```

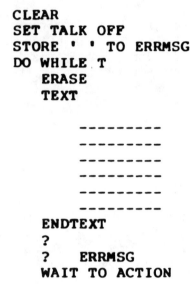 This is where you can design the screen layout
exactly as you want. Please note that in this case,
on account of the TEXT command, you should not
use the ? command but instead use only the exact
literals in the exact layout you want.

```
ENDTEXT
?
?    ERRMSG
WAIT TO ACTION
```

(proceed as before. . . .)

The TEXT command merely informs dBASE that whatever follows is to be sent up
on the screen exactly as formatted. Obviously, if you forget the ENDTEXT command,
the entire program will appear on the screen.

Let us now begin to complete the system. After all, the menu only initiates the
subprograms, and the subprograms are the ones written to do the real tasks. For our
previous INVENTORY CONTROL MENU system, we have to now write several
subprograms and a couple of report formats to complete the entire system.

PROGRAM A

This option has to identify items of inventory with an ONHAND balance below a certain
level which also will be specified by the operator. Since the menu itself should not be
cluttered up with these subsequent types of operator inputs, the option A itself should be
made to kick up a miniscreen, asking the operator to identify the level of inventory below
which items should be included in a report. Hence PGMA.CMD should be created as
follows:

```
ERASE

? "Option - A:  Report of ONHAND below a stated level:"
```

```
?
?
?
?   "What is the level of inventory below which you want to"
```

INPUT "receive a status" **TO** **LEVEL**

> **Note:** Since the question to be asked of the operator is lengthy, we break it up into two statements. The first of these program statements is the ? command, and we know that this only results in the literal being thrown back on the screen the way we have written it out. The second program statement is the INPUT statement. If you recall, the way this works is that the literal following the INPUT command is thrown up on the screen, the system waits for the operator's response, and the response is sent into a memory variable called, in this case, LEVEL. So if the operator enters the number 25 in response to this command, the number 25 comes to rest in the numeric memory variable called LEVEL. Remember that the type of variable created through the INPUT statement depends on the response (with or without quotes) made by the operator.

These commands produce the following results. The screen is ERASEd, the extraneous literals are presented on the screen, and the main question to be asked of the operator comes up on the screen in two lines. The system automatically waits for the response, and the response is placed into the numeric memory variable called LEVEL.

Let us continue with our program.

ERASE

> It is good practice to ERASE the screen after operator inputs have been received.

USE INVNTRY   **[INDEX .....]**

REPORT FORM   RPTA   **FOR**   **ONHAND ≤ LEVEL**   **[TO PRINT]**

WAIT

> Not necessary, if you are printing the report.

RETURN

> After the operator's response has been taken in, the program continues by ERASing the screen again, then pulling off a report format for those records whose ONHAND is less than the value keyed-in by the operator. The INVNTRY file may or may not be indexed, depending on the required report format. Note that after the report has been generated on the screen, you want to say WAIT, else the end of the report will be

followed immediately by the menu screen being sent up again, as soon as control is transferred back to the menu program. Of course, if the report is being sent TO PRINT, then you should not have the WAIT statement.

Now, you have to generate the appropriate REPORT FORMAT file, before this section of the system has been completed. Since report formats have been covered in great detail earlier, I refer you to Chapter 9 for review, if necessary. In this case, of course, the format and content of the report depends entirely on the requirements of the user of the system.

PROGRAM B

In this option, the PGMB program has to be created to pull off, in another report format, all those items of inventory for which a stock run-out is imminent. As you may appreciate, such timely reports are absolutely crucial for successful management of any business enterprise.

Let us see the following formula.

$$\text{QTY-ON-HAND is less than DAILY-USAGE * LEAD-TIME}$$
$$(50) \quad < \quad (5) \quad \times \quad (14)$$

If you had 50 pieces of an item in stock, and your average daily usage is 5 pieces, you know that at most you have 10 days worth of the items on hand. Now, if it takes 14 days, from requesting new supplies to getting them in stock, then you know that you are already in trouble, for that item.

Obviously, management needs to be informed of the potential for this kind of unwelcome situation before it presents itself. We need to be able to come up with a formula that will flag an item for action, providing us enough days of leeway during which an order for fresh supplies could be placed with the supplier, and also providing us with enough days for the item to be received in stock, from the supplier.

Let us check out the following formula:

$$\text{ONHAND is equal to or less than DAILY-USAGE * (LEAD-TIME + (Internal Processing))}$$
$$\text{<-----leeway----->}$$

Let us suppose, for now, that for any particular item, the DAILY-USAGE quantity is indeed a constant, and is not fluctuating. Suppose we had the following situation for an item:

$$\text{DAILY-USAGE} = 10 \text{ units, LEAD-TIME} = 20 \text{ days, IP} = 10 \text{ days}$$

From the above formula it follows that if the ONHAND value for this item falls to a level equal to (or below) 300, our program (to be provided later) will flag this item for action. For this particular item, we now have 10 days of leeway, during which an order for fresh supplies should be placed.

Please understand clearly that it is not my intention to provide a complete formula for this type of inventory control. Indeed, I am not qualified to provide such a formula. However, the intent here is to show you how you could use dBASE to provide for inventory control, presuming that you have access to some foolproof formula at your disposal.

Obviously, different items would require different amounts of leeway days for internal processing, and the inventory Master file could contain this factor as one more field of information for each item in inventory. The above formula will also hold good for those items whose DAILY-USAGE is not a constant, but fluctuates slightly. Obviously, such a DAILY-USAGE value is an average value.

PGMB should have the following lines of code:

ERASE
USE INVNTRY   **[INDEX.....]**

REPORT FORM RPTB <u>FOR</u> <u>ONHAND</u> <u><=</u> <u>USAGE</u> <u>*</u> <u>(LEAD+(IP))</u>

        IP stands for internal processing days.

WAIT
RETURN

Again, report form RPTB(.FRM) should be prepared, before this section of the system can be complete. The report format should be designed to provide, among other things, the maximum amount of leeway days provided for the item. You may also send this report TO PRINT.

PROGRAM C

This subprogram will provide a full Inventory report. The only entries in this kind of submodule would be as follows:

ERASE

USE INVNTRY   **[INDEX.....]**

REPORT FORM RPTC   **[TO PRINT]**

WAIT   Not necessary, if you are printing the report.

RETURN

Now RPTC.FRM should be prepared, for this section of the system to execute successfully.

The other options defined in our menu system will be covered after we learn to generate our own screen formats in the next section.

GENERATING SCREEN FORMATS

Learning the use of the Accept and Input commands helped in obtaining low-volume input from the operator during execution of a program. Menu-driven systems will go a long way towards establishing a complete dBASE-II system. But we will now enhance our programming capability by learning to write our own full-screen layouts. These full-screen layouts help in obtaining high-volume inputs from the operator, and these inputs can be edited/verified for accuracy, before acceptance as part of a new or changed record of information.

As an example of where we may want to use our own formats, recall the way the APPEND command works. It throws up the blank structure of any file in use and allows you to enter data. Each record is automatically added into the data-base.

To only send up a restricted structure to the screen, you would have to design your own screen format, accept the data entered by the operator, and then proceed to produce a new record of information in the Master file. Or, if you wanted to send up your own format and then edit the data keyed in by the operator (which the APPEND command, as it stands, does not let you do), then, too, you would have to design your own format and logic to edit the data.

We will now proceed to write a program which will send up a formatted screen. An example might look like the following.

```
            INVENTORY SYSTEM DATA-ENTRY SCREEN.
            ------------------------------------

ENTER THE FOLLOWING PIECES OF REQUIRED INFORMATION:
---------------------------------------------------

PART-NUMBER:            :
COST            :       :
SELLPRICE   :   :
ONHAND      :   :
ONORDER     :   :
USAGE       :   :
LEAD        :   :

Leave part-number field blank, and ctrl-W, to exit.
```

Having sent up this screen, the program will now wait for the operator to key in each piece of information. As the data entry proceeds, the program will place all the responses into memory variables.

Now the program will go ahead, and APPEND BLANK to the INVENTORY file. This will create a blank record at the end of the INVENTORY file, and more important, the record pointer will be positioned at the new, blank record. The program will now proceed to REPLACE all the appropriate fields of the blank record with the data that had been captured in the memory variables, thus appending a new record of data to the Inventory file.

The program will then proceed to send up the blank, formatted screen again, for the next record of information, and so on. In order to do this, we will proceed with an understanding of the @-----SAY command, some of which we have seen earlier. The @----SAY feature lets you put out specific information either onto a screen or onto a printer.

The general format of the @---SAY command is as follows:

@	coords	SAY	field-name from a file in use	or
			memory-variable	or
			literal	or
			expression	
		USING	<output edit-mask>	
		(to screen or the printer)		

and/or

		GET	field-name	or
			memory-variable	
		PICTURE	<input edit-mask>	
		(to/from the screen.)		

The coordinates refer either to screen coordinates (default) or to printer coordinates. When you first invoke dBASE, the default is SET FORMAT TO SCREEN. So by default, the coordinates refer to screen coordinates, and all the outputs of the @. . .SAY commands get thrown up on the screen. Screen coordinates are as follows:

24 LINES, numbered 0 through 23
80 COLUMNS, numbered 0 through 79

In the @ . . .SAY commands the coordinates always refer to: line, column. That is, @ 10, 15 . . . refers to the 11th line and the 16th column. Note, however, that if in the program, one of the statements is SET FORMAT TO PRINT then all the outputs of the @ . . .SAY commands get sent up on the printer. In this case, GET phrases are ignored.

It is important to understand that outputs to the screen can be sent up in any order. For example, you may SAY something at line 15 before you SAY something at line 10. However, outputs to the printer must be sent in order. Otherwise a page eject will take place between your SAY commands. For example, if you have SET FORMAT TO PRINT and you SAY something at line 10, and then you SAY something at line 5, dBASE will presume that you want line 5 on a new page, since the printer is already positioned beyond line 5 on the current page. The same caution applies to column specifications (when you have SET FORMAT TO PRINT). Failure to adhere to this caution will cause your printer to play some tricks on you.

Since you could SAY or GET either a field-name from a file in use or a memory variable existing at the time, please note that if you have a memory variable having the same name as one of the fields of the file in use, then dBASE will always pick up, by default, the field-name, and not the name of the memory variable.

A handy suggestion would be to start all your memory variables names with the letter M, so as to distinguish them from field-names from the file in use. For example, the memory variable to hold ITEM information could be called MITEM to differentiate it from the ITEM-field in the Inventory file.

Since the substance of our program is the initiation of a formatted screen for data entry by the operator, let us get down to the business of designing the screen layout shown earlier, for entering new records of data.

PROGRAM D

This program generates a format file and calling program for appending more records. Let us build up a file comprised of nothing but the following @---SAY commands. Such a file is called a format file. We will name it *LAYOUTD.FMT. Start with the following command:

.MODI COMM   LAYOUTD.FMT

The qualifier of .FMT is important, so don't ignore it. When the screen goes blank, we will enter the following @. . .SAY statements:

> **Note:** You may, if you like, provide blank lines within the format-file, for visual-aid/esthetic reasons.]

```
@ 2,25   SAY 'INVENTORY SYSTEM DATA-ENTRY SCREEN'
@ 3,25   SAY '--------- ------ ---- ----- ------'
@ 5,1    SAY 'ENTER THE FOLLOWING PIECES OF REQUIRED INFORMATION:'


@ 08,5   SAY  'PART-NUM ' GET MPART     PICTURE 'XXXXXX'
@ 10,5   SAY  'COST     ' GET MCOST     PICTURE '99999.99'
@ 12,5   SAY  'SELLPRICE' GET MSELL     PICTURE '99999.99'
@ 14,5   SAY  'ONHAND   ' GET MONHAND   PICTURE '999'
@ 16,5   SAY  'ONORDER  ' GET MONORDER  PICTURE '999'
@ 18,5   SAY  'USAGE    ' GET MUSAGE    PICTURE '99'
@ 20,5   SAY  'LEAD     ' GET MLEAD     PICTURE '99'
@ 23,1   SAY  'LEAVE PART-NUM FIELD BLANK, and  ctrl-W, TO EXIT'
```

Notice that all the literals have been provided the same length. While this is not at all necessary for the successful execution of the program, if all literals have the same length, then all variables start at the same relative columns on the screen, and this provides for a much more appealing screen, from an esthetic point of view.

> **Note:** The 'XXXXXX' or the '99999.99' is only a mask, specifying the type of data that will be expected to be entered in the field by the operator when the format file is activated. When the format comes up during execution, a pair of colons will signify the maximum length of the data expected in each field. The X in the picture mask of any field implies that a character (either alpha or numeric) will be accepted in place of each X. The picture mask for the UNIT-COST field obviously implies that only numeric data will be accepted as input for this field. Also, the operator will be forced to input data in the format specified. It

is up to you to ensure that your mask-size corresponds to the size of the individual fields in your Master file. After all, each complete screen entry by the operator will result in the creation of a new record of data in the Master file.

During execution, when the FORMAT-FILE is invoked, whatever literals have been specified come up on the screen. A READ command can now transfer the information entered by the operator, into the respective memory variables associated with the above GET statements.

Let us now build another command file, which will call the format file. This file will be called PGMD.CMD. If you remember, the menu program passes control to PGMD if the operator wants to select the APPEND option from the menu.

```
SET TALK OFF
ERASE
USE INVNTRY
DO WHILE T                    Start an infinite loop.

    STORE '      ' TO MPART
    STORE 0              TO MCOST
    STORE 0              TO MSELL
    STORE 0              TO MONHAND
    STORE 0              TO MONORDER
    STORE 0              TO MUSAGE
    STORE 0              TO MLEAD
```

Note: The calling program must initialize the memory variables to the exact length of the corresponding fields in the structure of the Master file. Hence the variable called MPART is defined as 6 characters since that variable will be used to replace the field called PART, which is defined as 6 characters, in the structure of the Inventory file.

SET FORMAT TO LAYOUTD

Note: This command activates the format file. Now the operator will see all the outputs of the SAY commands on the screen exactly as had been specified in the format file called LAYOUTD.

READ

Note: This will read the operator inputs into the memory variables as defined by the GET statements in the format file.

During execution, the READ command causes the cursor to skip from one GET field to the next as the operator keys-in the required entries. The entries are saved in the appropriate memory variables as defined by the GET statements of the FORMAT file. Cursor controls are identical to those we have studied for the APPEND mode in case you want to move the cursor around to make changes. After the last field is entered, program control takes off to execute the next instruction. If you want program control to take off with the next instruction without having to enter all the fields, enter Ctrl-W.

> **Note:** If you wish to ensure that the operator enters all UPPER-case characters for a character type field (e.g., PART-NUMBER field), then the mask should be defined as PICTURE '!!!!!!'. Now, any letter keyed in will be accepted in uppercase only. If numeric data is keyed in, it will, of course, be accepted. A PART-NUMBER field would usually require alphanumeric data to be entered. Also, if a field is to contain alphabetic data only in certain positions of the field, then the edit mask should be something like: PICTURE 'AXXAXA' or some such combination of the 'X' and the 'A', so that the 'X' will accept any character in its position, and the 'A' will only accept alphabetic input. You may have masks made up of required combinations of X and A and ! and 9.

```
IF  MPART  = '          '
    SET FORMAT TO                    Explained later.
    RETURN
ENDIF
```

Since the screen format specifies that the operator should leave the PART-NUMBER field blank to exit, our program must check the part-number field before proceeding. The RETURN statement will cause program execution to return to the menu screen again.

If a valid part number has been entered, proceed . ..

APPEND BLANK

This statement will cause a blank record to be appended to the bottom of the data-base and, more importantly, for the record pointer to point to the newly appended blank record!

At this point, the operator entries are in the memory variables, and the record pointer points to the blank record.

```
REPLACE PART WITH MPART;              Note the ; for continuation.
        COST WITH MCOST;
        SELLPRICE WITH MSELL;
        ONHAND WITH MONHAND;
        ONORDER WITH MONORDER;
        USAGE WITH MUSAGE;
        LEAD WITH MLEAD
```

The appropriate fields of the newly appended blank record now contain the data that was entered by the operator.

SET FORMAT TO

> **Note:** This command will deactivate the format file. This is important, since at some point in time, the operator will want to stop entering new records of information, and when this happens, you want to be out of this mode of operation without any format files active, else even a stand-alone command such as APPEND will cause the format-file format to appear on the screen, not the normal full-screen AP-PEND format you have seen so often! So you really want to deactivate this format file between screens.

ENDDO

The DO WHILE T and the ENDDO combination will cause this data-entry program to proceed for as long as the operator enters valid part numbers. Leaving the PART:NUM field blank and entering Ctrl-W will cause the RETURN statement to be executed, which will bring the menu up on the screen again.

Note that the STORE statements are within the DO loop, since the memory variables need to be initialized to blanks or zero for each new record to be appended.

> **Note:** To have your own SET CARRY ON type of effect for the above program, all you need to do is to have the STORE commands outside of the DO WHILE T loop. If this were done, then the memory variables would not get cleared between records, and you would be automatically "carrying on" data from one record to the next. Notice, however, that now the operator would have to blank-out the part-number field, in order to exit!
>
> **Note:** The IBM-PC and other computers will display items defined with a GET clause, in inverse video. Some others may display GET at normal intensity, and the SAY items at ½ intensity. To remove these effects, you may use the command: .SET INTENSITY OFF.
>
> **Note:** If you decide to interrupt program execution using the ESCAPE key, it is possible that the SET FORMAT TO instruction may not have executed. That is, the format file is still open. If you were to now say 'MODI COMM LAYOUTD.FMT', in an attempt to make some changes to the format file, dBASE will tell you that the file is still open. So you will have to execute a stand-alone instruction: .SET FORMAT TO before proceeding again.

To make further changes to an existing screen-format file, start off with the same syntax used for creating a new format file:

.MODI   COMM   LAYOUTD.FMT   <cr>

Now, if LAYOUTD.FMT exists, the screen comes up with the contents of the format file, and you can make changes at will, using the usual cursor controls learned earlier.

Advantages of Using a Format File

It is not mandatory that you should have a separate and distinct file called a format file, which will be invoked by a calling program. You can have all the @ ----SAY---GET statements for your format file right in the middle of your calling program, itself, in place of the statement: SET FORMAT TO LAYOUTD.

However, the advantages of having a format file distinct and separate from your calling program are many. For example, a change required to be made to the screen layout necessitates a change and a save of only the format file, instead of the entire program, which could be quite lengthy. More important, as we will see later on, some programs could be quite complex, and will necessitate the invoking of the screen format from different sections of the program. In such cases, if you had one gigantic module comprising of both format and program, you would end up repeating the @---SAY---GET collection of statements at several places in your program. To say the least, this could result in *terminal illness* for the programmer.

Edit Check Enhancement

The APPEND program we have just studied can be enhanced to provide an edit check on the data keyed in by the operator. For example, the COST of any item should not have exceeded $50.00. It is possible that a transformation error would have caused the operator to enter 63 for 36, and such errors should be trapped before the record is accepted. This is the subject of our enhancement.

The format file will be modified very slightly to provide for an error message on the screen.

```
@ 2,25   SAY 'INVENTORY SYSTEM DATA-ENTRY SCREEN'
@ 3,25   SAY '---------- ------- ---- ----- ------'
@ 5,1    SAY 'ENTER THE FOLLOWING PIECES OF REQUIRED INFORMATION:'


@ 08,5   SAY   'PART-NUM ' GET MPART      PICTURE 'XXXXXX'
@ 10,5   SAY   'COST     ' GET MCOST      PICTURE '99999.99'
@ 12,5   SAY   'SELLPRICE' GET MSELL      PICTURE '99999.99'
@ 14,5   SAY   'ONHAND   ' GET MONHAND    PICTURE '999'
@ 16,5   SAY   'ONORDER  ' GET MONORDER   PICTURE '999'
@ 18,5   SAY   'USAGE    ' GET MUSAGE     PICTURE '99'
@ 20,5   SAY   'LEAD     ' GET MLEAD      PICTURE '99'
@ 22,1   SAY 'LEAVE PART-NUM FIELD BLANK, and  ctrl-W, TO EXIT'
@ 23,1   SAY 'ERRMSGD'
```

Our calling program (PGMD.CMD) should be modified as follows:

```
SET TALK OFF
ERASE
USE INVNTRY
DO WHILE T          Start an infinite loop.

    STORE '      ' TO MPART
    STORE 0              TO MCOST
    STORE 0              TO MSELL
    STORE 0              TO MONHAND
```

```
        STORE 0                      TO MONORDER
        STORE 0                      TO MUSAGE
        STORE 0                      TO MLEAD
        STORE ' '                    TO ERRMSGD

    SET FORMAT TO LAYOUTD
    READ

    IF MPART  = '        '
        SET FORMAT TO
        RETURN
    ENDIF


    *                    BEGIN EDIT-CHECK ROUTINE !!

    STORE   T  TO NOGOOD                 So we can enter the "NOGOOD" loop.

    DO WHILE  NOGOOD
        STORE F TO NOGOOD

    IF MSELL < 5  .OR.  MSELL > 50
        STORE 'SELL PRICE ERROR' TO ERRMSGD
        STORE T TO NOGOOD
    ENDIF
    IF MCOST < 5 .OR. MCOST > 50
        STORE 'COST PRICE ERROR' TO ERRMSGD
        STORE T TO NOGOOD                  So we can remain in the loop.
    ENDIF


    IF  ----------------
        (similar checks for any field(s) input by the operator)
    ENDIF


    IF NOGOOD
        SET FORMAT TO LAYOUTD
        READ
    ENDIF
ENDDO

*                   END EDIT-CHECK ROUTINE !!
*.
*   If the edit check proves OK, the program will proceed with
*     the following instructions.

APPEND BLANK
REPLACE PART WITH MPART;
        COST WITH MCOST;
        SELLPRICE WITH MSELL;
        ONHAND WITH MONHAND;
        ONORDER WITH MONORDER;
```

USAGE WITH MUSAGE;
LEAD WITH MLEAD

SET FORMAT TO

ENDDO

Notice that since we have only provided for just the one error message on the screen, obviously if more than one field is in error, the second message will overlap the first one, and so on, down the line. Hence, the program logic checks the fields in the reverse order of output on the screen. That is, the program checks for valid data in field-2 before field-1, so if both fields are in error, the error message area highlights field-1 as being in error, etc.

> **Note:** While this book provides a great many programs for you to learn from, it is virtually impossible to produce, within the limitations of this book, all the possibilities one could encounter or may want to provide for, in these programs. For the sake of practicality, we will avoid producing the edit checks we mentioned here, for the other programs. We are very confident that you will be able to incorporate the shell of the edit checks just introduced into the remainder of the programs.
>
> At this stage, you may, perhaps, want to incorporate the duplicates-check we alluded to earlier (in the section on INDEXing). That is, as the operator proceeds to enter more data using your specially formatted screen, how do you ensure that a key data-item like PART-NUMBER is not being wrongly duplicated? If you can hold on a little longer, this extension will be explained to you after you have studied the section on Macros.

UNDERSTANDING MACROS

A *macro* is a short-hand notaton for specifying either an entire instruction, or merely a command out of an instruction, or a parameter of the instruction. For example, at the dBASE dot prompt, if we were to enter the following instruction:

.STORE "REPLACE ALL TOWN WITH 'ROCH' FOR ORG = 'BSG'" TO REPL

> **Note:** Double quotes were required, since the literal itself has single quotes embedded in it.

The above instruction will place a long-winded literal into a character memory variable called REPL. This long-winded literal also happens to resemble a dBASE command! Now, if at the dot prompt we were to specify the following type of instruction, dBASE would recall the previous instruction.

.&REPL   <cr>

dBASE will recognize the &REPL as being a *marco instruction* and will interpret this to be our lazy way of saying, "please execute the long-winded instruction in the REPL memory variable." The effect of the &REPL command would be as though you had typed, at the dot prompt, the entire REPLACE command yourself.

This means that you can STORE a command once and have it executed several times simply by using the macro version of the command. This saves us a lot of keystrokes at the keyboard.

Note: All macros are character memory variables, only!

The macros can also be used for parameters and are not limited to entire commands. For example:

.STORE "FOR ORG = 'BSG' .OR. ORG = 'GSD'" TO COND

This stores the literal in the character memory variable called COND. Now enter the following statement:

.REPLACE ALL TOWN WITH 'ROCH' &COND

It has the same effect as if you had typed out the following long-winded version:

.REPLACE ALL TOWN WITH 'ROCH' FOR ORG = 'BSG' .OR. ORG = 'GSD'
<------------&COND------------>

The important point to understand is that, depending on where in a statement the macro has been specified, it will be interpreted as being either a *command* or a *parameter* of a command. This feature is very handy, since it lets you specify variables entered by an operator during the execution of a program.

If we have the following instructions in a program, you can see how the operator's input becomes a macro and is used as a parameter.

ERASE
ACCEPT "Which Master-file do you want to use?" TO F
USE &F

During execution of the program, the operator's response for the file-name enters the character memory variable called F. The program will then use the contents of F to bring the appropriate file in USE. In this case, again, the &F is a macro that is used as a parameter and not as a command.

To highlight the use of a macro, let us take this extreme example:

.STORE "USE" TO M1
.STORE 'PERSNL' TO M2
.STORE 'DISP' TO M3
.STORE 'FOR' TO M4
.STORE "TOWN='ROCH'" TO M5

Now you can use the macros alone, as follows:

.&M1 &M2   (Use PERSNL)
.&M3 &M4 &M5   (DISP FOR TOWN='ROCH')

Using Macros in the Menu System

When you were learning how to build up a menu and check the option entered by the operator, I mentioned that at a later stage you would learn how to check for the operator option with just one command. Having studied the MACRO, I can now show you this solution for checking operator options:

```
- - - - - - - - - - - - -
- - - - - - - - - - - - -
IF !(ACTION) = 'P'        The check for exiting from the menu should made as usual.
USE
        RETURN
   ENDIF

IF !(ACTION)  $('ABCDEFGHIJKLMNO')        . . . . . . . . . . . . .  Ⓐ
        STORE ' ' TO ERRMSG
        STORE 'PGM' + !(ACTION)  TO   CHOICE. . . . . . . . .  Ⓑ
        DO   &CHOICE                      . . . . . . . . . .  Ⓒ
   ELSE
        STORE "INVALID OPTION SELECTED !!"   TO   ERRMSG
   ENDIF
ENDDO
```

The statement at (A) says, "If the uppercase version of the value in ACTION is to be found anywhere in the string ABCDEFGHIJKLMNO".......

The statement at (B) says: Store the literal PGM immediately followed by the uppercase version of the result of ACTION, to a memory variable called CHOICE. Hence if the operator chose the option A, then "PGMA" would be stored in the memory variable CHOICE. If the operator chose the option G, then "PGMG" would be stored in CHOICE, and so on.

The statement at (C) is, of course, our macro. As you can see, if the operator option is A, the statement would be: DO PGMA and if the option made was H, the statement would be: DO PGMH and so on. This is much more effective than typing out the multiple IF statements. However, the multiple IF statements may prove easier to understand.

Now we have the tools to be able to complete our previous programs. Among other things, we now want to enhance the APPEND program to check for duplicate keys inadvertently keyed in! First, however, we want to make a small but significant enhancement to one of our earlier programs.

Program A Revisited

We shall use our understanding of macros to put in a small, but significant enhancement to Program A. If you recall, Program A puts out a report which highlights those items for which the current ONHAND is less than a certain level input by the operator. Our enhancement provides for putting out that requested level in a special header in the report.

```
ERASE
? "Option – A:  Report of "ONHAND" below a stated level:"
```

220

```
?
?
?
? "What is the level of inventory below which you want to"
INPUT "receive a status"  TO  LEVEL

ERASE
USE INVNTRY [INDEX ....]

STORE STR(LEVEL,10) TO LVL

SET HEADING TO INVENTORY REPORT FOR ONHAND BELOW &LVL

REPORT FORM RPTA  FOR ONHAND < LEVEL  [TO PRINT]
WAIT
RETURN
```

The above program is identical to what we have seen before, with one exception. We have stored the contents of the numeric memory variable LEVEL into another character memory variable called LVL. Now, before the report gets generated, we have provided for a special header line, which reports on the level requested by the operator! Note the use of the macro, &LVL, in the special header line.

PROGRAM E

This program generates a format file and a calling program for appending new records and includes a duplicates check. The "guts" of this enhancement is the creation and use of an *index* built on the key-field that you want to check upon. The operator will key in new data for each new record to be appended, but before the program actually does the APPEND BLANK the program will use the FIND command to scan the indexed file to check for an already-existing key with the same value that the operator has entered for the new record key.

If the FIND command is successful in locating such an existing record, the built-in record number function (#) will contain the record number of the found record. If the FIND command could not find an already existing record with the key entered by the operator, the record number function will contain the value zero. This will be our basis for checking for duplicate keys.

We will first build up our format file, as usual, for the APPEND function: [LAYOUTE.FMT]

> **Note:** In order to make a copy of a format file, you could go through the same actions necessary for making copies of program files. Presuming you have a DUMMY file with only one field in its structure of length 80 characters but containing no data, enter the following:

```
.USE DUMMY
.APPEND FROM LAYOUTD.FMT    SDF
```

Remember that the format file is also a text file, just like a program file. At the end of the previous APPEND, the DUMMY database contains the format records out of LAYOUTD.FMT.

```
.COPY TO LAYOUTE.FMT     SDF
```

The COPY command will now create another file called LAYOUTE.FMT, as a text file. The file in use is still DUMMY, and so you should now enter the following:

```
.DELETE ALL     <cr>
.PACK           <cr>
```

You now have a clean DUMMY file for the next time around when you may want to make a copy of another program file or format file.

```
@ 2,10  SAY 'INVENTORY DATA-ENTRY SCREEN'
@ 3,10  SAY '---------------------------'
@ 4,10  SAY 'APPENDING NEW RECORDS, WITH DUPLICATES CHECK ON KEY-FIELD'

@ 6,1   SAY 'ENTER THE FOLLOWING ITEMS OF INFORMATION:'


@ 08,1  SAY 'PARTNUM   ' GET MPART PICTURE 'XXXXXX'
@ 10,1  SAY 'COST      ' GET MCOST PICTURE '99999.99'
@ 12,1  SAY 'SELLPRICE' GET MSELL PICTURE '99999.99'
@ 14,1  SAY 'ONHAND    ' GET MONHAND PICTURE '999'
@ 16,1  SAY 'ONORDER   ' GET MONORDER PICTURE '999'
@ 18,1  SAY 'USAGE     ' GET MUSAGE PICTURE '99'
@ 20,1  SAY 'LEAD      ' GET MLEAD PICTURE '99'
@ 22,10 SAY 'LEAVE PART-NUMBER FIELD BLANK, AND  ctrl-W,  TO EXIT.'
@ 23,1  SAY MWARN
```

Notice the introduction of one more memory variable in the format file which will hold a warning message to be displayed, in case the operator enters the wrong key value.

The "calling-program" (PGME.CMD) would be enhanced as follows:

```
SET TALK OFF
ERASE
USE INVNTRY INDEX PARTINDX
```

The use of the index feature has been explained earlier. The actual index file must already have been created prior to the execution of the program.

```
DO WHILE T                          Start an infinite loop . . . .


    STORE '        ' TO MPART
```

222

```
STORE 0 TO MCOST
STORE 0 TO MSELL
STORE 0 TO MONHAND
STORE 0 TO MONORDER
STORE 0 TO MUSAGE
STORE 0 TO MLEAD
STORE ' ' TO MWARN
SET FORMAT TO LAYOUTE
READ
IF MPART = '          '
    SET FORMAT TO
    RETURN
ENDIF
```

The above section of code will initialize all memory variables, bring up the screen, read-in the operate entries, and if the part-number field is blank, return to the primary menu screen.

DO WHILE # > 0

The above instruction is important to understand. We are attempting to repeat a loop for as long as the # function has a value greater than zero; that is, for as long as the duplicates check results in an existing duplicate key-value being found! So if this error persists, the loop will keep on repeating, until the operator enters a unique key value that causes the # function value to be zero, thus ending the loop. Obviously, for as long as the wrong key-value is being input, the program should keep sending up the formatted screen with the warning message in it.

Note that our entry into the loop for the first time is guaranteed, since the USE statement has placed control on record number 1, which ensures that the # function has a value greater than zero.

FIND &MPART

This statement will try and find the PART-NUMBER value the operator has entered.

IF # > 0

This statement determines if there is already a record with the same PART-NUMBER entered by the operator.

```
        STORE 'DUPLICATE KEY !' TO MWARN
        SET FORMAT TO LAYOUTE
        ? CHR(7)                        Ring a bell at the console.
        READ
    ENDIF
ENDDO
```

The previous DO WHILE . . . ENDDO loop will keep on repeating for as long as an invalid PART-NUMBER value is entered by the operator. If an acceptable PART-NUMBER value is entered, the following statements are executed:

```
APPEND BLANK
REPLACE PART WITH MPART;
        COST WITH MCOST;
        SELLPRICE WITH MSELL;
        ONHAND WITH MONHAND;
        ONORDER WITH MONORDER;
        USAGE WITH MUSAGE;
        LEAD WITH MLEAD
SET FORMAT TO
ENDDO
```

> **Note:** To have your own SET CARRY ON type of effect for the above program, all you need to do is to have the STORE commands outside of the DO WHILE T loop. If this were done, then the memory variables would not get cleared between records, and you would be automatically carrying on data from one record to the next. Notice, however, that now the operator would have to blank-out the part-number field, in order to exit!

EDITING EXISTING DATA

We can take advantage of format files to generate our own EDIT screens. That is, you could generate a screen layout and supporting program not only to produce the data entry covered earlier, but you could also produce the data edit ability. Now the operator could not only add new records but could also edit existing data either sequentially or at random. The operator could pick and choose the next record of existing data to be edited.

The biggest obvious difference between this requirement and that of the earlier one is that our format file GET statements should now refer to existing field-names from the file in use, and not to memory variables. If the GET statements refer to field-names, then the GET and READ combination will now not only bring up (GET) existing data from the current record on the screen, but will also automatically replace (READ) the data back into the fields of the current record of information.

Now if we don't need memory variables to be able to change existing data, it follows that we will not need the STORE statements that initialize the memory variables, nor the REPLACE commands to replace the field-names of the file with the contents of the memory variables.

Initially, we will proceed to create a format file and calling program to produce the sequential type of edit scenario, where the user can start editing at record #1 and proceed sequentially through the file. Later, we shall enhance the format file and the calling program to produce sequential edit capability with a check of the key-field value changes, to safeguard against duplicates.

We shall then proceed to provide the random edit capability, wherein the user could start editing at a specific record number and be able to specify the next record number to be edited at random. Later, still, we shall enhance this to provide the random edit capability with a check of the key-value changes, to safeguard against duplicates.

We shall also look at editing records at random based on key-values, not record numbers, again without/with the duplicates check, and finally look at deleting records at random, via key-values, and at scanning records at random, via key values. In other words, we have our work cut out for us, in the next few pages.

PROGRAM F

This program contains a format file and calling program for editing existing records sequentially. Let us build the format file first. Either make a copy of the previous format file, for quick changes (as explained for Program E), or start with the command, .MODI COMM   LAYOUTF.FMT, as usual.

```
@ 3,10  SAY 'INVENTORY DATA-EDIT SCREEN'
@ 4,10  SAY '-------------------------'.
@ 5,10  SAY 'EDIT RECORDS SEQUENTIALLY, NO CHANGES TO KEY-FIELD'

@ 08,1  SAY 'PARTNUM  '
@ 08,9  SAY PART USING   'XXXXXX'
@ 10,1  SAY 'COST     ' GET COST PICTURE '99999.99'
@ 12,1  SAY 'SELLPRICE' GET SELLPRICE PICTURE '99999.99'
@ 14,1  SAY 'ONHAND   ' GET ONHAND PICTURE '999'
@ 16,1  SAY 'ONORDER  ' GET ONORDER PICTURE '999'
@ 18,1  SAY 'USAGE    ' GET USAGE PICTURE '99'
@ 20,1  SAY 'LEAD     ' GET LEAD PICTURE '99'
@ 23,1  SAY 'MORE (Y/N) ?'  GET MMORE PICTURE 'X'
@ 23,30 SAY MLAST
```

Notice that now, in the GET commands, we are referring to field-names from the file in use and not to memory variables. Notice also, that since this program does not check for duplicate key entry, the format file does not permit any kind of changes to the PART-NUMBER field. If, for any field, you want to ensure that the cursor skips that field during the time of data-entry by the operator, in effect ensuring no changes in that field, you must not provide any GET clauses for the field in the format-file definition. Only SAY clauses should be provided for such fields. Notice the SAY parameter for the PART field! During screen functions, the cursor will come to rest in the COST field as the first GET field eligible for changes!

Let us now build another command file, which will call the format file. This file will be called PGMF.CMD. If you remember, the menu program passes control to PGMF in case the operator wants to select this EDIT option in the menu.

```
SET TALK OFF
ERASE
STORE ' ' TO MMORE
USE INVNTRY   [INDEX .....]
GO BOTT
STORE # TO LASTREC              Keeps track of the last record number in the file.
```

```
GO TOP
DO WHILE T
   IF !(MMORE) = 'N'
      SET FORMAT TO
      RETURN
   ENDIF
   IF # = LASTREC
```
If the current record we are on happens to be the last record number in our Master file . . .

```
      STORE 'LAST REC.!' TO MLAST
ELSE
      STORE ' ' TO MLAST
ENDIF
```

SET FORMAT TO LAYOUTF

This command activates the format file. Now the operator will see all the outputs of the SAY commands exactly as had been specified in the format file called LAYOUTF. That is, the literals and the data from the field-names of the current record will appear on the screen.

READ

This statement will read the operator inputs (the changes made, if any, by the operator) into the corresponding field-names as defined in the format file. During execution, the READ command causes the cursor to skip from one field to the next, as the operator keys-in the required changes, and the changed data is saved directly in the appropriate field-names of the current record as defined in the format file! Cursor controls are identical to those studied for the EDIT mode. After the last field is entered, the program control takes off to execute the next instruction. If you want program control to take off with the next instruction without having to enter all the fields, enter Ctrl-W.

SET FORMAT TO

SKIP Pass control to the next record. If the file was indexed, the next record will obviously appear in the order as defined by the index.

ENDDO

AN IMPORTANT CAUTION WHEN EDITING DATA IN AN INDEXED FILE

What we are about to discuss will not apply to the programs in this book but could very easily apply in other real-world situations. When dBASE deals with an indexed file, the SKIP command normally passes control to the very next record as ordained by the index. This, of course, is quite logical, normal and expected. However, there is a situation in which the SKIP command does not pass control to the very next record as defined in the index.

Let us suppose we have a Master file which contains, out of necessity, several records with the same key-field value. For example, in a PERSONNEL-FILE type of situation, if you have created an index on the ORGANIZATION field, you can obviously expect several duplicates, since there will always be more than just one record with the same organization. In this situation where you have duplicate keys, if you make no change at all, in any field of any record, and you are merely using the index to scan records in the order of the index, then the SKIP command will take you correctly through the index, from one record to the next, as defined in the index.

However—and this is the crux of the matter—if you make a change to any non-key field of a record, then dBASE makes a slight repositioning of the record in the index, and so the SKIP command does not provide you with the very next record, as you may have expected. For example, let us say we have the following 4 records in our indexed PERSNL file:

RECORD NUMBER	KEY-FIELD (ORG)	OTHER-FIELDS
000001	BSG	----- ----- ----- -----
000002	BSG	----- ----- ----- -----
000003	BSG	----- ----- ----- -----
000004	GSD	----- ----- ----- -----

Suppose you change any non-key field value, in record #1. As soon as the change is sensed, dBASE logically repositions the record after the last record that has the same key-value as the changed record. In our example, if record #1 has been changed in any non-key field, then this record is now repositioned after record #3, and hence the next record is record #4 and not record #2, as you may have expected.

If a key-field value had actually been altered, the record would have had to be reflected in a different location as per the index. In this example, the key-field in record #1, has not changed, and therefore the record cannot be totally repositioned too far off the BSG value in the key-field, and hence is repositioned after the last record that has the same key-field value.

In many situations, of course, this is unacceptable, since you would like to be able to SKIP sequentially through an indexed file which has duplicate keys and make changes to non-key-field values without having to omit any records along the way. To get the correct effect, when you provide the READ command, make sure the command specifies the following:

READ   NOUPDATE

The NOUPDATE parameter informs dBASE that the key-value has not been altered, and the current record should be left exactly where it had been found in the index. This parameter ensures that the SKIP command will, indeed, find the very next record as had been defined in the index.

In some situations, you may be altering the contents of a non-key field by replacing it with the contents of a memory variable. For example: REPLACE SALARY WITH MSAL. In this case, too, since a non-key-field value has been changed, you should take the caution of specifying:

.REPLACE <u>NOUPDATE</u> **SALARY WITH MSAL**

The NOUPDATE parameter plays the same role here, as outlined before.

This situation does not apply to the programs under discussion in this book, since we have made the presumption that an inventory file cannot (and definitely should not) have any records with duplicate part-number values in the PART key-field.

NOUPDATE says "don't update the index file". Obviously, this should be used only where you have duplicate keys in records that have to be accessed sequentially, and the keys are not to be altered! If keys have to be altered, you definitely want the index updated, so don't use this option. You realize, of course, that misuse of this option will result in the index not being updated, causing your data and index to be out of sync with each other.

PROGRAM G

Program G contains a format file and calling program for editing existing records sequentially and allowing changes to key-fields with a duplicates check.

Such programs, which allow the operator to make changes to key-values in Master files, are always tricky, to say the least. Let us understand what could possibly happen if we were to allow key-values to be changed.

> **Note:** Our format files will refer to the actual field-names from the record, and not to any memory variables. This has been fully explored, in previous sections. The program will, of course, have to use the indexed version of the Master file, for checking for duplicates.

Let us say that, upon initiation, the program will send up the formatted screen containing data from the first record of the indexed file. The operator makes changes to the data, and also, unfortunately, decides to change the key-field value! As soon as the SET FORMAT TO LAYOUTG and the READ commands have been executed, the first record has already been updated, and in effect, now, since the key-value was changed, the record is reflected in a different location, as per the index! Even if the new key-value was the duplicate of another key, the SET FORMAT TO LAYOUTG and the READ combination has already repositioned the new record after the existing record with the same key. Somehow, the program must be made to start with the first (indexed) record; keep a pointer to that current record; accept the changes to data and key-values; check the key for duplicates through the FIND command; reposition the new record if a valid key has been entered; flag an error if a duplicate key has been entered; and yet retain its position on the current record, and so on, and so on. In other words, we are going to be looking at a *slightly complicated* program. Nothing will be introduced here that we have not already covered, and liberal comments will be thrown in for your understanding. Programs that allow key-values to be changed are always a challenge.

> **Note:** Programming is an art, not a science, and the solutions provided here are by no means the only possible solutions to the problem.

Your best bet, of course, would be not to allow any changes to the key-field values by changing your format file slightly. If, for any field, you want to ensure that the cursor skips that field during the time of data-entry by the operator, in effect ensuring no changes in that field, you must not provide any GET clauses for the field in the format-file definition. Only SAY clauses should be provided for such fields.

In many situations, of course, it is imperative that access be provided to changing key-field values, and so we will not take the easy way out. Begin with the format file as usual: [LAYOUTG.FMT].

```
@ 3,10 SAY 'INVENTORY DATA-EDIT SCREEN'
@ 4,10 SAY '--------------------------'
@ 5,10 SAY 'EDIT SEQ., WITH DUP-CHECK'

@ 08,1 SAY 'PARTNUM  ' GET MPART PICTURE 'XXXXXX'
@ 10,1 SAY 'COST     ' GET COST PICTURE '99999.99'
@ 12,1 SAY 'SELLPRICE' GET SELLPRICE PICTURE '99999.99'
@ 14,1 SAY 'ONHAND   ' GET ONHAND PICTURE '999'
@ 16,1 SAY 'ONORDER  ' GET ONORDER PICTURE '999'
@ 18,1 SAY 'USAGE    ' GET USAGE PICTURE '99'
@ 20,1 SAY 'LEAD     ' GET LEAD PICTURE '99'
@ 23,1 SAY 'MORE (Y/N) ?'  GET MMORE PICTURE 'X'
@ 23,30 SAY MLAST PICTURE ' '
@ 23,60 SAY MWARN
```

Note: The biggest change is in the fact that the operator entry for the key-field will go into a memory variable and will not directly update the key-field of the current record. This is done since the operator entry for the key-value needs to be edited first for uniqueness before acceptance in the Master file.

The calling program for this purpose [PGMG.CMD] is as follows:

```
SET TALK OFF
ERASE
USE INVNTRY INDEX PARTINDX
GO BOTT
STORE # TO LASTREC                Keep track of the last record.
STORE ' ' TO MMORE
GO TOP
DO WHILE T                        Set pointer to first indexed record
   IF !(MMORE) = 'N'              Start an infinite loop . . .
      SET FORMAT TO
      RETURN
   ENDIF

   IF # = LASTREC                 If current record is last . .
      STORE 'LAST REC.!' TO MLAST
   ELSE
      STORE ' ' TO MLAST
   ENDIF
```

```
STORE ' ' TO MMORE
STORE '        ' TO MPART
STORE ' ' TO MWARN
STORE STR(#,6) TO CURRENT
```

Note the last instruction! We are storing the value in which is in the record pointer into a memory variable called CURRENT. That is, we want to keep track of our CURRENT position in the Master file. Since we want the memory variable called CURRENT to be a character memory variable (reason outlined later), we store the string value of the # function, to CURRENT.

STORE PART TO MPART

This statement stores the current record's PART-NUMBER into MPART.

SET FORMAT TO LAYOUTG

READ

Any changes to the PART-NUMBER would have gone directly into the memory variable called MPART.

DO WHILE MPART # PART .AND. MPART # '   '

If the operator had indeed changed the PART-NUMBER field, enter the loop.

FIND &MPART

```
IF # > 0
   STORE 'DUPLICATE KEY!' TO MWARN
   ? CHR(7)
   &CURRENT
```

We need to move the record pointer back to our current record, since in the attempt to FIND a record, the record pointer has moved all over the file. Hence the use of the macro &CURRENT. If you recall, all macros have to be defined as character memory variables and hence the use of the string function, when we first defined the memory variable called CURRENT.

```
   SET FORMAT TO LAYOUTG
   READ
```

ELSE

At this point, the key entry made by the operator was a unique value.

&CURRENT

Backup to our current record. See the previous explanation.

230

```
REPLACE PART WITH MPART
STORE '        ' TO MPART
```

This instruction is required to break out of the loop. If MPART = '   ', the loop ends, as per the definition of the DO WHILE statement.

```
   ENDIF

   ENDDO

   SET FORMAT TO

   SKIP
```
Passes control to the next record as defined by the index. However, since the new key entry was valid, the record has been repositioned as per the logical order of the index! Hence, the next record is now the one as defined by the new position in the index.

```
   ENDDO
```

PROGRAM H

Program H contains a format file and calling program for editing existing records randomly according to record number. This program does not allow changes to key-field values. Begin with the format-file as usual: [LAYOUTH.FMT].

```
@ 3,10   SAY 'INVENTORY DATA-EDIT SCREEN'
@ 4,10   SAY '-------------------------'
@ 5,10   SAY 'RANDOM EDIT, ON RECORD NUMBERS'
@ 6,10   SAY 'NO CHANGES TO KEY-FIELD !'
@ 8,1    SAY 'CURRENT RECORD'
@ 8,16   SAY MCURR

@ 09,1   SAY 'PARTNUM'
@ 09,9   SAY PART USING 'XXXXXX'
@ 10,1   SAY 'COST     ' GET COST PICTURE '99999.99'
@ 11,1   SAY 'SELLPRICE' GET SELLPRICE PICTURE '99999.99'
@ 12,1   SAY 'ONHAND   ' GET ONHAND PICTURE '999'
@ 13,1   SAY 'ONORDER  ' GET ONORDER PICTURE '999'
@ 14,1   SAY 'USAGE    ' GET USAGE PICTURE '99'
@ 15,1   SAY 'LEAD     ' GET LEAD PICTURE '99'
@ 16,1   SAY 'NEXT RECORD-NUMBER ?' GET MNEXT PICTURE 'XXXXXX'
@ 16,50  SAY '(LEAVE BLANK, TO EXIT)'
@ 20,1   SAY MWARN1
@ 21,1   SAY MWARN2
```

Our calling-program (PGMH.CMD) will look something like this:

```
SET TALK OFF
STORE '        ' TO MCURR
USE INVNTRY
STORE 'BAD' TO RECNUM

DO WHILE RECNUM = 'BAD'
   ERASE

   ? "RECORD-NUMBER TO START EDITING ON ?       (LEAVE BLANK, TO EXIT)"
   ACCEPT TO MNEXT

   IF VAL(MNEXT) = 0
      RETURN
   ENDIF
```

If the numerical value provided by the memory variable called MNEXT = zero, i.e., if the operator enters alphas in response to the question, then we want to return to the menu screen.

```
IF ' ' $(MNEXT)
   LOOP
ENDIF
```

If there is a blank anywhere in the MNEXT variable, i.e., if the operator makes an entry like 2 5 instead of 25, then the LOOP command will cause control to be transferred back to the DO WHILE statement. In effect, the question: RECORD NUMBER TO START EDITING ON ? will appear on the screen again.

If a valid starting number has been provided then the following occurs:

```
GO BOTT
STORE # TO TOTRECS
IF VAL(MNEXT) > TOTRECS
```

This sequence checks if the valid start number is more than the number of records in the Master file.

```
      ? CHR(7)
      @ 5,15 SAY 'RECORD OUT OF RANGE.'
      @ 6,15 SAY 'YOU ONLY HAVE' + STR(#,6) + '    ' + 'RECORDS IN YOUR FILE'
      WAIT
      LOOP
   ELSE
      STORE 'GOOD' TO RECNUM
   ENDIF
ENDDO
```

At this point, we have a good start number which falls within the range of records in our file.

```
DO WHILE T
   STORE ' ' TO MWARN1
   STORE ' ' TO MWARN2

   IF MNEXT = '        '
      SET FORMAT TO
```

232

```
     RETURN
ENDIF

   ERASE
   IF VAL(MNEXT) > TOTRECS
      STORE 'RECORD OUT OF RANGE' TO MWARN1
      STORE 'YOU ONLY HAVE'+STR(TOTRECS,6)+'   '+'RECORDS IN YOUR FILE';
            TO MWARN2
      ? CHR(7)
      SET FORMAT TO LAYOUTH
      READ
      SET FORMAT TO
      LOOP
   ENDIF
```

The first time through, control will pass to this point since we had started with a good record within the range of the Master file. Subsequent outcomes will depend on the next record number requested by the operator.

```
      &MNEXT                       --------------------(A)
      STORE MNEXT TO MCURR
      STORE '       ' TO MNEXT
      SET FORMAT TO LAYOUTH
      READ
      SET FORMAT TO
ENDDO
```

When the program starts executing, the operator will respond to the question posed by the ACCEPT command, and the required starting record number will enter the memory variable called MNEXT. The program makes a check of the start number to ensure its validity. The &MNEXT at point (A) is a macro. Since this macro is in the position where a command is usually entered, dBASE will interpret that record number as a command, and in effect, during execution, the record pointer will be positioned at the number specified in the MNEXT memory variable!

When the LAYOUTH file is activated, since the GET commands in the LAYOUTH file refer to field-names, the appropriate contents of the field-names from that current record will be brought to the screen. The operator will then make any changes, if required. The operator will also specify the next record number to be edited. The READ command will change the existing data in the appropriate fields of the current record directly, and the operator's response for the next record enters the memory variable called MNEXT.

When the program loops back to the DO WHILE statement, the program checks the contents of the MNEXT variable to ensure a record number within the range of the records in the file, and then the &MNEXT statement will again be interpreted as a command, a new position is taken up in the data-base, and the cycle of events will be repeated. In this way, you can proceed from record to record, editing at random.

PROGRAM I

This program contains a format file and calling program for editing existing records randomly by record number. It includes a duplicate check. Begin with the format file as usual: [LAYOUTI.FMT].

```
@ 3,10    SAY 'INVENTORY DATA-EDIT SCREEN'
@ 4,10    SAY '----------------------------'
@ 5,10    SAY 'RANDOM EDIT ON RECORD NUMBERS, WITH DUP-CHECK'
@ 7,1     SAY 'CURRENT RECORD'
@ 7,16    SAY MCURR
@ 08,1    SAY 'PARTNUM  ' GET MPART PICTURE 'XXXXXX'
@ 10,1    SAY 'COST     ' GET COST PICTURE '99999.99'
@ 11,1    SAY 'SELLPRICE' GET SELLPRICE PICTURE '99999.99'
@ 12,1    SAY 'ONHAND   ' GET ONHAND PICTURE '999'
@ 13,1    SAY 'ONORDER  ' GET ONORDER PICTURE '999'
@ 14,1    SAY 'USAGE    ' GET USAGE PICTURE '99'
@ 15,1    SAY 'LEAD     ' GET LEAD PICTURE '99'
@ 16,1    SAY 'NEXT RECORD-NUMBER ?'  GET MNEXT PICTURE 'XXXXXX'
@ 16,50   SAY '(LEAVE BLANK, TO EXIT)'
@ 20,1    SAY MWARN1
@ 21,1    SAY MWARN2
```

Our calling program (PGMI.CMD) will look something like this:

```
SET TALK OFF
STORE '          ' TO MCURR
USE INVNTRY INDEX PARTINDX
STORE 'BAD' TO RECNUM

DO WHILE RECNUM = 'BAD'

    ERASE
    ? 'RECORD NUMBER TO START EDITING ON ?          (LEAVE BLANK, TO EXIT)'
    ACCEPT TO MNEXT

    IF VAL(MNEXT) = 0
       RETURN
    ENDIF

    IF ' ' $(MNEXT)
       LOOP
    ENDIF
    GO BOTT
    STORE # TO TOTRECS
    IF VAL(MNEXT) > TOTRECS
        ? CHR(7)
        @ 5,15 SAY 'RECORD OUT OF RANGE.'
        @ 6,15 SAY 'YOU ONLY HAVE' + STR(#,6) + '    ' + 'RECORDS IN YOUR FILE'
        WAIT
        LOOP
    ELSE
        STORE 'GOOD' TO RECNUM
    ENDIF
ENDDO
```

At this point, we have a good starting record number.

```
DO WHILE T
    STORE '        ' TO MPART
    STORE ' ' TO MWARN1
    STORE ' ' TO MWARN2
  IF MNEXT = '        '
     SET FORMAT TO
     RETURN
  ENDIF
```

The first time through, control will reach this point, since we had a good start number within the range of records in the Master file.

```
&MNEXT
STORE MNEXT TO MCURR
STORE '        ' TO MNEXT
STORE PART TO MPART          Save the part-number out of the current rec-
                             ord.
SET FORMAT TO LAYOUTI
READ

DO WHILE MPART#PART .OR. VAL(MNEXT) > TOTRECS
```

This DO loop is entered if either the part number was changed, or the next record requested is outside of the range of records in the Master file.

```
STORE ' ' TO MWARN1
STORE ' ' TO MWARN2
IF MPART # PART
```

If it was the part number that had been changed then the following sequence occurs:

```
    FIND &MPART
    IF # > 0
       STORE 'DUPLICATE KEY!' TO MWARN1
       &MCURR
       ? CHR(7)
       SET FORMAT TO LAYOUTI
       READ
       LOOP
    ELSE
       &MCURR
       REPLACE PART WITH MPART
       LOOP
    ENDIF
ENDIF
```

ELSE it is the next record number as requested by the operator, that is out of range.

```
      &MCURR
      STORE PART TO MPART
      STORE 'RECORD OUT OF RANGE' TO MWARN1
      STORE 'YOU ONLY HAVE'+STR(TOTRECS,6)+'    '+'RECORDS IN YOUR FILE';
            TO MWARN2
      ? CHR(7)
      SET FORMAT TO LAYOUTI
      READ
      LOOP
   ENDDO
ENDDO
```

PROGRAM J

Program J contains a format file and calling program for editing existing records randomly via key-field. No changes can be made to the key-field. Begin with the format file as before: [LAYOUTJ.FMT].

```
@ 1,20   SAY 'INVENTORY DATA-EDIT SCREEN'
@ 2,20   SAY '--------------------------'
@ 4,20   SAY 'Random processing on key-field values'
@ 7,1    SAY 'CURRENT RECORD-KEY'
@ 7,20   SAY MCURR

@ 08,1   SAY 'PARTNUM'
@ 08,9   SAY MPART USING 'XXXXXX'

@ 10,1   SAY 'COST     ' GET COST PICTURE '99999.99'
@ 12,1   SAY 'SELLPRICE' GET SELLPRICE PICTURE '99999.99'
@ 14,1   SAY 'ONHAND   ' GET ONHAND PICTURE '999'
@ 16,1   SAY 'ONORDER  ' GET ONORDER PICTURE '999'
@ 18,1   SAY 'USAGE    ' GET USAGE PICTURE '99'
@ 20,1   SAY 'LEAD     ' GET LEAD PICTURE '99'
@ 21,10  SAY MWARN1
@ 23,1   SAY 'NEXT FULL-KEY ?'  GET MNEXT PICTURE 'XXXXXX'
@ 23,50  SAY 'LEAVE BLANK, TO EXIT'
```

No changes are expected to be made to the key-field value. Our calling program (PGMJ.CMD) will look something like this:

```
SET TALK OFF
STORE '      ' TO MCURR
STORE '      ' TO MNEXT
USE INVNTRY INDEX PARTINDX
STORE 'BAD' TO RECKEY

DO WHILE RECKEY = 'BAD'

   ERASE
   ? 'WHICH RECORD-KEY TO START EDITING ON ?    GENERIC-KEY, O.K.'
```

236

```
?
? 'LEAVE BLANK, TO EXIT'
?
ACCEPT TO MNEXT

IF VAL(MNEXT) = 0
   RETURN
ENDIF

IF ' ' $(MNEXT)
   LOOP
ENDIF


FIND &MNEXT
IF # = 0
   @ 10,10 SAY 'NO SUCH RECORD-KEY.  RE-ENTER FULL/GENERIC KEY'
   ? CHR(7)
   WAIT
   LOOP
ELSE
   STORE 'GOOD' TO RECKEY
   STORE STR(#,6) TO CURRENT
   STORE PART TO MNEXT
ENDIF
ENDDO
```

At this point, we have entered a good starting key-value, and the record number of that starting record has been saved into a memory variable called current.

```
DO WHILE T

   IF MNEXT = '          '
      SET FORMAT TO
      RETURN
   ENDIF

   STORE ' ' TO MWARN1

   FIND &MNEXT
   IF # = 0
      STORE 'NO SUCH RECORD KEY !  RE-ENTER FULL KEY, OR LEAVE BLANK TO EXIT';
            TO MWARN1
      &CURRENT
      STORE PART TO MCURR
      STORE PART TO MPART
      ? CHR(7)
      SET FORMAT TO LAYOUTJ
      READ
      SET FORMAT TO
   ELSE
```

The first time through, since a good start key had been found, program control will come here.

237

```
        STORE '       ' TO MNEXT
        STORE PART TO MCURR
        STORE PART TO MPART
        STORE STR(#,6) TO CURRENT
        SET FORMAT TO LAYOUTJ
        READ
    ENDIF
ENDDO
```

PROGRAM K

Program K contains a format file and calling program for editing existing records randomly on the key-field value. It includes a duplicates check. Begin with the format file as before: [LAYOUTK.FMT].

```
@ 3,10   SAY 'INVENTORY DATA-EDIT SCREEN'
@ 4,10   SAY '---------------------------'
@ 5,10   SAY 'RANDOM EDIT ON KEY-FIELD, WITH DUP-CHECK'
@ 6,1    SAY 'CURRENT RECORD-KEY'
@ 6,20   SAY MCURR

@ 08,1   SAY 'PARTNUM  ' GET MPART PICTURE 'XXXXXX'
@ 10,1   SAY 'COST     ' GET COST PICTURE '99999.99'
@ 11,1   SAY 'SELLPRICE' GET SELLPRICE PICTURE '99999.99'
@ 12,1   SAY 'ONHAND   ' GET ONHAND PICTURE '999'
@ 13,1   SAY 'ONORDER  ' GET ONORDER PICTURE '999'
@ 14,1   SAY 'USAGE    ' GET USAGE PICTURE '99'
@ 15,1   SAY 'LEAD     ' GET LEAD PICTURE '99'
@ 16,1   SAY 'NEXT FULL-KEY ?' GET MNEXT PICTURE 'XXXXXX'
@ 16,50  SAY '(LEAVE BLANK TO EXIT.)'
@ 20,1   SAY MWARN1
@ 21,1   SAY MWARN2
```

Our calling program (PGMK.CMD) will look something like this:

```
SET TALK OFF
STORE '       ' TO MCURR
USE INVNTRY INDEX PARTINDX
STORE 'BAD' TO RECKEY

DO WHILE RECKEY = 'BAD'

    ERASE
    ? 'WHICH RECORD-KEY TO START EDITING ON ?    GENERIC-KEY, O.K.'
    ?
    ? 'LEAVE BLANK, TO EXIT'
    ?
    ACCEPT TO MNEXT
```

238

```
       IF VAL(MNEXT) = 0
          RETURN
       ENDIF
       IF ' ' $(MNEXT)
          LOOP
       ENDIF

       FIND &MNEXT
       IF # = 0
          @ 10,10 SAY 'NO SUCH RECORD-KEY.  RE-ENTER FULL/GENERIC KEY'
          ? CHR(7)
          WAIT
          LOOP
       ELSE
          STORE 'GOOD' TO RECKEY
       ENDIF
   ENDDO
```

At this stage, we have entered a valid start-record key.

```
DO WHILE T
   STORE '          ' TO MPART
   STORE ' ' TO MWARN1
   STORE ' ' TO MWARN2

   IF MNEXT = '          '
      SET FORMAT TO
      RETURN
   ENDIF


   FIND &MNEXT
   IF # = 0
      STORE 'NO SUCH RECORD KEY !  RE-ENTER FULL KEY, OR LEAVE BLANK TO EXIT';
          TO MWARN1
      &CURRENT
      STORE PART TO MPART
      ? CHR(7)
      SET FORMAT TO LAYOUTK
      READ
      LOOP
   ELSE
```

The first time through, control comes here, since we had ensured a good start key-value.

```
      STORE STR(#,6) TO CURRENT
   ENDIF



   &CURRENT
   STORE PART   TO MCURR
   STORE '          ' TO MNEXT
```

```
STORE PART TO MPART
SET FORMAT TO LAYOUTK
READ

DO WHILE MPART#PART
    FIND &MPART
    IF # > 0
        STORE 'DUPLICATE KEY!' TO MWARN1
        &CURRENT
        ? CHR(7)
        SET FORMAT TO LAYOUTK
        READ
        LOOP
    ELSE
```

The changed key-value is also a unique value.

```
        &CURRENT
        REPLACE PART WITH MPART
    ENDIF
ENDDO
ENDDO
```

PROGRAM L

Program L contains a format file and calling program for deleting existing records randomly on the key-field value. Begin with the format file, as usual: [LAYOUTL.FMT].

```
@ 3,10  SAY 'INVENTORY DATA-EDIT SCREEN'
@ 4,10  SAY '---------------------------'
@ 5,10  SAY 'DELETE RECORDS RANDOMLY, ON KEY-FIELD'
@ 10,5  SAY 'PARTNUM'
@ 10,25 SAY PART USING    'XXXXXX'
@ 12,5  SAY 'COST'
@ 12,25 SAY COST USING    '99999.99'
@ 14,5  SAY 'SELLPRICE'
@ 14,25 SAY SELLPRICE USING   '99999.99'
@ 16,5  SAY 'ONHAND'
@ 16,25 SAY ONHAND USING   '999'
@ 18,5  SAY 'ONORDER'
@ 18,25 SAY ONORDER USING   '999'
@ 20,5  SAY 'USAGE'
@ 20,25 SAY USAGE USING    '999'
@ 21,5  SAY 'LEAD'
@ 21,25 SAY LEAD USING    '999'
@ 22,5  SAY 'DELETE (Y/N) ?'  GET MANSWER PICTURE 'X'
@ 22,50 SAY 'NEXT RECORD-KEY ?' GET MNEXT PICTURE 'XXXXXX'
```

```
@ 23,6   SAY MWARN1
@ 23,50 SAY 'LEAVE BLANK, TO EXIT'
```

All the fields will appear on the screen. However, there will be no updating taking place, since we have only SAY commands in our format file layout. The cursor will stop in the field that asks for a confirmation of the delete, for the current record.

Notice also, that this time our mask for the USAGE and LEAD fields contains '999' instead of just '99' (both fields are defined as 2-digits each). This has been done only to line-up the numeric variables which will always be right justified on the screen, again, for visual aid reasons. If you remember, the mask must be at least as long as the data coming in, and could always be longer.

Our calling program (PGML.CMD) will look something like this:

```
SET TALK OFF
USE INVNTRY INDEX PARTINDX
STORE 'BAD' TO RECKEY

DO WHILE RECKEY = 'BAD'

    ERASE
    ? 'WHICH RECORD-KEY TO START DELETING ON ?     GENERIC-KEY, O.K.'
    ?
    ? 'LEAVE BLANK, TO EXIT'
    ?
    ACCEPT TO MNEXT

    IF VAL(MNEXT) = 0.
        RETURN
    ENDIF

    IF ' ' $(MNEXT)
        LOOP
    ENDIF

    FIND &MNEXT
    IF # = 0
        @ 10,10 SAY 'NO SUCH RECORD-KEY.   RE-ENTER FULL/GENERIC KEY'
        ? CHR(7)
        WAIT
        LOOP
    ELSE
        STORE 'GOOD' TO RECKEY
    ENDIF
ENDDO
```

We start off with a good valid record-key.

```
        STORE ' ' TO DELETE:FLG
        DO WHILE T

            IF MNEXT = '        '
```

241

At the end of all the delete operations use the following:

```
SET FORMAT TO
ERASE
IF DELETE:FLG = '*'
```

It implies that there has been at least one record deleted.

```
    STORE ' ' TO MANSWER
    @ 5,10 SAY 'DO YOU WANT THE FILE PACKED ?  (Y/N)' GET MANSWER
    READ
    IF MANSWER = 'Y'
        @ 10,10 SAY 'PACK OPERATION IN PROGRESS ! DO NOT INTERRUPT !'
        PACK
    ELSE
        @ 10,10 SAY 'RECORDS DELETED, FILE NOT PACKED !'
    ENDIF
    WAIT
  ENDIF
  RETURN
ENDIF
```

If another key-value has been supplied then the following code is used.

```
STORE ' '  TO MWARN1
STORE ' ' TO MANSWER
FIND &MNEXT
IF # = 0
   STORE 'NO SUCH RECORD KEY !  RE-ENTER FULL KEY, OR LEAVE BLANK TO EXIT';
        TO MWARN1
   &CURRENT
   ? CHR(7)
   SET FORMAT TO LAYOUTL
   READ
   LOOP
ELSE
```

The record-key entered is that of a valid record, and so we will save the current record number; go to the current record; display the formatted record on the screen; and delete the record, if so requested.

```
    STORE STR(#,6) TO CURRENT
```

```
ENDIF
```

```
    &CURRENT
    STORE '         ' TO MNEXT
    SET FORMAT TO LAYOUTL
    READ

    IF MANSWER = 'Y'
```

```
        DELETE
        STORE '*' TO DELETE:FLG
     ENDIF
  ENDDO
```

PROGRAM M

Program M contains a format file and calling program for scanning existing records sequentially. The format-file looks like this [LAYOUTM.FMT]:

```
@ 3,10   SAY 'INVENTORY DATA-EDIT SCREEN'
@ 4,10   SAY '----------------------------'
@ 5,10   SAY 'SCAN RECORDS SEQUENTIALLY'
@ 7,5    SAY 'CURRENT REC-NUMBER'
@ 7,25   SAY MCURR
@ 9,50   SAY 'PROCEED ?  (Y/N)'  GET  MPROCEED PICTURE 'X'
@ 10,5   SAY 'PARTNUM'
@ 10,25  SAY PART USING 'XXXXXX'
@ 12,5   SAY 'COST'
@ 12,25  SAY COST USING '99999.99'
@ 14,5   SAY 'SELLPRICE'
@ 14,25  SAY SELLPRICE USING '99999.99'
@ 16,5   SAY 'ONHAND'
@ 16,25  SAY ONHAND USING '999'
@ 18,5   SAY 'ONORDER'
@ 18,25  SAY ONORDER USING '999'
@ 20,5   SAY 'USAGE'
@ 20,25  SAY USAGE USING '999'
@ 21,5   SAY 'LEAD'
@ 21,25  SAY LEAD USING '999'
@ 23,1   SAY MWARN1
```

Again, since there is no editing contemplated, we have only SAY parameters for the fields of our file. Note that, again, the USAGE and LEAD items have been provided a slightly longer mask of '999' instead of '99', to line up these numeric, right justified items with the others on the screen.

Our 'calling-program' (PGM.CMD) will look like this:

```
SET TALK OFF
STORE ' ' TO MPROCEED
STORE ' ' TO MWARN1
ERASE
USE INVNTRY
GO BOTT
STORE # TO LASTREC          Save the last record number.
GO TOP
```

243

```
DO WHILE .NOT. EOF
    STORE # TO MCURR        Store the current-record into MCURR.

    IF # = LASTREC
        STORE 'LAST RECORD !' TO MWARN1
    ENDIF
    SET FORMAT TO LAYOUTM
    READ
    IF !(MPROCEED)= 'N'
        SET FORMAT TO
        RETURN
    ENDIF

    SKIP
ENDDO
RETURN
```

PROGRAM N

This program contains a format file and calling program for scanning existing records randomly on the key-field value. Begin with the format file, as usual: [LAYOUTN.FMT].

```
@ 3,10   SAY 'INVENTORY DATA-EDIT SCREEN'
@ 4,10   SAY '---------------------------'
@ 5,10   SAY 'SCAN RECORDS RANDOMLY, ON KEY-FIELD'
@ 7,5    SAY 'CURRENT RECORD-KEY'
@ 7,25   SAY MCURR
@ 09,5   SAY 'PARTNUM'
@ 09,25  SAY PART USING 'XXXXXX'
@ 10,5   SAY 'COST'
@ 10,25  SAY COST USING '99999.99'
@ 11,5   SAY 'SELLPRICE'
@ 11,25  SAY SELLPRICE USING '99999.99'
@ 12,5   SAY 'ONHAND'
@ 12,25  SAY ONHAND USING '999'
@ 13,5   SAY 'ONORDER'
@ 13,25  SAY ONORDER USING '999'
@ 14,5   SAY 'USAGE'
@ 14,25  SAY USAGE USING '999'
@ 15,5   SAY 'LEAD'
@ 15,25  SAY LEAD USING '999'
@ 17,5   SAY MWARN1
@ 20,1   SAY 'NEXT FULL RECORD-KEY ?' GET MNEXT PICTURE 'XXXXXX'
@ 20,50  SAY '(LEAVE BLANK, TO EXIT)'
```

Our calling program (PGMN.CMD) will look like this:

```
SET TALK OFF
STORE '        ' TO MCURR
```

```
USE INVNTRY INDEX PARTINDX
STORE 'BAD' TO RECKEY

DO WHILE RECKEY = 'BAD'

   ERASE
   ? 'WHICH RECORD-KEY TO START EDITING ON ?     GENERIC-KEY, O.K.'
   ?
   ? 'LEAVE BLANK, TO EXIT'
   ?


ACCEPT TO MNEXT

IF VAL(MNEXT) = 0
   RETURN
ENDIF

IF ' ' $(MNEXT)
   LOOP
ENDIF

   FIND &MNEXT
   IF # = 0
  ` @ 10,10 SAY 'NO SUCH RECORD-KEY.   RE-ENTER FULL/GENERIC KEY'
      ? CHR(7)
      WAIT
      LOOP
   ELSE
      STORE 'GOOD' TO RECKEY
   ENDIF
ENDDO          Start off with a good, valid record-key value.

DO WHILE T

   IF MNEXT = '         '
      SET FORMAT TO
      RETURN
   ENDIF


FIND &MNEXT
IF # = 0
   STORE 'NO SUCH RECORD KEY !  RE-ENTER FULL KEY, OR LEAVE BLANK TO EXIT';
        TO MWARN1
   &CURRENT
   STORE PART TO MPART
   ? CHR(7)
   SET FORMAT TO LAYOUTN
   READ
   LOOP
ELSE
   STORE STR(#,6) TO CURRENT
ENDIF
```

Program control will come here for every valid record-key value entered by the operator.

```
      STORE ' ' TO MWARN1
      &CURRENT
      STORE PART  TO MCURR
      STORE '       ' TO MNEXT
      SET FORMAT TO LAYOUTN
      READ
ENDDO
```

PROGRAM O

Program O can be used for removal of duplicate-key records in the event that some duplicates have crept into your Master file. I am providing this program as a utility in case you have been entering new data or editing existing data without regard for duplicate key-values and find yourself with sufficient duplicate records as to make a physical, manual check quite inappropriate.

The following program will scan your indexed file for records that have duplicate values in the key-field, and delete those records, and then pack in your Master file. The first record, of any series of duplicate records, will be presumed to be the correct one, and retained. The others will be deleted. As you can imagine, this is quite a simple program.

```
ERASE
USE INVNTRY INDEX  PARTINDX
STORE PART TO MPART
STORE 0 TO COUNTER
SKIP
DO WHILE  .NOT.  EOF
   IF  PART = MPART
      DELETE
      STORE COUNTER+1  TO COUNTER
   ELSE
      STORE PART TO MPART
   ENDIF
   SKIP
ENDDO
IF COUNTER = 0
   RETURN
ENDIF
PACK
ERASE

@ 10,15 SAY 'NUMBER OF DELETED RECORDS = '
@ 10,50 SAY COUNTER  USING  '99999'
WAIT
RETURN
```

CONCLUDING OBSERVATIONS

You may have noticed that some preceding programs asked for a generic starting-key value, but the same programs wanted subsequent keys provided in full. This is so since, in our programs, the ACCEPT command was used to generate the memory variable containing the starting key, and we know that the variable created with the ACCEPT command is itself variable in length. However, the memory variable used for obtaining the subsequent key values was defined with the STORE command, which defines a fixed-length variable. So a starting key of P12 is good enough to reach part-number P12345, whereas a subsequent entry of P12 would generate the value 'P12 ' as the key, which does not exist.

The previous programs also highlighted the necessary program code to effect changes in the key-field of a record. We did this with the presumption that we did not have any deleted records in our file, since the REPLACE command which is necessary to change values in key-fields has no effect on deleted records! If we use the replace command on the key-field of a deleted record, dBASE goes off into a never-ending loop. This hangs up the system and requires the use of the ESC key to break the loop.

If you do have deleted records in your file, you should proceed as outlined in following shell, before attempting the REPLACE:

```
-----
-----
-----
IF   (KEY-HAS-TO-BE-CHANGED)
      IF .NOT.*
          REPLACE       ..............
      ELSE
           RECALL
           REPLACE       ..............
           DELETE
      ENDIF
ENDIF
-----
-----
-----
```

The record would first have to be activated before attempting the REPLACE command.

SUMMARY

To emphasize a point made before, the previous menu system was an overkill, for the purposes of learning some of the various options available. One obviously needs to pick and choose those options most suited to a particular application.

As you can see from the preceding few pages, writing a menu system comprises several steps.

1. Writing the menu program itself.
2. Writing the subprograms that the menu transfers control to.

3. Writing the screen formats that the subprograms may refer to.
4. Writing the report formats that the subprograms may refer to.

You can build the format file right into the calling program. However, creating a separate format file leaves your program less cluttered, especially when the screen format needs to be invoked several times in a program. You also have the advantage of making changes to your format file without having to edit and save your entire program if you create a separate file.

You can, of course, come up with any number of functions for a menu system. Only the very real factors of time and system requirements will be the constraints restricting you from giving full rein to your imagination. Programming is an art, not a science, and you should feel free to invert your own routines for doing exotic things with your computer and with dBASE.

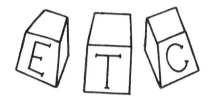

11. Additional Tips and Techniques

I n this chapter, I will explain several programming concepts that you may find useful. these concepts can be used in any number of useful ways in your programming tasks. Study them carefully so that you understand the reasoning behind their use. They can make a hard to program task very simple.

COMBINING MULTIPLE FILES

When we studied the DISPLAY and the REPORT feature of dBASE, we learned how we could obtain a display or a report from two data-bases, by designating our files as primary and secondary. We can use a similar setup, along with our knowledge of programming, to extend this ability to combine multiple files and produce reports or other files.

When we specify primary and secondary files to dBASE, it maintains separate and distinct current record pointers for each data-base. By using the SELECT PRIM or SELECT SECO statements, we can switch back and forth between data-bases, each time picking up where we left off in that data-base.

Our scenario is as follows: suppose you have an Inventory Master file, with TPART:NUM as the key-field. Let us suppose there are two other Master files which have, among other fields, a PART:NUM key-field, so you can tie one Master file to any of the others. Obviously, each Master file has some pieces of information not found in any of the others. It is our task to combine a Master file record with its various counterparts to produce another file having in its structure all the fields we would like to see together. Our presumption is that all the files are indexed on their key-fields.

"Master-1" file structure: PART-NUM UNIT:COST DESC
"Master-2" file structure: PART:NUM CGC
"Master-3" file structure: PART:NUM ONHAND
"OUTPUT"   file structure: PART:NUM UNIT:COST DESC CGC ONHAND

We shall proceed as follows: starting with "Master-1" as primary, we store PART:NUM, UNIT:COST and DESC items into memory variables. Now, we designate, "Master-2" as secondary, and try and find a secondary record with the same PART:NUM key as obtained in the primary record. If successful, we store the CGC field of that record into a memory variable. Now we redesignate Master-3 as the new secondary, and repeat the find command. If successful, we store the ONHAND field from that record into a memory variable.

Having obtained all the items we want for any one PART:NUM into the memory variables (which, of course, may still be blank), we now designate our Output file as the secondary file and proceed with the APPEND BLANK command to create a new record of data, the details of which we have covered before.

The program has been provided here.

```
SET TALK OFF
ERASE
@ 10,15 SAY "Program has commenced linking the files."
@ 11,15 SAY "Do not interrupt !!"
SELE PRIM
USE F1 INDEX P1INDX
```

> **Note:** This file F1 does not necessarily have to be indexed. If file F1 is indexed, the output-file records will be created in the indexed order of file F1. However, the other (secondary) files will have to be indexed, since we will be using the FIND command against these files.

```
DO WHILE .NOT. EOF
    STORE PART:NUM TO MPARTNUM
    STORE UNIT:COST TO MUNIT
    STORE DESC TO MDESC

    STORE ' ' TO MCGC
    STORE ' ' TO MONHAND
    SELE SECO
```

> **Note:** Until we SELE PRIM again, we will continue to use all files in the "secondary" area.

```
    USE F2 INDEX P2INDX
    FIND &MPARTNUM
    IF # > 0
        STORE CGC TO MCGC
```

```
ENDIF
USE F3 INDEX P3INDX
FIND &MPARTNUM
IF # > 0
   STORE ONHAND TO MONHAND
ENDIF
USE OUTPUT
APPEND BLANK
REPLACE PART:NUM WITH MPARTNUM;
        UNIT:COST WITH MUNIT;
        DESC WITH MDESC;
        CGC WITH MCGC;
        ONHAND WITH MONHAND
```

SELE PRIM This sends us back to the primary file at the record we had left off.

```
SKIP
ENDDO
USE
```
USE This closes the primary.

SELE SECO

USE This closes the secondary.

RETURN If part of a menu-system.

ENHANCED SCREEN LAYOUTS

We can incorporate a touch of pizazz into our screen formats, by using the screen's inverse video option. The condition to be satisfied is, obviously, that your particular terminal supports inverse video. Also, the codes provided here for producing the inverse video effect apply to the Xerox 820-II computer system. You will have to scan your system's reference book for the codes that produce this effect on your particular terminal.

Most CRTs can support the following types of visual display: Normal (regular) and Special (Inverse, Blink, Low, Graphic, etc.). When you want the display to change from one type to another, you have to initiate a sequence of codes that informs the hardware of your intentions. This sequence of codes usually starts off with the ESCAPE character.

The CHR function helps to set these codes in the case of 8-bit processors. The CHR function refers to the character defined by a specific decimal value. For example, the command ? CHR(42) results in the * as the answer, and ? CHR(36) results in the $ sign being produced. Every character that your computer system can work with has a decimal equivalent. Numbers beyond 127 have not been assigned any defined character standard, and so different computer systems will produce different characters for the same decimal equivalent beyond 127. ? CHR(42) can be read as, "What is the character produced by the decimal-number 42."

We will revisit PGMD, our program to append data into the data-base. This time, PGMD will be enhanced to produce a couple of edit checks on the data entered by the operator. The screen inverse video effect will be brought into play in the case of er-

251

roneous entry by the operator. There's nothing like the entire screen going into in-verse video, to wake up an operator!

```
SET TALK OFF
ERASE
USE INVENTORY
DO WHILE T
    ? CHR(27)+'('
    STORE '        ' TO MPART
    STORE 0 TO MCOST
    STORE 0 TO MSELL
    STORE 0 TO MONHAND
    STORE 0 TO MONORDER
    STORE 0 TO MUSAGE
    STORE 0 TO MLEAD
    STORE ' ' TO ERRMSG
    SET FORMAT TO LAYOUTD          "LAYOUTDA" is identical to "LAYOUTD"
    READ                           with the exception of one more entry at the
    IF MPART = '        '          bottom of the screen for ERRMSG.
        SET FORMAT TO
        RETURN
    ENDIF

    STORE T TO NOGOOD

    DO WHILE NOGOOD
    STORE F TO NOGOOD
        IF MSELL < 10 .OR. MSELL > 30
            STORE 'SELL PRICE ERROR !!!' TO ERRMSG
            STORE T TO NOGOOD
        ENDIF
        IF MCOST < 10 .OR. MCOST > 30
            STORE 'COST PRICE ERROR !!!' TO ERRMSG
            STORE T TO NOGOOD
        ENDIF
        IF NOGOOD
            ? CHR(27)+')'+CHR(27)+'7'....... (A)
            SET FORMAT TO LAYOUTD
            READ
        ENDIF
    ENDDO

    APPEND BLANK

    REPLACE PART WITH MPART;
            COST WITH MCOST;
            SELLPRICE WITH MSELL;
            ONHAND WITH MONHAND;
            ONORDER WITH MONORDER;
            USAGE WITH MUSAGE;
            LEAD WITH MLEAD
    SET FORMAT TO
ENDDO
```

Notice that I provide two edit checks; one each for selling price and for cost price (you may include any number of such checks, of course). If an error has been found in either of these fields, the sequence of codes is executed to signal inverse video to the hardware before the screen is brought up again.

Since I have only provided for one error message on the screen at a time, obviously if more than one field is in error, the second message will overlap the first one, and so on, down the line. Hence, the program logic checks the fields in the reverse order of output on the screen. That is, the program checks for valid data in field-2 before field-1. If both fields are in error, field-1 is high lighted as the one in error.

The following illustration explains point (A) in the previous program:

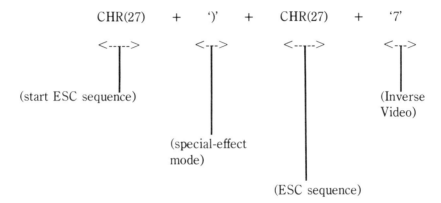

The combination of the above STRING informs the hardware that you want an inverse-video effect. Once the above string is executed, the inverse video remains in effect, unless reset by the following:

The next illustration explains point (B) in the above program:

CHR(27) + '('   (ESC sequence, followed by Regular display mode.)

These codes are valid for the Xerox 820-II microcomputer system. You will have to obtain the unique sequence of codes for your own terminal from your reference book.

Is it necessary to memorize the sequence of codes for particular functions? It is always a plus, in your favor, if you do have these sequence codes memorized; however, this is not at all necessary, and we shall now show you an easier, more comprehensible, method of producing the above result.

The sequence of codes could be placed into memory variables.

These memory variables could be invoked as the parameters of the ? command! For example, you could string together all those codes required for the inverse-video effect into a memory variable called Inverse. Then ? &INVERSE would produce the inverse-video effect.

```
.STORE "CHR(27)+')'+CHR(27)+'5' "  TO GRAPHICS        <cr>
.STORE "CHR(27)+')'+CHR(27)+'7' "  TO INVERSE         <cr>
.STORE "CHR(27)+')'+CHR(27)+'6' "  TO BLINK           <cr>
.STORE "CHR(27)+'(' "              TO NORMAL          <cr>
```

Having created these memory variables, we now store them all together in a memory file on our disk so they are always available in the future.

.SAVE TO SPECIALS   \<cr>

This command saves all the memory variables into a file called SPECIALS.MEM. You may, of course, provide any name you want to the memory file.

.RESTORE FROM SPECIALS ADDITIVE   \<cr>

This command will reload all the memory variables from disk into memory. Obviously, they should be available in memory, before they can be successfully used as macroparameters. The additive (add-on) parameter ensures that other, existing memory variables are left intact.

Now, the following version of PGMD is identical to the one before. The only change is, of course, in the restoration and use of the memory variables in the form of macroparameters to go into and out of the inverse-video mode.

```
SET TALK OFF
ERASE
RESTORE FROM SPECIALS ADDITIVE        . . . . . . . . . . (A)
USE INVENTORY
DO WHILE T
     ? &NORMAL                        . . . . . . . . . . (B)
     STORE '          ' TO MPART
     STORE 0 TO MCOST
     STORE 0 TO MSELL
     STORE 0 TO MONHAND
     STORE 0 TO MONORDER
     STORE 0 TO MUSAGE
     STORE 0 TO MLEAD
     STORE ' ' TO ERRMSG
     SET FORMAT TO LAYOUTD
     READ
     IF MPART = '          '
        SET FORMAT TO
        RETURN
     ENDIF

     STORE T TO NOGOOD

     DO WHILE NOGOOD
     STORE F TO NOGOOD
        IF MSELL < 10 .OR. MSELL > 30
           STORE 'SELL PRICE ERROR !!!' TO ERRMSG
           STORE T TO NOGOOD
        ENDIF
        IF MCOST < 10 .OR. MCOST > 30
           STORE 'COST PRICE ERROR !!!' TO ERRMSG
           STORE T TO NOGOOD
        ENDIF
```

254

```
        IF  NOGOOD
            ?  &INVERSE                            . . . . . . . . (C)
            SET  FORMAT  TO  LAYOUTD
            READ
        ENDIF
    ENDDO


    APPEND BLANK

    REPLACE  PART  WITH  MPART;
             COST  WITH  MCOST;
             SELLPRICE  WITH  MSELL;
             ONHAND  WITH  MONHAND;
             ONORDER  WITH  MONORDER;
             USAGE  WITH  MUSAGE;
             LEAD  WITH  MLEAD
    SET  FORMAT  TO
ENDDO
```

Notice that in this version our program is restoring all the memory variables from the SPECIALS.MEM file into memory. The command at (A) performs this task. The command line at (B) executes the ? command to produce the normal effect. You would want the normal effect before each new record was entered.

The command line at (C) executes the ? command to produce the inverse-video effect in case of operator error. This inverse video remains in effect until reset, and hence the next command: .SET FORMAT TO LAYOUTD will bring up the entire screen in full inverse video! As per our program instructions, the inverse video mode remains in effect for as long as there are data entry errors by the operator.

TABLE LOOKUP

Let us suppose you have entered two tables into memory variables, as follows:

.STORE '01 02 03 04 05 06 07 08 09 10 11 12 ' TO CODE
.STORE 'JANFEBMARAPRMAYJUNJULAUGSEPOCTNOVDEC' TO MONTH

Notice that there is a one-to-one correspondence between the arguments (the codes) and the functions (the months). That is, each argument and each function is built up to take 3 locations in memory. Suppose we have to look up the appropriate letters of the month for the number 05. That is, we have to convert this 05 to MAY from the table. The following command provides a means for this kind of table lookup:

Note: If you remember, to substring a character string use the following format:

$(name-of-string,start-location,number-of-locations)
Example: $(TOWN,2,3)

For our table lookup, we want to equate the '05' to the month MAY.

. ? $(MONTH, ('05',CODE),3)

Start
Location

number of
locations

The ('05',CODE) should be read as follows: "At the position where we can find a '05' in the memory variable called CODE . . ." The result of this @ command is the numerical value 13, since the 0 of the 05 begins in the 13th location, in the string called CODE. The expression breaks down to the following resultant:

? $(MONTH,13,3)

This resultant should be read as: "What is the substring to be obtained from MONTH, starting at the 13th location, for 3 locations?" The answer, of course, is MAY. You could have also provided the name of a character memory variable in place of the numeric literal 05. That is, you could have asked the operator to provide a number for the month:

.ACCEPT "Please enter month-number" TO ANSWER

The ACCEPT command will automatically create a character memory variable. The following command will produce the appropriate letters of the month.

. ? $(MONTH, (ANSWER,CODE),3)

The above statement could be read as: "What is the substring to be obtained from the variable MONTH, starting at that location provided by the start of the value found in the variable ANSWER, in the string CODE, for 3 locations?"

UPDATE COMMAND

Suppose you have a Master file and a Transaction file, and you want the records of the Transaction file to be used for updating the Master. The transactions are usually either to: ADD new records to the Master file, or to CHANGE existing records of the Master in some of the fields, or to DELETE existing Master records.

Since the APPEND and DELETE commands are two powerful commands to Add and Delete records from a Master file, the UPDATE command does not handle these features. You can only make changes to existing data records in the Master file with UPDATE.

The Master file has to be INDEXED on some key field. The Transaction file may or may not be physically sorted on the key. If the TRANS file is physically sorted, then the following sequence will work:

```
.USE MASTER INDEX INVINDX
.UPDATE FROM TRANS ON PART:NUM  ADD ONHAND;
                                REPL COST
```

If the Transaction file was not sorted use this command:

```
.UPDATE FROM TRANS  ON  PART:NUM  RANDOM;
                        ADD  ONHAND  REPLACE  COST
```

From the way the above instructions have been written, it follows that the fields called PART:NUM, ONHAND and COST must exist in the structures of both Master and Transaction files. Hopefully, their corresponding TYPEs and LENGTHs will also match.

In these instructions, if a PART:NUM from the Master file is equal to the PART:NUM from the transaction file, then dBASE will ADD the ONHAND in the transaction record to the ONHAND in the Master record, thus updating the ONHAND field in the Master record, and dBASE will REPLACE the COST field in the Master record with the contents of the COST field from the transaction record.

An example of the before and after picture follows:

Master Before	Transaction	Master After
ONHAND: 500	ONHAND: 50	ONHAND: 550
COST : 50.00	COST : 55.00	COST : 55.00

The UPDATE command only provides the opportunity to ADD the contents of two fields. Suppose the ONHAND in the above example experiences a shortfall of, say, 20 units, through deterioration. How would you be able to subtract this 20 from the ONHAND in the Master file? Try specifying the transaction quantity as being negative! This will automatically provide the algebraic subtraction operation desired.

The negative entry in the transaction-file fields has the added advantage of your being able to list out all the negative transactions from a transaction-file, without the necessity of any special codes.

```
.LIST FOR  ONHAND < 0    <cr>
```

This command will produce a listing of all negative entries in the ONHAND field in the transaction file.

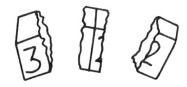

12. Shattering the Myth of the 32-Field Structure Limitation

DBASE-II users are acutely aware of, and continually lament, a limitation of the product. You can only define a maximum of 32-fields in the structure of any one data-base. Other software vendors have capitalized on this limitation of dBASE by advertising their product as being capable of supporting many more than 32-fields in the structure. This limitation has caused many users to break up a large file structure into two files, one primary and the other secondary, and then try and connect these two physical files into one logical data-base. While this can, of course, be done, as has been amply demonstrated in the preceding pages, this can lead to problems with programming, data consistency, maintenance, and documentation of the separate files. The problems compound for more than two physical files for any one logical file.

How would you like to be able a define a dBASE-II data-base comprising, say, 50 fields in the structure? Or how about 75 fields, or 300 fields, or 400 fields? If you are willing to stay within the limitation of 1000 characters for the structure length, you can define any number of fields you want for the file while letting dBASE think it is still working within the limitation of 32-fields.

Not only is it possible to define such a structure, you can now work with that structure just as you would with any other normal structure. You could index such a data-base on multiple ascending/descending indexes, you could pull off reports with totals/subtotals, etc.

In short, I am going to present to you this innovative approach to using dBASE-II to maximum advantage by removing one of the most-lamented obstacles out of our way—that of the 32-field limitation. You will need all of the programming skills you have learned so far, including skills with the special functions presented earlier, to be able to make use of this approach. Obviously, it follows that the novice at dBASE-II will have to live within the limitation of 32-fields in the structure of any one data-base.

I am hoping that this topic will serve to enhance the utility-value of dBASE-II.

The trick to this entire scenario is defining any number of fields you want while letting dBASE-II think it is living within the 32-field limitation. That means, you will have to *group together* several fields of information as *one field*, store the actual data as such, and then separate the information at the time of usage for indexing or reporting, etc. Theoretically, you could store 50 fields of information all in one field. Your data-base would have just the one field in its structure.

This grouping and separating of information necessitates that you are able to write computer programs to do the job for you. We shall now see exactly how this may be done.

CREATING

Let us go back to our PERSNL file data. This file contains several fields of information. We shall take the extreme case, and decide that we want to store the entire structure as just one field of information.

First create a file containing just one field in its structure of length equal to the combined lengths of the various fields of data to be stored. Let us presume you have created a file called PERSNL containing a field called ONEFIELD of length 49 characters.

Now, let us write a computer program to put out a formatted screen asking for "EMP-NUM", "EMP-NAME", "ORG", etc. When the entries have been made by the operator, this program will go ahead and create one record out of this information, and store this record into the one field of the data-base defined earlier.

The format-file (LAYOUTB.FMT) is shown below:

```
@ 10,1 SAY 'EMP-NUMBER        ' GET MEMPNUM   PICT 'XXXXXX'
@ 12,1 SAY 'EMP-NAME          ' GET MEMPNAME  PICT 'XXXXXXXXXXXXXX'
@ 14,1 SAY 'TOWN              ' GET MTOWN     PICT 'XXXXXXXXXXX'
@ 16,1 SAY 'ORG               ' GET MORG      PICT 'XXX'
@ 18,1 SAY 'EXEMPT            ' GET MEXEMPT   PICT 'X'
@ 20,1 SAY 'YEAR OF HIRE      ' GET MYEAR     PICT '9999'
@ 22,1 SAY 'SALARY            ' GET MSALARY   PICT '99999.99'
```

The calling program is shown next.

```
SET TALK OFF
USE PERSNL
DO WHILE T
    STORE '        ' TO MEMPNUM
    STORE '              ' TO MEMPNAME
    STORE '           ' TO MTOWN
    STORE '    ' TO MORG
    STORE ' ' TO MEXEMPT
    STORE 0 TO MYEAR
    STORE 0 TO MSALARY
```

```
SET FORMAT TO LAYOUTB
READ
IF MEMPNUM = '          '
    SET FORMAT TO
    RETURN

ENDIF

APPEND BLANK
```

Note that we are treating the EXEMPT field as a character field, not as a logical field. At this point in time, all operator entries have been placed into memory variables, and the record pointer has been positioned at the newly appended blank record. Now the program has to go ahead, and store all these fields as one field into the structure of the file in use.

```
REPLACE ONEFIELD WITH MEMPNUM+MEMPNAME+MTOWN+MORG+MEXEMPT;

                    +STR(MYEAR,4)+STR(MSALARY,8,2)
```

```
ENDDO
```

The above REPLACE command does the trick of concatenating the various individual memory variables into ONEFIELD. Remember also, that the + function applies only to character fields, and so the YEAR:OF:HIRE and the SALARY fields have to be specified as string versions. This is the same reason why the EXEMPT field was stored as a character field.

Note that the inherent structure of this one field is as follows:

(field-name)	(start-location)	(number-of-locations)
EMP:NUM	1	6
EMP:NAME	7	15
TOWN	22	12
ORG	34	·3
EXEMPT	37	1
YEAR/HIRE	38	4
SALARY	42	8

Also, since all the fields have been concatenated into one big character field, each piece of data in that field is considered to be character data, regardless of user-interpretation of that data!

SEQUENCING

Now, let us suppose we wanted to index such records:

.INDEX ON $(ONEFIELD,34,3)   TO XYZ

This would produce the index on the ORG field. After the creation of such an index, further actions would affect the index, as usual. For example, an APPEND would ensure that the new records are automatically placed in their correct logical positions in the index.

.INDEX ON VAL($(ONEFIELD,42,8))   TO XYZ

This would produce the normal ascending sequence on the SALARY field. Note that the VAL function refers to the numerical value obtained from a character string, in this case, the subcharacter string data pertaining to SALARY.

.INDEX ON $(ONEFIELD,34,3)+STR(VAL($(ONEFIELD,42,8)),8,2) TO XYZ

> **Note:** The above expression extracts the SALARY portion from
> ONEFIELD and treats it as numeric data through the VAL function.
> Now we have to produce an index on a combination of a character field
> (the extract of ORG) and a numeric field, and so the numeric field has to
> be expressed as a string function!

While the above expression may seem complex, if you can logically step through the process as we have attempted to explain it, it should not prove too difficult. This expression would produce the index on ORG and ascending SALARY. Note that the SALARY data is actually stored as character information. After the creation of such an index, further actions would affect the index, as usual. For example, an APPEND would ensure that the new records are automatically placed in their correct logical positions in the index.

If you wanted to index on descending sequence of the salary field, this command would work.

.INDEX ON 99999.99-(VAL($(ONEFIELD,42,8))) TO XYZ

If you recall, the VAL function refers to the numeric value obtained from any character field, in this case, the substring character field representing the salary data.

If you wanted the index on ORG and descending SALARY, then the following command would do the trick:

.INDEX ON
  $(ONEFIELD,34,3)+STR(99999.99-(VAL($(ONEFIELD,42,8,))),8,2)

Study the breakdown of this command from right to left.

$(ONEFIELD,42,8) is the SALARY extract.
VAL(< --->) is the numerical value
                                                                    of this extract.

99999.99-(< -->) is the descending
numerical value of
this extract.

STR(< -->)8,2) is necessary as
we are indexing on a
combination of a
character and a
numeric.

REPORTING

Reporting from such a file is no problem, either! Let us pull off three reports, to clarify how this can be done. The first report is done without totals.

.REPORT FORM RPT1 NEXT 5

```
ENTER OPTIONS, M=LEFT MARGIN, L=LINES/PAGE, W=PAGE WIDTH
PAGE HEADING? (Y/N) Y
ENTER PAGE HEADING: REPORT 1
DOUBLE SPACE REPORT? (Y/N) N
ARE TOTALS REQUIRED? (Y/N) N
COL     WIDTH,CONTENTS
001     6,$(ONEFIELD,1,6)          Note this statement!
ENTER HEADING: EMPNOS
002     15,$(ONEFIELD,7,15)          Note!
ENTER HEADING: <EMP-NAMES
003     3,$(ONEFIELD,34,3)          Note!
ENTER HEADING: ORG
004     8,$(ONEFIELD,42,8)          Note!
ENTER HEADING: >SALARY
005
```

```
PAGE NO.  00001
07/01/84
                                           REPORT 1


EMPNOS EMP-NAMES          ORG    SALARY

070707 NINA  BHARUCHA     BSG 36300.00
7545AD PETE  JOHNSON      BSG 30349.00
987178 GLORIA PATEL       RMG 27500.00
232430 MAX  LEVENSKY      RMG 27550.00
0989SD KIM  BRANDT        RMG 36000.00
```

The second report is done with totals.

.REPORT FORM RPT2 NEXT 5

ENTER OPTIONS, M=LEFT MARGIN, L=LINES/PAGE, W=PAGE WIDTH
PAGE HEADING? (Y/N) Y
ENTER PAGE HEADING: REPORT 2;WITH TOTALS
DOUBLE SPACE REPORT? (Y/N) N
ARE TOTALS REQUIRED? (Y/N) Y
SUBTOTALS IN REPORT? (Y/N) N
COL   WIDTH,CONTENTS
001   6,$(ONEFIELD,1,6)
ENTER HEADING: EMPNOS
002   15,$(ONEFIELD,7,15)
ENTER HEADING: <EMP-NAMES
003   3,$(ONEFIELD,34,3)
ENTER HEADING: ORG
004   8,VAL($(ONEFIELD,42,8))   Note this statement!!
ENTER HEADING: >SALARY   We are asking for the
ARE TOTALS REQUIRED? (Y/N) Y   VAL resultant (numeric)
005   of the salary data.

PAGE NO. 00001
07/01/84
                                    REPORT 2

                                WITH TOTALS

EMPNOS EMP-NAMES   ORG   SALARY

070707 NINA BHARUCHA   BSG   36300
7545AD PETE JOHNSON   BSG   30349
987178 GLORIA PATEL   RMG   27500
232430 MAX LEVENSKY   RMG   27550
0989SD KIM BRANDT   RMG   36000
** TOTAL **
                                   157699

The last report is done with subtotals.

.REPORT FORM RPT3 NEXT 5

ENTER OPTIONS, M=LEFT MARGIN, L=LINES/PAGE, W=PAGE WIDTH
PAGE HEADING? (Y/N) Y
ENTER PAGE HEADING: REPORT 3;WITH TOTALS & SUBTOTALS
DOUBLE SPACE REPORT? (Y/N) N
ARE TOTALS REQURIED? (Y/N) Y

SUBTOTALS IN REPORT? (Y/N) Y
ENTER SUBTOTALS FIELD: $(ONEFIELD,34,3)
SUMMARY REPORT ONLY? (Y/N) N
EJECT PAGE AFTER SUBTOTALS? (Y/N) N
ENTER SUBTOTAL HEADING: SUB-TOTALS FOR ORG
COL   WIDTH,CONTENTS
001   6,$(ONEFIELD,1,6)
ENTER HEADING: MEPNOS
002   15,$(ONEFIELD,7,15)
ENTER HEADING: <EMP-NAMES
003   3,$(ONEFIELD,34,3)
ENTER HEADING: ORG
004   8,VAL($(ONEFIELD,42,8))
ENTER HEADING: >SALARY
ARE TOTALS REQUIRED? (Y/N) Y
005

```
PAGE NO.  00001
07/01/84
                                        REPORT 3

                             WITH TOTALS & SUBTOTALS


EMPNOS EMP-NAMES          ORG   SALARY

* SUB-TOTALS FOR ORG BSG
070707 NINA BHARUCHA      BSG      36300
7545AD PETE JOHNSON       BSG      30349
** SUBTOTAL **
                                   66649


* SUB-TOTALS FOR ORG RMG
987178 GLORIA PATEL       RMG      27500
232430 MAX LEVENSKY       RMG      27550
0989SD KIM BRANDT         RMG      36000
** SUBTOTAL **
                                   91050

** TOTAL **
                                  157699
```

EDITING

Editing such a file is very easy, too. Let us now write a small edit program, similar to the one seen before, to edit each record sequentially. The format-file (LAYOUTR.FMT) is shown here:

```
@ 10,1 SAY 'EMP-NUMBER          ' GET MEMPNUM   PICT 'XXXXXX'
@ 12,1 SAY 'EMP-NAME            ' GET MEMPNAME  PICT 'XXXXXXXXXXXXXXX'
@ 14,1 SAY 'TOWN               ' GET MTOWN     PICT 'XXXXXXXXXXXX'
@ 16,1 SAY 'ORG                ' GET MORG      PICT 'XXX'
@ 18,1 SAY 'EXEMPT             ' GET MEXEMPT   PICT 'X'
@ 20,1 SAY 'YEAR OF HIRE       ' GET MYEAR     PICT '9999'
@ 22,1 SAY 'SALARY             ' GET MSALARY   PICT '99999.99'
@ 23,1 SAY 'CARRY ON   (Y/N) ?' GET MNEXT     PICT 'X'
```

The calling program is shown next.

```
SET TALK OFF
ERASE
USE PERSNL
*  The above statement places record # 1 under your control
*
STORE ' ' TO MNEXT
DO WHILE T

    STORE $(ONEFIELD,1,6) TO MEMPNUM
    STORE $(ONEFIELD,7,15) TO MEMPNAME
    STORE $(ONEFIELD,22,12) TO MTOWN
    STORE $(ONEFIELD,34,3) TO MORG
    STORE $(ONEFIELD,37,1) TO MEXEMPT
    STORE VAL($(ONEFIELD,38,4)) TO MYEAR
    STORE VAL($(ONEFIELD,42,8)) TO MSALARY
    SET FORMAT TO LAYOUTR
    READ
```

At this point, the altered data has again been placed into the same memory variables they were obtained from.

```
    REPLACE ONEFIELD WITH MEMPNUM+MEMPNAME+MTOWN+MORG+MEXEMPT;
                        +STR(MYEAR,4)+STR(MSALARY,8,2)
```

```
*  Note that we make the change first, and then we check the
*  operator response for proceeding ahead.

    IF MNEXT = 'N'
        SET FORMAT TO
        RETURN
    ENDIF
    SKIP
ENDDO
```

I have shown, in these few pages, how you could have gone about storing all seven fields of information in the PERSNL file in just one field of data. You could have extended this process to include many more fields, if necessary. You could also pick and choose the fields you want lumped together, and as such you could have stored, say, 200 logical fields into a total of 20 physical fields by simply concatenating 10 logical fields into each physical field. As far as dBASE-II is concerned, it would be working with 20 fields in such a structure, but you now have access to 200 logical fields in such a file.

SUMMARY

Well, this is it! If you have managed to reach this far successfully, you can consider yourself rather good with dBASE. If you were to try and sum it all up, I think you would reach the conclusion that dBASE-II is a powerful data-base management system. Its proper usage to maximum advantage requires that you sit down and study it. This, of course, is true of any piece of software that provides the same amount of power and flexibility as dBASE-II.

Appendices

Appendix A

The Report Program

The Report Program.

```
ERASE
DO         Accepts
ERASE
DO         Hdr
STORE 0 TO MSALARY
STORE 0 TO RECORDCNT
USE PERSNL
SET FORMAT TO PRINT
DO WHILE  .NOT.  EOF
   'IF !(TOWN) = !(MTOWN)  .AND.  !(ORG) = !(MORG)
      @ LINECNT,10 SAY EMP:NUM
      @ LINECNT,25 SAY EMP:NAME
      @ LINECNT,38 SAY YR:OF:HIRE
      @ LINECNT,43 SAY SALARY
      STORE RECORDCNT+1  TO RECORDCNT
      STORE MSALARY + SALARY   TO   MSALARY
      STORE LINECNT+1 TO LINECNT
      IF   LINECNT > 55
           DO  Hdr
      ENDIF
   ENDIF
   SKIP
ENDDO
STORE LINECNT+3 TO LINENT
@ LINECNT,10 SAY "SALARY TOTAL:"
@ LINECNT,25 SAY MSALARY
STORE LINECNT+1 TO LINECNT
@ LINECNT,10 SAY "TOTAL RECORDS"
@ LINECNT,25 SAY RECORDCNT
STORE LINECNT+1 TO LINECNT
@ LINECNT,10 SAY "AVERAGE SALARY:"
@ LINECNT,25 SAY (MSALARY/RECORDCNT)
```

"Accepts" Program:

```
Accept "Please enter a town name"  to  mtown
Erase
```

```
Accept "Now please enter an organization name"  to  morg
Erase
Return


"Hdr" Program:
-------------


EJECT
@ 2,28 SAY "REPORT AS OF JUNE 15, 1984"
@ 2,70 say DATE()
@ 3,28 say "--------------------------"
@ 5,10 say "EMP-NUMBER"
@ 5,25 say "EMP-NAME"
@ 5,35 say "YR/HIRE"
@ 5,45 say "SALARY"
Store 8 to linecnt
Return
```

Appendix B

The Menu Programs

MENU PROGRAM

```
CLEAR
SET TALK OFF
STORE ' ' TO ERRMSG
DO    WHILE    T
    ERASE
    ? "                          INVENTORY CONTROL MENU"
    ? "                          ---------------------"
    ?
    ?
    ? "    A  -   Report of items with ONHAND below a stated level"
    ?
    ? "    B  -   Report of items in danger of a stock-runout"
    ?
    ? "    C  -   Full inventory report."
    ?
    ? "    D  -   Add more data into the Inventory data-base"
    ? "    E  -   Add more data        with duplicates-check"
    ?
    ? "    F  -   Edit existing data - Sequentially"
    ? "    G  -   Edit Sequentially    with duplicates-check"
    ?
    ? "    H  -   Edit existing data - Random, by record-numbers"
    ? "    I  -   Edit Random on rec-numbers, with duplicates-check"
    ?
    ? "    J  -   Edit Random  based on the KEY-value"
    ? "    K  -   Edit Random on KEY    with duplicates-check"
    ?
    ? "    L  -   Delete records at Random, by KEY-value"
    ?
    ? "    M  -   Scan records Sequentially"
    ? "    N  -   Scan records at Random, by KEY-value"
    ? "    O  -   Remove duplicate records from master file"
    ? "    P  -   Exit from this menu"
    ?
    ? ERRMSG
    WAIT    TO    ACTION
    IF  !(ACTION) = 'A'
        DO PGMA
    ENDIF
    IF  !(ACTION) = 'B'
        DO PGMB
    ENDIF
    IF  !(ACTION) = 'C'
        DO PGMC
    ENDIF
    IF  !(ACTION) = 'D'
        DO PGMD
    ENDIF
    IF  !(ACTION) = 'E'
        DO PGME
    ENDIF
    IF  !(ACTION) = 'F'
        DO PGMF
    ENDIF
    IF  !(ACTION) = 'G'
        DO PGMG
    ENDIF
```

```
IF !(ACTION) = 'H'
DO PGMH
ENDIF
IF !(ACTION) = 'I'
   DO PGMI
ENDIF
IF !(ACTION) = 'J'
   DO PGMJ
ENDIF
IF !(ACTION) = 'K'
   DO PGMK
ENDIF
IF !(ACTION) = 'L'
   DO PGML
ENDIF
IF !(ACTION) = 'M'
   DO PGMM
ENDIF
IF !(ACTION) = 'N'
   DO PGMN
ENDIF
IF !(ACTION) = 'O'
   DO PGMO
ENDIF
IF !(ACTION) = 'P'
   USE RETURN

   ENDIF
   IF ACTION < 'A'  .OR.  !(ACTION) > 'P'
      STORE 'INVALID OPTION SELECTED !!'   TO   ERRMSG
   ELSE
      STORE ' ' TO ERRMSG
   ENDIF
ENDDO
```

   Checking the results of operator action - short process.

```
   ------
   ------
   ------
   IF !(ACTION) = 'P'
       USE RETURN
    ENDIF
   IF !(ACTION)  $('ABCDEFGHIJKLMNO')
       STORE ' ' TO ERRMSG
       STORE 'PGM' + !(ACTION)  TO  CHOICE
       DO  &CHOICE
   ELSE
       STORE "INVALID OPTION SELECTED !!"  TO  ERRMSG
   ENDIF
ENDDO
```

   PROGRAM-A   REPORT OF ITEMS WITH AN ONHAND BALANCE BELOW
   A STATED LEVEL.

```
   ERASE
   ? "Option - A:  Report of "ONHAND" below a stated level:"
```

```
?
?
?
? "What is the level of inventory below which you want to"
INPUT "receive a status"  TO   LEVEL
ERASE
USE INVNTRY    [INDEX .....]
REPORT FORM   RPTA     FOR  ONHAND < LEVEL  [TO PRINT]
WAIT
RETURN
```

Program-A re-visited, briefly.

```
ERASE
? "Option - A:  Report of "ONHAND" below a stated level:"
?
?
?
? "What is the level of inventory below which you want to"
INPUT "receive a status"  TO   LEVEL
ERASE
USE INVNTRY [INDEX ....]
STORE STR(LEVEL,10) TO LVL
SET HEADING TO INVENTORY REPORT FOR ONHAND BELOW &LVL
REPORT FORM RPTA  FOR ONHAND < LEVEL  [TO PRINT]
WAIT
RETURN
```

PROGRAM-B   REPORT OF ITEMS IN DANGER OF STOCK RUN-OUT.

```
ERASE
USE INVNTRY      [INDEX.....]
REPORT FORM RPTB FOR ONHAND <=USAGE * (LEAD+IP)
WAIT
RETURN
```

PROGRAM-C   FULL INVENTORY REPORT.

```
ERASE
USE INVENTRY [INDEX.....]
REPORT FORM RPTC [TO PRINT]
WAIT
RETURN
```

Program "D".

GENERATING FORMAT FILE AND "CALLING PROGRAM"

FOR APPENDING MORE RECORDS.

```
@ 2,25   SAY 'INVENTORY SYSTEM DATA-ENTRY SCREEN'
@ 3,25   SAY '--------- ------ ---- ----- ------'
@ 5,1    SAY 'ENTER THE FOLLOWING PIECES OF REQUIRED INFORMATION:'
@ 08,5   SAY 'PART-NUM ' GET MPART      PICTURE 'XXXXXX'
@ 10,5   SAY 'COST     ' GET MCOST      PICTURE '999.99'
@ 12,5   SAY 'SELLPRICE' GET MSELL      PICTURE '999.99'
@ 14,5   SAY 'ONHAND   ' GET MONHAND    PICTURE '999'
@ 16,5   SAY 'ONORDER  ' GET MONORDER   PICTURE '999'
@ 18,5   SAY 'USAGE    ' GET MUSAGE     PICTURE '99'
@ 20,5   SAY 'LEAD     ' GET MLEAD      PICTURE '99'
@ 23,1   SAY 'LEAVE PART-NUM FIELD BLANK, and  ctrl-W, TO EXIT'

SET TALK OFF
ERASE
USE INVNTRY
DO WHILE T
   STORE '      ' TO MPART
   STORE 0                 TO MCOST
   STORE 0                 TO MSELL
   STORE 0                 TO MONHAND
   STORE 0                 TO MONORDER
   STORE 0                 TO MUSAGE
   STORE 0                 TO MLEAD
   SET FORMAT TO LAYOUTD
   READ
   IF MPART  = '       '
      SET FORMAT TO
      RETURN
   ENDIF
   APPEND BLANK
   REPLACE PART WITH MPART;
           COST WITH MCOST;
           SELLPRICE WITH MSELL;
           ONHAND WITH MONHAND;
           ONORDER WITH MONORDER;
           USAGE WITH MUSAGE;
           LEAD WITH MLEAD
   SET FORMAT TO
ENDDO
```

Edit check enhancement.

```
@ 2,25   SAY 'INVENTORY SYSTEM DATA-ENTRY SCREEN'
@ 3,25   SAY '--------- ------ ---- ----- ------'
@ 5,1    SAY 'ENTER THE FOLLOWING PIECES OF REQUIRED INFORMATION:'
@ 08,5   SAY 'PART-NUM ' GET MPART      PICTURE 'XXXXXX'
@ 10,5   SAY 'COST     ' GET MCOST      PICTURE '999.99'
@ 12,5   SAY 'SELLPRICE' GET MSELL      PICTURE '999.99'
@ 14,5   SAY 'ONHAND   ' GET MONHAND    PICTURE '999'
@ 16,5   SAY 'ONORDER  ' GET MONORDER   PICTURE '999'
@ 18,5   SAY 'USAGE    ' GET MUSAGE     PICTURE '99'
@ 20,5   SAY 'LEAD     ' GET MLEAD      PICTURE '99'
@ 22,1   SAY 'LEAVE PART-NUM FIELD BLANK, and  ctrl-W, TO EXIT'
@ 23,1   SAY 'ERRMSGD'

SET TALK OFF
ERASE
USE INVNTRY
```

```
DO WHILE T
   STORE '       ' TO MPART
   STORE 0                    TO MCOST
   STORE 0                    TO MSELL
   STORE 0                    TO MONHAND
   STORE 0                    TO MONORDER
   STORE 0                    TO MUSAGE
   STORE 0                    TO MLEAD
   STORE ' '                  TO ERRMSGD
   SET FORMAT TO LAYOUTD
   READ
   IF MPART = '        '
      SET FORMAT TO
      RETURN
   ENDIF
*                  BEGIN EDIT-CHECK ROUTINE !!
   STORE  T  TO NOGOOD
   DO WHILE  NOGOOD
      STORE F TO NOGOOD
      IF MSELL < 5  .OR.  MSELL > 50
         STORE 'SELL PRICE ERROR' TO ERRMSGD
         STORE T TO NOGOOD
      ENDIF
      IF MCOST < 5 .OR. MCOST > 50
         STORE 'COST PRICE ERROR' TO ERRMSGD
         STORE T TO NOGOOD
      ENDIF
      IF  ----------------
         (similar checks for any field(s) input by the operator)
      ENDIF
      IF NOGOOD
         SET FORMAT TO LAYOUTD
         READ
      ENDIF
   ENDDO
*                  END EDIT-CHECK ROUTINE !!
*.
*   If the edit check proves OK, the program will proceed with
*   the following instructions.

   APPEND BLANK
   REPLACE PART WITH MPART;
          COST WITH MCOST;
          SELLPRICE WITH MSELL;
          ONHAND WITH MONHAND;
          ONORDER WITH MONORDER;
          USAGE WITH MUSAGE;
          LEAD WITH MLEAD
   SET FORMAT TO
ENDDO
```

Program "E".

GENERATING FORMAT FILE AND "CALLING PROGRAM"

FOR APPENDING NEW RECORDS,

WITH DUPLICATES-CHECK.

```
@ 2,10   SAY 'INVENTORY DATA-ENTRY SCREEN'
@ 3,10   SAY '---------------------------'
@ 4,10   SAY 'APPENDING NEW RECORDS, WITH DUPLICATES CHECK ON KEY-FIELD'
@ 6,1    SAY 'ENTER THE FOLLOWING ITEMS OF INFORMATION:'
@ 08,1   SAY 'PARTNUM  ' GET MPART PICTURE 'XXXXXX'
@ 10,1   SAY 'COST     ' GET MCOST PICTURE '999'
@ 12,1   SAY 'SELLPRICE' GET MSELL PICTURE '99999.99'
@ 14,1   SAY 'ONHAND   ' GET MONHAND PICTURE '999'
@ 16,1   SAY 'ONORDER  ' GET MONORDER PICTURE '999'
@ 18,1   SAY 'USAGE    ' GET MUSAGE PICTURE '99'
@ 20,1   SAY 'LEAD     ' GET MLEAD PICTURE '99'
@ 22,10  SAY 'LEAVE PART-NUMBER FIELD BLANK, AND  ctrl-W,  TO EXIT.'
@ 23,1   SAY MWARN

SET TALK OFF
ERASE
USE INVNTRY INDEX PARTINDX
DO WHILE T
    STORE '      ' TO MPART
    STORE 0 TO MCOST
    STORE 0 TO MSELL
    STORE 0 TO MONHAND
    STORE 0 TO MONORDER
    STORE 0 TO MUSAGE
    STORE 0 TO MLEAD
    STORE ' ' TO MWARN
    SET FORMAT TO LAYOUTE
    READ
    IF MPART = '        '
        SET FORMAT TO
        RETURN
    ENDIF
    DO WHILE # > 0
        FIND &MPART
        IF # > 0
            STORE 'DUPLICATE KEY !' TO MWARN
            SET FORMAT TO LAYOUTE
            ? CHR(7)
            READ
        ENDIF
    ENDDO
    APPEND BLANK
    REPLACE PART WITH MPART;
            COST WITH MCOST;
            SELLPRICE WITH MSELL;
            ONHAND WITH MONHAND;
            ONORDER WITH MONORDER;
            USAGE WITH MUSAGE;
            LEAD WITH MLEAD
    SET FORMAT TO
ENDDO



Program "F".
----------


            GENERATING FORMAT FILE AND "CALLING PROGRAM"

            FOR EDITING EXISTING RECORDS SEQUENTIALLY
            ------------------------------------------
```

```
@ 3,10   SAY 'INVENTORY DATA-EDIT SCREEN'
@ 4,10   SAY '---------------------------'
@ 5,10   SAY 'EDIT RECORDS SEQUENTIALLY, NO CHANGES TO KEY-FIELD'
@ 08,1   SAY 'PARTNUM  '
@ 08,9   SAY PART USING   'XXXXXX'
@ 10,1   SAY 'COST     ' GET COST PICTURE '999.99'
@ 12,1   SAY 'SELLPRICE' GET SELLPRICE PICTURE '999.99'
@ 14,1   SAY 'ONHAND   ' GET ONHAND PICTURE '999'
@ 16,1   SAY 'ONORDER  ' GET ONORDER PICTURE '999'
@ 18,1   SAY 'USAGE    ' GET USAGE PICTURE '99'
@ 20,1   SAY 'LEAD     ' GET LEAD PICTURE '99'
@ 23,1   SAY 'MORE (Y/N) ?'  GET MMORE PICTURE 'X'
@ 23,30 SAY MLAST

SET TALK OFF
ERASE
STORE ' ' TO MMORE
USE INVNTRY  [INDEX .....]
GO BOTT
STORE # TO LASTREC
1
DO WHILE T
   IF !(MMORE) = 'N'
      SET FORMAT TO
      RETURN
   ENDIF
   IF # = LASTREC
      STORE 'LAST REC.!' TO MLAST
   ELSE
      STORE ' ' TO MLAST
   ENDIF
   SET FORMAT TO LAYOUTF
   READ
   SET FORMAT TO
   SKIP
ENDDO
```

Program "G".

GENERATING FORMAT FILE AND "CALLING PROGRAM"

FOR EDITING EXISTING RECORDS SEQUENTIALLY

ALLOWING CHANGES TO KEY-FIELDS, WITH DUPLICATES-CHECK.

```
@ 3,10 SAY 'INVENTORY DATA-EDIT SCREEN'
@ 4,10 SAY '---------------------------'
@ 5,10 SAY 'EDIT SEQ., WITH DUP-CHECK'
@ 08,1 SAY 'PARTNUM  ' GET MPART PICTURE 'XXXXXX'
@ 10,1 SAY 'COST     ' GET COST PICTURE '999.99'
@ 12,1 SAY 'SELLPRICE' GET SELLPRICE PICTURE '999.99'
@ 14,1 SAY 'ONHAND   ' GET ONHAND PICTURE '999'
@ 16,1 SAY 'ONORDER  ' GET ONORDER PICTURE '999'
```

```
@ 18,1 SAY 'USAGE    ' GET USAGE PICTURE '99'
@ 20,1 SAY 'LEAD     ' GET LEAD PICTURE '99'
@ 23,1 SAY 'MORE (Y/N) ?'  GET MMORE PICTURE 'X'
@ 23,30 SAY MLAST PICTURE ' '
@ 23,60 SAY MWARN

SET TALK OFF
ERASE
USE INVNTRY INDEX PARTINDX
GO BOTT
STORE # TO LASTREC
STORE ' ' TO MMORE
GO TOP
DO WHILE T
    IF !(MMORE) = 'N'
       SET FORMAT TO
       RETURN
    ENDIF
    IF # = LASTREC
       STORE 'LAST REC.!' TO MLAST
    ELSE
       STORE ' ' TO MLAST
    ENDIF
    STORE ' ' TO MMORE
    STORE '        ' TO MPART
    STORE ' ' TO MWARN
    STORE STR(#,6) TO CURRENT
    STORE PART TO MPART
    SET FORMAT TO LAYOUTG
    READ
    DO WHILE MPART # PART .AND. MPART # '        '
       FIND &MPART
       IF # > 0
          STORE 'DUPLICATE KEY!' TO MWARN
          ? CHR(7)
          &CURRENT
          SET FORMAT TO LAYOUTG
          READ
       ELSE
          &CURRENT
          REPLACE PART WITH MPART
          STORE '        ' TO MPART
       ENDIF
    ENDDO
    SET FORMAT TO
    SKIP
ENDDO
```

Program "H".

GENERATING FORMAT FILE AND "CALLING PROGRAM"

FOR EDITING EXISTING RECORDS R A N D O M L Y ON RECORD-NUMBER,

NO CHANGES TO KEY-FIELD VALUES.

```
@ 3,10   SAY 'INVENTORY DATA-EDIT SCREEN'
@ 4,10   SAY '-------------------------'
@ 5,10   SAY 'RANDOM EDIT, ON RECORD-NUMBERS'
@ 6,10   SAY 'NO CHANGES TO KEY-FIELD !'
@ 8,1    SAY 'CURRENT RECORD'
@ 8,16   SAY MCURR
@ 09,1   SAY 'PARTNUM'
@ 09,9   SAY PART USING 'XXXXXX'
@ 10,1   SAY 'COST     ' GET COST PICTURE '999.99'
@ 11,1   SAY 'SELLPRICE' GET SELLPRICE PICTURE '999.99'
@ 12,1   SAY 'ONHAND   ' GET ONHAND PICTURE '999'
@ 13,1   SAY 'ONORDER  ' GET ONORDER PICTURE '999'
@ 14,1   SAY 'USAGE    ' GET USAGE PICTURE '99'
@ 15,1   SAY 'LEAD     ' GET LEAD PICTURE '99'
@ 16,1   SAY 'NEXT RECORD-NUMBER ?'  GET MNEXT PICTURE 'XXXXXX'
@ 16,50  SAY '(LEAVE BLANK, TO EXIT)'
@ 20,1   SAY MWARN1
@ 21,1   SAY MWARN2

SET TALK OFF
STORE '      ' TO MCURR
USE INVNTRY
STORE 'BAD' TO RECNUM
DO WHILE RECNUM = 'BAD'
   ERASE
   ? "RECORD-NUMBER TO START EDITING ON ?      (LEAVE BLANK, TO EXIT)"
   ACCEPT TO MNEXT
   IF VAL(MNEXT) = 0
      RETURN
   ENDIF
   IF ' ' $(MNEXT)
      LOOP
   ENDIF
   GO BOTT
   STORE # TO TOTRECS
   IF VAL(MNEXT) > TOTRECS
      ? CHR(7)
      @ 5,15 SAY 'RECORD OUT OF RANGE.'
      @ 6,15 SAY 'YOU ONLY HAVE' + STR(#,6) + '    ' + 'RECORDS IN YOUR FILE'
      WAIT
      LOOP
   ELSE
      STORE 'GOOD' TO RECNUM
   ENDIF

ENDDO
DO WHILE T
   STORE ' ' TO MWARN1
   STORE ' ' TO MWARN2
   IF MNEXT = '      '
      SET FORMAT TO
      RETURN
   ENDIF
   ERASE
   IF VAL(MNEXT) > TOTRECS
      STORE 'RECORD OUT OF RANGE' TO MWARN1
      STORE 'YOU ONLY HAVE'+STR(TOTRECS,6)+'   '+'RECORDS IN YOUR FILE';
         TO MWARN2
      ? CHR(7)
      SET FORMAT TO LAYOUTH
      READ
```

285

```
        SET FORMAT TO
        LOOP
     ENDIF
     &MNEXT
     STORE MNEXT TO MCURR
     STORE '       ' TO MNEXT
     SET FORMAT TO LAYOUTH
     READ
     SET FORMAT TO
ENDDO
```

Program "I".

GENERATING FORMAT FILE AND "CALLING PROGRAM"

FOR EDITING EXISTING RECORDS R A N D O M L Y ON RECORD-NUMBER,

WITH DUPLICATES-CHECK.

```
@ 3,10   SAY 'INVENTORY DATA-EDIT SCREEN'
@ 4,10   SAY '--------------------------'
@ 5,10   SAY 'RANDOM EDIT ON RECORD-NUMBERS, WITH DUP-CHECK'
@ 7,1    SAY 'CURRENT RECORD'
@ 7,16   SAY MCURR
@ 08,1   SAY 'PARTNUM ' GET MPART PICTURE 'XXXXXX'
@ 10,1   SAY 'COST    ' GET COST PICTURE '999.99'
@ 11,1   SAY 'SELLPRICE' GET SELLPRICE PICTURE '999.99'
@ 12,1   SAY 'ONHAND  ' GET ONHAND PICTURE '999'
@ 13,1   SAY 'ONORDER ' GET ONORDER PICTURE '999'
@ 14,1   SAY 'USAGE   ' GET USAGE PICTURE '99'
@ 15,1   SAY 'LEAD    ' GET LEAD PICTURE '99'
@ 16,1   SAY 'NEXT RECORD-NUMBER ?'  GET MNEXT PICTURE 'XXXXXX'
@ 16,50  SAY '(LEAVE BLANK, TO EXIT)'
@ 20,1   SAY MWARN1
@ 21,1   SAY MWARN2

SET TALK OFF
STORE '        '. TO MCURR
USE INVNTRY INDEX PARTINDX
STORE 'BAD' TO RECNUM
DO WHILE RECNUM = 'BAD'
     ERASE
     ? 'RECORD-NUMBER TO START EDITING ON ?              (LEAVE BLANK, TO EXIT)'
     ACCEPT TO MNEXT
     IF VAL(MNEXT) = 0
        RETURN
     ENDIF
     IF ' ' $(MNEXT)
        LOOP
     ENDIF
     GO BOTT
     STORE # TO TOTRECS
     IF VAL(MNEXT) > TOTRECS
        ? CHR(7)
        @ 5,15 SAY 'RECORD OUT OF RANGE.'
```

286

```
                @ 6,15 SAY 'YOU ONLY HAVE' + STR(#,6) + '    ' + 'RECORDS IN YOUR FILE'
                WAIT
                LOOP
        ELSE
                STORE 'GOOD' TO RECNUM
        ENDIF
ENDDO
DO WHILE T
        STORE '        ' TO MPART
        STORE ' ' TO MWARN1
        STORE ' ' TO MWARN2
        IF MNEXT = '        '
                SET FORMAT TO
                RETURN
        ENDIF
        &MNEXT
        STORE MNEXT TO MCURR
        STORE '        ' TO MNEXT
        STORE PART TO MPART
        SET FORMAT TO LAYOUTI
        READ
        DO WHILE MPART#PART .OR. VAL(MNEXT) > TOTRECS
                STORE ' ' TO MWARN1
                STORE ' ' TO MWARN2
                IF MPART # PART
                        FIND &MPART
                        IF # > 0
                                STORE 'DUPLICATE KEY!' TO MWARN1
                                &MCURR
                                ? CHR(7)
                                SET FORMAT TO LAYOUTI
                                READ
                                LOOP
                        ELSE
                                &MCURR
                                REPLACE PART WITH MPART
                                LOOP
                        ENDIF
                ENDIF
                &MCURR
                STORE PART TO MPART
                STORE 'RECORD OUT OF RANGE' TO MWARN1
                STORE 'YOU ONLY HAVE'+STR(TOTRECS,6)+'    '+'RECORDS IN YOUR FILE';
                        TO MWARN2
                ? CHR(7)
                SET FORMAT TO LAYOUTI
                READ
                LOOP
        ENDDO
ENDDO
```

Program "J".

GENERATING FORMAT FILE AND "CALLING PROGRAM"

FOR EDITING EXISTING RECORDS R A N D O M L Y

VIA KEY-FIELD VALUE,

NO CHANGES TO BE MADE TO THE KEY-FIELD.

```
@ 1,20   SAY 'INVENTORY DATA-EDIT SCREEN'
@ 2,20   SAY '-------------------------'
@ 4,20   SAY 'Random processing on key-field values'
@ 7,1    SAY 'CURRENT RECORD-KEY'
@ 7,20   SAY MCURR
@ 08,1   SAY 'PARTNUM'
@ 08,9   SAY MPART USING 'XXXXXX'
@ 10,1   SAY 'COST     ' GET COST PICTURE '999.99'
@ 12,1   SAY 'SELLPRICE' GET SELLPRICE PICTURE '999.99'
@ 14,1   SAY 'ONHAND   ' GET ONHAND PICTURE '999'
@ 16,1   SAY 'ONORDER  ' GET ONORDER PICTURE '999'
@ 18,1   SAY 'USAGE    ' GET USAGE PICTURE '99'
@ 20,1   SAY 'LEAD     ' GET LEAD PICTURE '99'
@ 21,10  SAY MWARN1
@ 23,1   SAY 'NEXT FULL-KEY ?' GET MNEXT PICTURE 'XXXXXX'
@ 23,50  SAY 'LEAVE BLANK, TO EXIT'


SET TALK OFF
STORE '       ' TO MCURR
STORE '       ' TO MNEXT
USE INVNTRY INDEX PARTINDX
STORE 'BAD' TO RECKEY
DO WHILE RECKEY = 'BAD'
    ERASE
    ? 'WHICH RECORD-KEY TO START EDITING ON ?   GENERIC-KEY, O.K.'
    ?
    ? 'LEAVE BLANK, TO EXIT'
    ?
    ACCEPT TO MNEXT
    IF VAL(MNEXT) = 0
       RETURN
    ENDIF
    IF ' ' $(MNEXT)
       LOOP
    ENDIF
    FIND &MNEXT
    IF # = 0
       @ 10,10 SAY 'NO SUCH RECORD-KEY.  RE-ENTER FULL/GENERIC KEY'
       ? CHR(7)
       WAIT
       LOOP
    ELSE
       STORE 'GOOD' TO RECKEY
       STORE STR(#,6) TO CURRENT
       STORE PART TO MNEXT
    ENDIF
ENDDO
DO WHILE T
    IF MNEXT = '       '
       SET FORMAT TO
       RETURN
    ENDIF
    STORE ' ' TO MWARN1
    FIND &MNEXT
    IF # = 0
```

288

```
      STORE 'NO SUCH RECORD KEY !  RE-ENTER FULL KEY, OR LEAVE BLANK TO EXIT';
           TO MWARN1
      &CURRENT
      STORE PART TO MCURR
      STORE PART TO MPART
      ? CHR(7)
      SET FORMAT TO LAYOUTJ
      READ
      SET FORMAT TO
  ELSE
      STORE '      ' TO MNEXT
      STORE PART TO MCURR
      STORE PART TO MPART
      STORE STR(#,6) TO CURRENT
      SET FORMAT TO LAYOUTJ
      READ
  ENDIF

  ENDDO
```

Program "K".

GENERATING FORMAT FILE AND "CALLING PROGRAM"

FOR EDITING EXISTING RECORDS R A N D O M L Y

ON THE KEY-FIELD VALUE, WITH DUPLICATES-CHECK.

```
      @ 3,10  SAY 'INVENTORY DATA-EDIT SCREEN'
      @ 4,10  SAY '-------------------------'
      @ 5,10  SAY 'RANDOM EDIT ON KEY-FIELD, WITH DUP-CHECK'
      @ 6,1   SAY 'CURRENT RECORD-KEY'
      @ 6,20  SAY MCURR
      @ 08,1  SAY 'PARTNUM  ' GET MPART PICTURE 'XXXXXX'
      @ 10,1  SAY 'COST     ' GET COST PICTURE '999.99'
      @ 11,1  SAY 'SELLPRICE' GET SELLPRICE PICTURE '999.99'
      @ 12,1  SAY 'ONHAND   ' GET ONHAND PICTURE '999'
      @ 13,1  SAY 'ONORDER  ' GET ONORDER PICTURE '999'
      @ 14,1  SAY 'USAGE    ' GET USAGE PICTURE '99'
      @ 15,1  SAY 'LEAD     ' GET LEAD PICTURE '99'
      @ 16,1  SAY 'NEXT FULL-KEY ?' GET MNEXT PICTURE 'XXXXXX'
      @ 16,50 SAY '(LEAVE BLANK TO EXIT.)'
      @ 20,1  SAY MWARN1
      @ 21,1  SAY MWARN2
  SET TALK OFF
  STORE '      ' TO MCURR
  USE INVNTRY INDEX PARTINDX
  STORE 'BAD' TO RECKEY
  DO WHILE RECKEY = 'BAD'
      ERASE
      ? 'WHICH RECORD-KEY TO START EDITING ON ?      GENERIC-KEY, O.K.'
      ?
      ? 'LEAVE BLANK, TO EXIT'
      ?
      ACCEPT TO MNEXT
```

```
            IF VAL(MNEXT) = 0
               RETURN
            ENDIF
            IF ' ' $(MNEXT)
               LOOP
            ENDIF
            FIND &MNEXT
            IF # = 0
               @ 10,10 SAY 'NO SUCH RECORD-KEY.  RE-ENTER FULL/GENERIC KEY'
               ? CHR(7)
               WAIT
               LOOP
            ELSE
               STORE 'GOOD' TO RECKEY
            ENDIF
      ENDDO             .
      DO WHILE T
         STORE '            ' TO MPART
         STORE ' ' TO MWARN1
         STORE ' ' TO MWARN2
         IF MNEXT = '          '
            SET FORMAT TO
            RETURN
         ENDIF
         FIND &MNEXT
         IF # = 0
            STORE 'NO SUCH RECORD KEY !  RE-ENTER FULL KEY, OR LEAVE BLANK TO EXIT';
                  TO MWARN1
            &CURRENT
            STORE PART TO MPART
            ? CHR(7)
            SET FORMAT TO LAYOUTK
            READ
            LOOP
         ELSE
            STORE STR(#,6) TO CURRENT
         ENDIF
         &CURRENT
         STORE PART  TO MCURR
         STORE '          ' TO MNEXT
         STORE PART TO MPART
         SET FORMAT TO LAYOUTK
         READ
         DO WHILE MPART#PART
            FIND &MPART
            IF # > 0
               STORE 'DUPLICATE KEY!' TO MWARN1
               &CURRENT
               ? CHR(7)
               SET FORMAT TO LAYOUTK
               READ
               LOOP
            ELSE
               &CURRENT
               REPLACE PART WITH MPART
            ENDIF
         ENDDO
      ENDDO
```

Program "L".

GENERATING FORMAT FILE AND "CALLING PROGRAM"

FOR DELETING EXISTING RECORDS RANDOMLY

ON THE KEY-FIELD VALUE.

```
@ 3,10  SAY 'INVENTORY DATA-EDIT SCREEN'
@ 4,10  SAY '--------------------------'
@ 5,10  SAY 'DELETE RECORDS RANDOMLY, ON KEY-FIELD'
@ 10,5  SAY 'PARTNUM'
@ 10,25 SAY PART USING    'XXXXXX'
@ 12,5  SAY 'COST'
@ 12,25 SAY COST USING    '999.99'
@ 14,5  SAY 'SELLPRICE'
@ 14,25 SAY SELLPRICE USING   '999.99'
@ 16,5  SAY 'ONHAND'
@ 16,25 SAY ONHAND USING   '999'
@ 18,5  SAY 'ONORDER'
@ 18,25 SAY ONORDER USING   '999'
@ 20,5  SAY 'USAGE'
@ 20,25 SAY USAGE USING    '999'
@ 21,5  SAY 'LEAD'
@ 21,25 SAY LEAD USING    '999'
@ 22,5  SAY 'DELETE (Y/N) ?'  GET MANSWER PICTURE 'X'
@ 22,50 SAY 'NEXT RECORD-KEY ?' GET MNEXT PICTURE 'XXXXXX'
@ 23,6  SAY MWARN1
@ 23,50 SAY 'LEAVE BLANK, TO EXIT'

SET TALK OFF
USE INVNTRY INDEX PARTINDX
STORE 'BAD' TO RECKEY
DO WHILE RECKEY = 'BAD'
   ERASE
   ? 'WHICH RECORD-KEY TO START DELETING ON ?     GENERIC-KEY, O.K.'
   ?
   ? 'LEAVE BLANK, TO EXIT'
   ?
   ACCEPT TO MNEXT
   IF VAL(MNEXT) = 0
     RETURN
   ENDIF
   IF ' ' $(MNEXT)
     LOOP
   ENDIF
   FIND &MNEXT
   IF # = 0
     @ 10,10 SAY 'NO SUCH RECORD-KEY.  RE-ENTER FULL/GENERIC KEY'
     ? CHR(7)
     WAIT
     LOOP
   ELSE
     STORE 'GOOD' TO RECKEY
   ENDIF
```

```
ENDDO
STORE ' ' TO DELETE:FLG
DO WHILE T
    IF MNEXT = '          '
        SET FORMAT TO
        ERASE
        IF DELETE:FLG = '*'
            STORE ' ' TO MANSWER
            @ 5,10 SAY 'DO YOU WANT THE FILE PACKED ?  (Y/N)' GET MANSWER
            READ
            IF !(MANSWER) = 'Y'
                @ 10,10 SAY 'PACK OPERATION IN PROGRESS ! DO NOT INTERRUPT !'
                PACK
            ELSE
                @ 10,10 SAY 'RECORDS DELETED, FILE NOT PACKED !'
            ENDIF
            WAIT
        ENDIF
        RETURN
    ENDIF
    STORE ' '  TO MWARN1
    STORE ' ' TO MANSWER
    FIND &MNEXT
    IF # = 0
        STORE 'NO SUCH RECORD KEY !  RE-ENTER FULL KEY, OR LEAVE BLANK TO EXIT';
              TO MWARN1
        &CURRENT
        ? CHR(7)
        SET FORMAT TO LAYOUTL
        READ
        LOOP
    ELSE
        STORE STR(#,6) TO CURRENT
    ENDIF
    &CURRENT
    STORE '        ' TO MNEXT
    SET FORMAT TO LAYOUTL
    READ
    IF !(MANSWER) = 'Y'
        DELETE
        STORE '*' TO DELETE:FLG
    ENDIF
ENDDO
```

Program "M".

GENERATING FORMAT FILE AND "CALLING PROGRAM"

FOR SCANNING EXISTING RECORDS SEQUENTIALLY

```
@ 3,10   SAY 'INVENTORY DATA-EDIT SCREEN'
@ 4,10   SAY '---------------------------'
@ 5,10   SAY 'SCAN RECORDS SEQUENTIALLY'
@ 7,5    SAY 'CURRENT REC-NUMBER'
@ 7,25   SAY MCURR
```

```
@ 9,50   SAY 'PROCEED ?  (Y/N)' GET  MPROCEED PICTURE 'X'
@ 10,5   SAY 'PARTNUM'
@ 10,25 SAY PART USING 'XXXXXX'
@ 12,5   SAY 'COST'
@ 12,25 SAY COST USING '999.99'
@ 14,5   SAY 'SELLPRICE'
@ 14,25 SAY SELLPRICE USING '999.99'
@ 16,5   SAY 'ONHAND'
@ 16,25 SAY ONHAND USING '999'
@ 18,5   SAY 'ONORDER'
@ 18,25 SAY ONORDER USING '999'
@ 20,5   SAY 'USAGE'
@ 20,25 SAY USAGE USING '999'
@ 21,5   SAY 'LEAD'
@ 21,25 SAY LEAD USING '999'
@ 23,1   SAY MWARN1

SET TALK OFF
STORE ' ' TO MPROCEED
STORE ' ' TO MWARN1
ERASE
USE INVNTRY
GO BOTT
STORE # TO LASTREC
GO TOP
DO WHILE .NOT. EOF
    STORE # TO MCURR
    IF # - LASTREC
       STORE 'LAST RECORD !' TO MWARN1
    ENDIF
    SET FORMAT TO LAYOUTM
    READ
    IF !(MPROCEED) = 'N'
       SET FORMAT TO
       RETURN
    ENDIF
    SKIP
ENDDO
RETURN
```

Program "N".

GENERATING FORMAT FILE AND "CALLING PROGRAM"

FOR SCANNING EXISTING RECORDS RANDOMLY

ON THE KEY-FIELD VALUE.

```
@ 3,10  SAY 'INVENTORY DATA-EDIT SCREEN'
@ 4,10  SAY '-------------------------'
@ 5,10  SAY 'SCAN RECORDS RANDOMLY, ON KEY-FIELD'
@ 7,5   SAY 'CURRENT RECORD-KEY'
@ 7,25  SAY MCURR
@ 09,5  SAY 'PARTNUM'
```

```
@ 09,25 SAY PART USING 'XXXXXX'
@ 10,5   SAY 'COST'
@ 10,25 SAY COST USING '999.99'
@ 11,5   SAY 'SELLPRICE'
@ 11,25 SAY SELLPRICE USING '999.99'
@ 12,5   SAY 'ONHAND'
@ 12,25 SAY ONHAND USING '999'
@ 13,5   SAY 'ONORDER'
@ 13,25 SAY ONORDER USING '999'
@ 14,5   SAY 'USAGE'
@ 14,25 SAY USAGE USING '999'
@ 15,5   SAY 'LEAD'
@ 15,25 SAY LEAD USING '999'
@ 17,5   SAY MWARN1
@ 20,1   SAY 'NEXT FULL RECORD-KEY ?' GET MNEXT PICTURE 'XXXXXX'
@ 20,50 SAY '(LEAVE BLANK, TO EXIT)'

SET TALK OFF
STORE '        ' TO MCURR
USE INVNTRY INDEX PARTINDX
STORE 'BAD' TO RECKEY
DO WHILE RECKEY = 'BAD'
    ERASE
    ? 'WHICH RECORD-KEY TO START EDITING ON ?     GENERIC-KEY, O.K.
    ?
    ? 'LEAVE BLANK, TO EXIT'
    ?
    ACCEPT TO MNEXT
    IF VAL(MNEXT) = 0
       RETURN
    ENDIF
    IF ' ' $(MNEXT)
       LOOP
    ENDIF
    FIND &MNEXT
    IF # = 0
       @ 10,10 SAY 'NO SUCH RECORD-KEY.  RE-ENTER FULL/GENERIC KEY
       ? CHR(7)
       WAIT
       LOOP
    ELSE
       STORE 'GOOD' TO RECKEY
    ENDIF
ENDDO
DO WHILE T
    IF MNEXT = '       '
       SET FORMAT TO
       RETURN
    ENDIF
    FIND &MNEXT
    IF # = 0
       STORE 'NO SUCH RECORD KEY !  RE-ENTER FULL KEY, OR LEAVE BLANK TO EXIT';
             TO MWARN1
       &CURRENT
       STORE PART TO MPART
       ? CHR(7)
       SET FORMAT TO LAYOUTN
       READ
       LOOP
    ELSE
```

294

```
          STORE STR(#,6) TO CURRENT
      ENDIF
      STORE ' ' TO MWARN1
      &CURRENT
      STORE PART  TO MCURR
      STORE '        ' TO MNEXT
      SET FORMAT TO LAYOUTN
      READ
ENDDO
```

Program "O".

PROGRAM FOR REMOVAL OF DUPLICATE-KEY RECORDS,

in case some duplicates have crept into your master file.

```
ERASE
USE INVNTRY INDEX  PARTINDX
STORE PART TO MPART
STORE 0 TO COUNTER
SKIP
DO WHILE  .NOT.  EOF
   IF PART = MPART
      DELETE
      STORE COUNTER+1  TO COUNTER
   ELSE
      STORE PART TO MPART
   ENDIF
   SKIP
ENDDO
IF COUNTER = 0
   RETURN
ENDIF
PACK
ERASE
@ 10,15 SAY 'NUMBER OF DELETED RECORDS = '
@ 10,50 SAY COUNTER  USING  '99999'
WAIT
RETURN
```

COMBINING MULTIPLE FILES, THROUGH PROGRAMMING.

"Master-1" file structure:	PART:NUM	UNIT:COST	DESC
"Master-2" file structure:	PART:NUM	CGC	
"Master-3" file structure:	PART:NUM	ONHAND	

"OUTPUT"   file structure: PART:NUM UNIT:COST DESC CGC ONHAND

```
        SET TALK OFF
        ERASE
        @ 10,15 SAY "Program has commenced linking the files."
        @ 11,15 SAY "Do not interrupt !!"
        SELE PRIM
        USE F1 INDEX P1INDX
        DO WHILE .NOT. EOF
           STORE PART:NUM TO MPARTNUM
           STORE UNIT:COST TO MUNIT
           STORE DESC TO MDESC
           STORE ' ' TO MCGC
           STORE ' ' TO MONHAND
           SELE SECO
           USE F2 INDEX P2INDX
           FIND &MPARTNUM
           IF # > 0
              STORE CGC TO MCGC
           ENDIF
           USE F3 INDEX P3INDX
           FIND &MPARTNUM
           IF # > 0
              STORE ONHAND TO MONHAND
           ENDIF

           USE OUTPUT
           APPEND BLANK
           REPLACE PART:NUM WITH MPARTNUM;
                   UNIT:COST WITH MUNIT;
                   DESC WITH MDESC;
                   CGC WITH MCGC;
                   ONHAND WITH MONHAND
           SELE PRIM
           SKIP
        ENDDO
        USE
        SELE SECO
        USE
        RETURN
```

ENHANCED SCREEN-LAYOUTS.

Send screen into inverse-video, if input-error.

```
SET TALK OFF
ERASE
USE INVENTORY
DO WHILE T
     ? CHR(27)+'('
     STORE '       ' TO MPART
     STORE 0 TO MCOST
     STORE 0 TO MSELL
```

```
             STORE 0 TO MONHAND
             STORE 0 TO MONORDER
             STORE 0 TO MUSAGE
             STORE 0 TO MLEAD
             STORE ' ' TO ERRMSG
             SET FORMAT TO LAYOUTDA
             READ
             IF MPART = '        '
                SET FORMAT TO
                RETURN
             ENDIF
             STORE T TO NOGOOD
             DO WHILE NOGOOD
             STORE F TO NOGOOD
                IF MSELL < 10 .OR. MSELL > 30
                   STORE 'SELL PRICE ERROR !!!' TO ERRMSG
                   STORE T TO NOGOOD
                ENDIF
                IF MCOST < 10 .OR. MCOST > 30
                   STORE 'COST PRICE ERROR !!!' TO ERRMSG
                   STORE T TO NOGOOD
                ENDIF
                IF NOGOOD
                   ? CHR(27)+')'+CHR(27)+'7'
                   SET FORMAT TO LAYOUTDA
                   READ
                ENDIF
             ENDDO
             APPEND BLANK
             REPLACE PART WITH MPART;
                     COST WITH MCOST;
                     SELLPRICE WITH MSELL;
                     ONHAND WITH MONHAND;
                     ONORDER WITH MONORDER;
                     USAGE WITH MUSAGE;
                     LEAD WITH MLEAD
             SET FORMAT TO
ENDDO
```

ENHANCED SCREEN LAYOUTS – contd.

(Extended with the use of memory-variables)

```
.STORE "CHR(27)+')'+CHR(27)+'5'"    TO GRAPHICS
.STORE "CHR(27)+')'+CHR(27)+'7'"    TO INVERSE
.STORE "CHR(27)+')'+CHR(27)+'6'"    TO BLINK
.STORE "CHR(27)+'('"                TO NORMAL
.SAVE TO SPECIALS
```

```
SET TALK OFF
ERASE
```

RESTORE FROM SPECIALS ADDITIVE

(The command: **.RESTORE FROM SPECIALS ADDITIVE**   <cr>
will reload all the memory-variables from disk into memory.
Obviously, they should be available in memory, before they can be
successfully used as macro-parameters. The "additive" ("add-on")
parameter ensures that other, **existing** memory-variables are left
intact.)

```
USE INVENTORY
DO WHILE T
     ? &NORMAL
     STORE '          ' TO MPART
     STORE 0 TO MCOST
     STORE 0 TO MSELL
     STORE 0 TO MONHAND
     STORE 0 TO MONORDER
     STORE 0 TO MUSAGE
     STORE 0 TO MLEAD
     STORE ' ' TO ERRMSG
     SET FORMAT TO LAYOUTDA
     READ
     IF MPART = '          '
        SET FORMAT TO
        RETURN
     ENDIF

     STORE T TO NOGOOD

     DO WHILE NOGOOD
     STORE F TO NOGOOD
        IF MSELL < 10 .OR. MSELL > 30
           STORE 'SELL PRICE ERROR !!!' TO ERRMSG
           STORE T TO NOGOOD
        ENDIF
        IF MCOST < 10 .OR. MCOST > 30
           STORE 'COST PRICE ERROR !!!' TO ERRMSG
           STORE T TO NOGOOD
        ENDIF
        IF NOGOOD
           ? &INVERSE
           SET FORMAT TO LAYOUTDA
           READ
        ENDIF
     ENDDO
     APPEND BLANK
     REPLACE PART WITH MPART;
             COST WITH MCOST;
             SELLPRICE WITH MSELL;
             ONHAND WITH MONHAND;
             ONORDER WITH MONORDER;
             USAGE WITH MUSAGE;
             LEAD WITH MLEAD
     SET FORMAT TO
ENDDO
```

SHATTERING THE 32-FIELD LIMITATION MYTH.

The format-file (LAYOUTB.FMT) is shown below:

```
@ 10,1 SAY 'EMP-NUMBER         ' GET MEMPNUM  PICT 'XXXXXX'
@ 12,1 SAY 'EMP-NAME           ' GET MEMPNAME PICT 'XXXXXXXXXXXXXX'
@ 14,1 SAY 'TOWN               ' GET MTOWN    PICT 'XXXXXXXXXXXX'
@ 16,1 SAY 'ORG                ' GET MORG     PICT 'XXX'
@ 18,1 SAY 'EXEMPT             ' GET MEXEMPT  PICT 'X'
@ 20,1 SAY 'YEAR OF HIRE       ' GET MYEAR    PICT '9999'
@ 22,1 SAY 'SALARY             ' GET MSALARY  PICT '99999.99'

SET TALK OFF
USE PERSNL
DO WHILE T
   STORE '      ' TO MEMPNUM
   STORE '               ' TO MEMPNAME
   STORE '            ' TO MTOWN
   STORE '   ' TO MORG
   STORE ' ' TO MEXEMPT
   STORE 0 TO MYEAR
   STORE 0 TO MSALARY
   SET FORMAT TO LAYOUTB
   READ
   IF MEMPNUM = '      '
      SET FORMAT TO
      RETURN
   ENDIF
   APPEND BLANK
   REPLACE ONEFIELD WITH MEMPNUM+MEMPNAME+MTOWN+MORG+MEXEMPT;
                         +STR(MYEAR,4)+STR(MSALARY,8,2)
ENDDO
```

The format-file (LAYOUTR.FMT) is shown here:

```
@ 10,1 SAY 'EMP-NUMBER         ' GET MEMPNUM  PICT 'XXXXXX'
@ 12,1 SAY 'EMP-NAME           ' GET MEMPNAME PICT 'XXXXXXXXXXXXXX'
@ 14,1 SAY 'TOWN               ' GET MTOWN    PICT 'XXXXXXXXXXXX'
@ 16,1 SAY 'ORG                ' GET MORG     PICT 'XXX'
@ 18,1 SAY 'EXEMPT             ' GET MEXEMPT  PICT 'X'
@ 20,1 SAY 'YEAR OF HIRE       ' GET MYEAR    PICT '9999'
@ 22,1 SAY 'SALARY             ' GET MSALARY  PICT '99999.99'
@ 23,1 SAY 'CARRY ON   (Y/N) ?' GET MNEXT    PICT 'X'

SET TALK OFF
ERASE
USE PERSNL
STORE ' ' TO MNEXT
DO WHILE T
   STORE $(ONEFIELD,1,6) TO MEMPNUM
   STORE $(ONEFIELD,7,15) TO MEMPNAME
   STORE $(ONEFIELD,22,12) TO MTOWN
   STORE $(ONEFIELD,34,3) TO MORG
   STORE $(ONEFIELD,37,1) TO MEXEMPT
   STORE VAL($(ONEFIELD,38,4)) TO MYEAR
```

299

```
      STORE VAL($(ONEFIELD,42,8)) TO MSALARY
      SET FORMAT TO LAYOUTR
      READ
      REPLACE ONEFIELD WITH MEMPNUM+MEMPNAME+MTOWN+MORG+MEXEMPT;
                              +STR(MYEAR,4)+STR(MSALARY,8,2)

      IF MNEXT = 'N'
         SET FORMAT TO
         RETURN
      ENDIF
      SKIP
ENDDO
```

Index

Index

OTHER POPULAR TAB BOOKS OF INTEREST

TAB   TAB BOOKS Inc.

Blue Ridge Summit. Pa. 17214

Send for FREE TAB Catalog describing over 750 current titles in print.